SONOMA COUNTY
LIBRARY
OFFICIAL
DISCARD

THE HISTORY OF CASTLES

FORTIFICATIONS AROUND THE WORLD

The History of Castles

FORTIFICATIONS AROUND THE WORLD

CHRIS GRAVETT

THE LYONS PRESS
GUILFORD, CT
AN IMPRINT OF THE GLOBE PEQUOT PRESS

The History of Castles—Fortifications Around the World

First Lyons Press edition 2001

The Lyons Press is an imprint of the Globe Pequot Press.

Printed and bound in Italy by Milanostampa SpA

ISBN 1-58574-435-2

Project Editor: Warren Lapworth
Design: Roger Kean, Oliver Frey
Illustrations: Oliver Frey
Four-Color Separation: Michael Parkinson

Picture Acknowledgments
Hemera: 1; Matthew Uffindell: 2–3
Picture research by Thalamus Studios and Image Select International Limited
Lesley & Roy Adkins: 47 (bottom), 58 (top), 58 (bottom); Agence France Presse - Anatoly Maltsev: 144; Agence Photographique de la Réunion des Musées Nationaux: 26, 180 (top); AKG London: 6, 12; AKG London/Camoisson 154; Art Archive: 138, 170, 180 (bottom), 181; Austrian Views/Bohnecker 89; Austrian Views/Jezierzanski: 84; Austrian Views/Simoner: 86; Austrian Views/Trumler: 88; Austrian Views/H. Wiesenhofer: 91 (top); B&U International Picture Service: 78, 79 (bottom left), 79 (bottom right), 81 (top), 83; Belgian Tourist Office - Brussels & Ardennes 79 (top); Luigi Bertello 119; Corbis: 157; Corbis/Paul Almasy: 7, 16, 21, 80, 107 (top), (bottom left), 140, 141, 150, 156; Corbis/James L. Amos: 70; Corbis/Craig Aurness 183; Corbis/Hal Beral: 99; Corbis/Yann Arthus-Bertrand: 128, 160, 163; Corbis/William A Blake: 175; Corbis/Chris Bland: 45 (right); Corbis/Dr Christian Brandstätter: 75; Corbis/Michael Busselle: 104, 108; Corbis/Eric Chalker: 30; Corbis/Michelle Chaplow: 103; Corbis/Elio Ciol: 162; Corbis/Stephanie Colasanti: 124; Corbis/Sheldan Collins: 162; Corbis/Dean Conger: 147; Corbis/Richard A, Cooke: 168 (bottom); Corbis/Araldo de Luca: 161; Corbis/Ric Ergenbright: 56; Corbis/Eye Ubiquitous: 98; Corbis/Macduff Everton: 53, 55, 106; Corbis/John Farmar: 47; Corbis/Franz-Marc Frei: 25, 55, 115, 136; Corbis/Farel Grehan: 62; Corbis/Alison Hall: 22; Corbis/Richard Hamilton: 19; Corbis/John Heseltine: 124, 125; Corbis/Jeremy Horner: 163; Corbis/Peter Horree: 125, 127; Corbis/Harald A. Jahn - Viennaslide Photoagency: 24; Corbis/Wolfgang Kaehler: 68; Corbis/Kea Publishing Services Ltd: 82; Corbis/Michael John Kielty: 187; Corbis/Bob Krist: 73, 77, 177; Corbis/Charles & Josette Lenars: 20, 155, 168 (top), 187; Corbis/Chris Lisle: 131; Corbis/Abilio Lope: 10; Corbis/Dennis Marsico: 124; Corbis/Stephanie Maze: 107; Corbis/Peter Mertz: 91; Corbis/Beebe - Morton: 93; Corbis/Yiorgos Nikiteas: 41 (bottom); Corbis/Richard T Nowitz: 49 (top), 154, 157 159 (top), 159 (center); Corbis/Gianni Dagli Orti: 169; Corbis/Papilio: 36, 148; Corbis/Chris Parker: 41 (top); Corbis/José F Poblete: 27; Corbis/Carl Purcell: 165; Corbis/Enzo & Paolo Ragazzini: 101, 109 (bottom), 123; Corbis/Steve Raymer: 146; Corbis/Carmen Redondo: 126; Corbis/Hans Georg Roth: 115 (top right); 112, 115, 116; Corbis/Kim Sayer: 123; Corbis/Phil Schermeister: 143; Corbis/Gregor M. Schmid: 85, 145; Corbis/Joseph Sohm: 179; Corbis/Paul A Souders: 130; Corbis/Michael St. Maur Shiel: 63, 64, 65; Corbis/Sandy Stockwell: 39; Corbis/Keren Su: 165; Corbis/Roger Tidman: 57; CorbisVanni Archive: 101 (bottom); Corbis/Sandro Vannini: 57, 97, 121, 134, 142; Corbis/Patrick Ward: 74; Corbis/Westerman: Kurt-Michael 87; Corbis/Nik Wheeler: 114; Corbis;Terry Whittaker: 38; Corbis/Roger Wood: 151; Corbis/Adam Woolfitt: 31, 45 (top), 49 (bottom); 50; 90, 100, 10, 135, 175, 179, 189 (bottom); Corbis/Michael S Yamashita: 167 (top), 167 (bottom left); Corbis/Felix Zaska: 60; Maurizio di Stefano: 118, 120, 122 (right); Dúchas, The Heritage Service 61 (top); E.T. Archive 35 (top); Oliver Frey/Thalamus Studios: 14, 15, 17, 171, 172, 173, 184 (top); Fyntour: 132; German National Tourist Office: 66, 67, 76; Christopher Gravett: 36 (left), 51 (top); Nicholas Hall, Royal Armouries: 182; Hemera: 1, 9, 11, 32, 34, 36 (bottom), 40, 46, 48, 49 (top), 51 (bottom), 51 (center), 65 (top), 72, 75 (top), 81 (bottom), 95, 111, 131 (top), 153, 164, 166, 167 (bottom right), 169 (top), 182 (top), 188, 189 (top); Image Select: 42, 186; Image Select/Ann Ronan: 13; Jarold: 43 (bottom); A. Martinuzzi: 126 (bottom); J. Barry Mittan: 35 (bottom); Photri-Microstock: 184 (bottom), 185 (left), 185 (right); Scuol Tourismus: 97 (top); Skyscan Balloon Photography: 176; Spectrum Colour Library: 8, 10, 18, 19 (top), 23 (bottom), 28, 29, 33, 37, 43 (top), 44. 52, 61 (right), 113, 117, 143 (top), 149, 152, 159 (bottom), 174; Swiss-Image GmbH: 94, 96; Thalamus Publishing: 23 (top), 92, 93 (top), 99, 102 (center), 105, 109 (top), 122 (left), 133, 136 (top), 139, 145 (top), 146 (left), 147 (inset), 158; Matthew Uffindell: 2–3; Wales Tourist Board Photo Library: 45.

Every effort has been made to correctly acknowledge and contact the copyright holder of each picture. Thalamus Publishing apologises for any unintentional errors or omissions which will be corrected in future editions of this book.

title page: Schloss Königstein, Saxony, Germany—precipitously perched on the edge of the mountain.

previous spread: Over nine hundred years old, Ludlow castle greets the dawn of a new Millennium over the medieval English town.

facing: Plan showing the domestic quarters of Tarascon, situated on the Rhône below Avignon, France (*see page 27*).

Contents

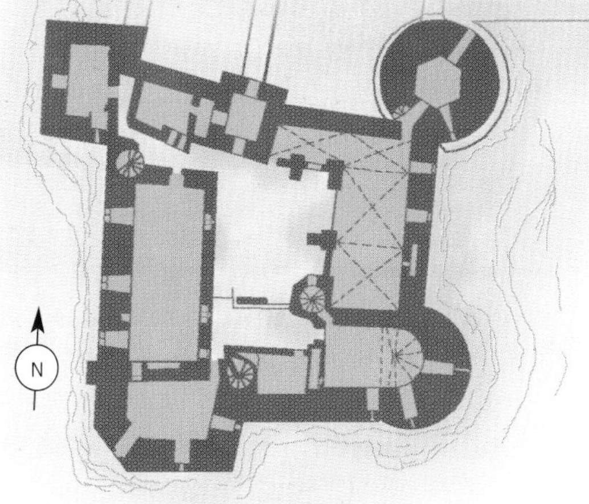

Introduction

above: Castles often have a history inextricably mixed with the fortified town beside it. An invader could not seize a land until he captured its castles, for their garrisons could cut off supply lines and harry his men.

Castles are the stuff of romance, with the power to fascinate the modern mind. They are often seen as places crammed with armored knights, where dank dungeons house chained prisoners. Castles are symbols of power; the larger and taller the towers, the more they seem to proclaim domination and lordship.

In their era, castles were centers for administration and the dispensation of justice, often constructed along borders, roads, or rivers, or in a stretched line to communicate with one another. Sometimes a site was chosen because of ideal terrain or because the lord wished to control an immediate area, perhaps following its seizure.

A single castle commanded a radius of about 10 miles—a day's ride out and back. Rather than risk pitched battles, encroaching armies often sent soldiers to pillage, destroying the local economy while feeding their own men. A castle was a threat to this tactic, protecting the countryside and starving the enemy of supplies. An invader could not seize a land until he captured its castles, for their garrisons could cut off supply lines and harry his men, or act as a base for massing troops for counterattack. The more castles there are in an area, the more that area is likely to have been disputed.

Many castles housed only a small number of people on a day-to-day basis. Moreover, there is often little evidence for large numbers of prisoners or the torture of those whose presence is recorded. Since these were secure buildings, it made sense to house prisoners within their walls, a function often maintained after a castle's military role ended.

A Measured Study

This book is not a guide to every castle—a whole series would be required to catalog them all—and many castles were small-scale affairs or survive chiefly as earthworks. It cannot do justice to all the worthy fortifications that can be found and which, again, have been excluded purely due to lack of space.

It does, however, provide an overview of castles and fortifications to demonstrate how regional diversity is found in the use of styles of defense and decoration. Equally, the intercourse in ideas from one area, or one culture, to another, has resulted in some breathtaking examples of fortification. The importance of terrain also plays a part in molding the form of strongholds most common to certain areas.

Each country featured in this book is divided into sections, each of which deals with a type of castle. Many castles have features common to more than one section and are therefore relevant to two or three different areas.

Although this book mainly concerns castles, it looks both back to antiquity and forward to the time after the decline of castles. The fortifications of antiquity, though not technically castles, were often vast and the technology of superior quality. The use of strong walls to protect a community continued in one form or another right through the era of the castle—indeed castles often have a history inextricably mixed with the fortified town beside it.

Castles themselves—which at the beginning of the period were often simple structures—grew in sophistication to become breathtaking strongholds with every defensive trick. At the same time as military ideas developed, older styles remained in use or were adapted.

After the demise of the castle, military architects did not cease to plan defensive structures, even with the advent of modern weapons capable of mass destruction. Across the world different cultures have built defenses of various kinds. All these must be explored if the form and functions of the castle are to be understood and placed within the history of man.

below: Castles are symbols of power; the larger and taller the towers, the more they seem to proclaim domination and lordship—Peñafiel castle near Valladolid, Spain (*see page 107*).

Chapter One:

Early Fortifications

The predecessors of castles were not buildings but defensive walls, surrounding prosperous towns and cities. Few of them remain, but they can be visited as sites and ruins, surviving towers showing where envious rivals were spotted and repelled.

The oldest city yet discovered is Jericho, adjacent to the modern town. Two sets of walls have been excavated: the outer wall is dated to 8000 BC and constructed from carefully set stones from a nearby river bed, smaller than those of the inner wall of 7000 BC, which probably once stood over 15 feet high. The outer wall is 6 feet wide and survives to almost 20 feet.

Beyond is an enormous ditch 27 feet wide and 9 feet deep. A solid stone tower over 30 feet in diameter at its base survives to 30 feet high.

Sumer

Over 4,000 years ago the Sumerians in Mesopotamia surrounded their cities with mud brick walls. At three sites between Karachi and the Iranian border, rectangular towers and walls 30 feet thick protected the inhabitants from seaborne attack.

Troy

Troy had nine cities, one below the other, dating from 3000–2560 BC. The Sixth City is probably that of the Homeric epics. The walls, set with

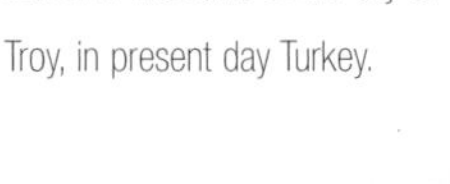

below: The ruins of the city of Troy, in present day Turkey.

towers, still reach 20 feet in height and have a steep batter or slope. The gate, on the inside face of the curtain wall, is reached by passing between two sections of wall, making it difficult to see from the outside.

Babylon

The original city walls of Babylon may be even earlier than those of Atchana, near Antioch, which date to the 19th century BC. Building on flat lands, the Babylonians surrounded their walls with moats. In the 6th century BC Nebuchadrezzar rebuilt the walls; about 23 feet thick and buttressed with towers, Herodotus said a four-horse chariot could turn on them. The western wall rose from the Euphrates, also forming a flood barrier. Above rose the Tower of Babylon, or Babel.

The Hittites

The militaristic Hittites ruled an area from the Aegean Sea to the borders of Mesopotamia. In the 14th–13th centuries BC they expanded their capital of Hattusa, which had been settled since 1650 BC. The walls were extended and ran 4 miles across hills and low points, making Hattusa the largest fortified city anywhere. The walls, 26 feet thick in places, sat on tiers of huge stones, many so smooth that mortar was unnecessary.

There were five main gates with probably copper-covered wooden doors, and twin gate towers with internal cross-walls, the gaps filled with rubble. The King's Gate had two double-doors closing inward—the guard left by rope or ladder to the wall above.

At Carchemish on the Euphrates are two lines of defense and a citadel, and drawings show battlemented wall and tower tops at the city of Dapur.

Egypt

Near Wadi Halfa are three border fortresses dating to c.2000 BC. Egyptian temples were also surrounded by fortifications. The Ramesseum (1280 BC) has a rectangular group of buildings inside a wall and is entered via a huge gate. At Medinet Habu (1200 BC) the inner gate has three stories and flanking towers, with two tiers of chambers above the gate. Rounded crenellations survive on the walls, similar to those seen in Hittite and Assyrian drawings.

above left: Reconstruction of the ceremonial Ishtar Gate at Babylon, built of kiln-dried bricks cemented with pitch and an outer shell of enamelled brick.

above: The massive walls of the Ramesseum, the funerary temple of Ramses II at Thebes.

Mycenae

The acropolis at Mycenae (the citadel of Agamemnon) is built on a rocky hilltop surrounded by a single wall on average 16 feet thick and originally about 32 feet high. The outer gate has a solid stone lintel carved with two lions. The palace ruins are on the summit—the Greeks built on hills where possible.

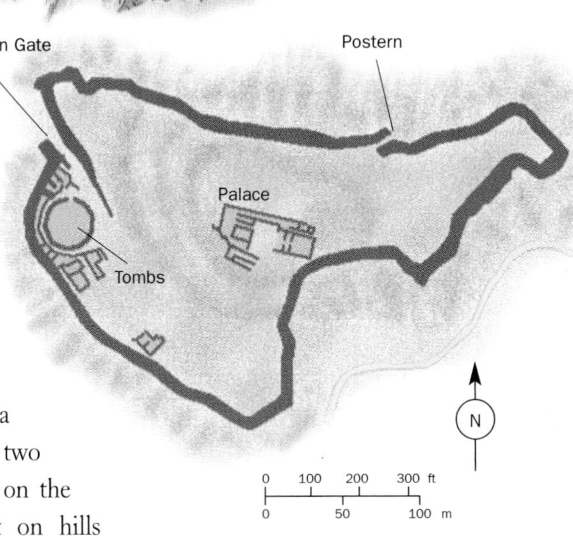

above: Reconstruction and plan of Mycenae.

Assyria

In 1600 bc the Assyrians built the curtain wall of Ashur in modern Iraq. During their ascendancy they built a number of cities similar in form to the Hittites'. Khorsabad, near Mosul, was built 722–705 BC on a rectangular plan and had walls 79 feet thick, set with towers. Each gateway had rectangular twin flanking towers.

Ancient Walls

All early fortifications were communal. They protected a large number of people and were defended by warriors as the state instructed. They were not the private residences of a king or emperor, even though he might reside within the walls.

below: Maiden Castle, Dorset, England, as it appears today, with a reconstructed view of the fortification c.100 BC .

Greece

The acropolis remained the center of a town's defense until the sixth century, when walls were added around whole towns. Rubble work or mud walls gave way to stone blocks. By the fifth century towers were spaced along the walls, not just at gates and weak spots. Athens built a double wall 4 miles long to encompass the port of Piraeus.

During the late fifth–early fourth century BC, Athens built frontier posts, such as Eleutherae, with two-story towers jutting out. In the fourth–third centuries battlements were replaced by shuttered loopholes for archers and ballistae, and the walls were thickened and heightened. From the mid-fourth century BC walls and towers were given loopholes for artillery.

Towers, now sometimes five stories high, had heavy artillery at second-floor level and lighter ones at the top; battlements were replaced by a tilted roof. Ditches were dug in front, the inner with artillery emplacements, the outer with palisades and thorn hedges. Archimedes used five tall pylons in his defenses at Euryalus to defend the approaches and cover the ditches.

Rome

Roman defenses along the Rhine consisted of auxiliary and legionary forts, supported by signal and watch towers. The Danube defenses included a ditch and palisade (sometimes replaced by a wall and turrets) running from Bonn to Regensburg.

In Britain, Hadrian built a wall from east to west, 75 miles long, with 80 mile castles, about 160 turrets, and a fort every 5 or 6 miles. The walls of Pompeii, destroyed in AD 79 , are backed by an earth rampart, and appear to have had wing walls, where special buttresses protected archers.

Roman cities often had D-shaped towers that flanked gates; Philo of Byzantium suggests gypsum walls at least 15 feet thick and 30 feet high. Battlements might have had temporary timber wall-walks that could be removed to prevent an attacker reaching the wall top. Curtain walls were about 90 feet from houses to allow space for siege engines, reinforcements, and trenches if necessary.

In about 30 BC Herod the Great built Masada in Israel rather like a medieval fortress, on high ground for the protection of himself and his followers.

The Celts

In western Europe the Celts built communal hill forts, either using the natural defenses to cut off a section with ditches and ramparts, or by surrounding the compound with them, as at Maiden Castle in Dorset, England. In Gaul, Julius Caesar described cities protected by strong walls of stone and earth. In Scotland broch forts have stone towers with battered plinths, some of which may be prehistoric. The best preserved is at Mousa in Shetland. At Tarragona, Spain, impressive Celtic walls, gateways, and towers may date to 210 BC.

above: Reconstruction Clickhimin Broch, Shetland, as it would have looked early in the 1st century AD.

Byzantium

As the Eastern Roman Empire, the Byzantines used their inherited skills to produce an awesome defense system around Constantinople in the fifth century. The landward walls are up to 25 feet thick. A 60-foot moat that could be flooded with pipes led to a low wall, behind which was a 27-foot wall set with towers, 192 in total. Towers in the third line of walls were 70 feet high.

Anglo-Saxons and Vikings

The Saxons and Vikings used ditches and palisades to surround towns and to build defensive enclosures called burhs. These were communal structures, their upkeep and defense a part of a service agreed by the king.

Carolingians

The Franks, who settled in western Europe after the Romans, gradually built an empire under Charlemagne. Aping Rome, they produced large palaces such as Aachen, or Ingelheim, shaped like a basilica with colonnaded internal galleries. Square forts were used in wars against the Saxons, smaller successors to Roman buildings.

below: Hadrian's wall, built between AD 122 and 130, spans the north of Britain from Bowness-on-Solway in the east to Wallsend on the Tyne in the west.

Chapter Two:

Gazetteer

Building a Castle

The construction of a castle required planning and the marshalling of great numbers of men and materials. Stone and brick castles called for enormous expenditure, financially for the workforce and materials, and physically to bring everything to the ordained building site-which was often in enemy territory. Yet this was achieved time and again.

The first task was to choose a suitable site. Wherever possible, natural advantages were utilized, hence we find many castles on hilltops, cliffs, or mountain crags. A rock foundation was always best, for it deterred enemies from mining underneath. Rivers not only offered the opportunity of a moat, again deterring mining, they were also a lifeline during sieges and an obstacle in themselves. If there was good pasture or woodland nearby, even better.

Selection of the site devolved to the lord, perhaps with his knights and masons. Some master masons built impressive reputations, such as Master James of St. George, who for a long time worked for Edward I on his castles in north Wales.

A formal ceremony normally signaled the choosing of a site. On rare occasions the plan for a new castle survives, though sometimes the masons simply appear to have worked from measurements. Usually the cost of labor and materials fell to the lord, though the mason might pay for some of the latter.

Freemasons would cut squared ashlar, moldings, and tracery; roughmasons usually laid stone, while layers built walls and hewers worked in the quarries. Diggers were necessary to create the ditch or moat.

A lord might also employ: miners, quarriers, hodmen, carpenters, woodcutters, hammerers, levelers, foundation workers, well-diggers, fencing workers, lime-burners, mortar-makers, porters, smiths, plasterers, glass-makers, ditchers, carters, carriers, barrow-men, water-carriers, and pickaxe-men. On a large castle the numbers of workmen could run to

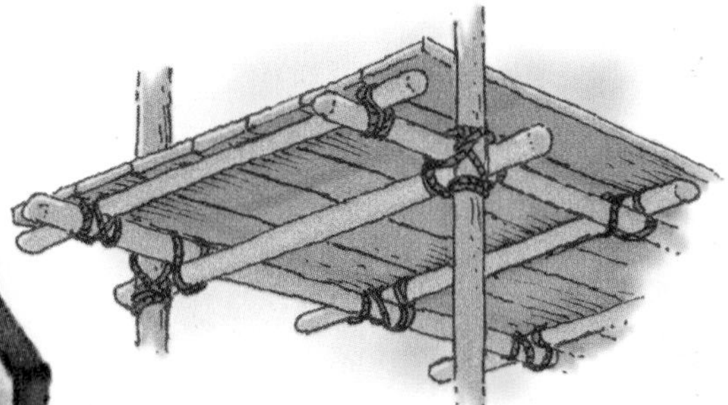

left: Builders at work, from a 14th-century manuscript.

The Celts

In western Europe the Celts built communal hill forts, either using the natural defenses to cut off a section with ditches and ramparts, or by surrounding the compound with them, as at Maiden Castle in Dorset, England. In Gaul, Julius Caesar described cities protected by strong walls of stone and earth. In Scotland broch forts have stone towers with battered plinths, some of which may be prehistoric. The best preserved is at Mousa in Shetland. At Tarragona, Spain, impressive Celtic walls, gateways, and towers may date to 210 BC.

Byzantium

As the Eastern Roman Empire, the Byzantines used their inherited skills to produce an awesome defense system around Constantinople in the fifth century. The landward walls are up to 25 feet thick. A 60-foot moat that could be flooded with pipes led to a low wall, behind which was a 27-foot wall set with towers, 192 in total. Towers in the third line of walls were 70 feet high.

Anglo-Saxons and Vikings

The Saxons and Vikings used ditches and palisades to surround towns and to build defensive enclosures called burhs. These were communal structures, their upkeep and defense a part of a service agreed by the king.

Carolingians

The Franks, who settled in western Europe after the Romans, gradually built an empire under Charlemagne. Aping Rome, they produced large palaces such as Aachen, or Ingelheim, shaped like a basilica with colonnaded internal galleries. Square forts were used in wars against the Saxons, smaller successors to Roman buildings.

above: Reconstruction Clickhimin Broch, Shetland, as it would have looked early in the 1st century AD.

below: Hadrian's wall, built between AD 122 and 130, spans the north of Britain from Bowness-on-Solway in the east to Wallsend on the Tyne in the west.

Chapter Two:

Gazetteer

Building a Castle

The construction of a castle required planning and the marshalling of great numbers of men and materials. Stone and brick castles called for enormous expenditure, financially for the workforce and materials, and physically to bring everything to the ordained building site-which was often in enemy territory. Yet this was achieved time and again.

The first task was to choose a suitable site. Wherever possible, natural advantages were utilized, hence we find many castles on hilltops, cliffs, or mountain crags. A rock foundation was always best, for it deterred enemies from mining underneath. Rivers not only offered the opportunity of a moat, again deterring mining, they were also a lifeline during sieges and an obstacle in themselves. If there was good pasture or woodland nearby, even better.

Selection of the site devolved to the lord, perhaps with his knights and masons. Some master masons built impressive reputations, such as Master James of St. George, who for a long time worked for Edward I on his castles in north Wales.

A formal ceremony normally signaled the choosing of a site. On rare occasions the plan for a new castle survives, though sometimes the masons simply appear to have worked from measurements. Usually the cost of labor and materials fell to the lord, though the mason might pay for some of the latter.

Freemasons would cut squared ashlar, moldings, and tracery; roughmasons usually laid stone, while layers built walls and hewers worked in the quarries. Diggers were necessary to create the ditch or moat.

A lord might also employ: miners, quarriers, hodmen, carpenters, woodcutters, hammerers, levelers, foundation workers, well-diggers, fencing workers, lime-burners, mortar-makers, porters, smiths, plasterers, glass-makers, ditchers, carters, carriers, barrow-men, water-carriers, and pickaxe-men. On a large castle the numbers of workmen could run to

left: Builders at work, from a 14th-century manuscript.

nearly 3,000. Though some labor services were customarily required in some areas, paid work was usual.

Timber and Stone

Wood was copiously used. Shuttering for molding concrete, roofs, beams, and flooring, doors, window shutters, and room paneling-all were made from wood, as was all scaffolding. Holes in the walls-putlog holes-were left for the insertion of scaffolding beams, and below battlements for wooden hoarding. Spiral scaffolding was brought to England from Savoy by Edward I's masons.

Where timber was not used, stone was the most common material. Occasionally stone from ditches could be used for buildings, but usually local material was only fit for use in rubble walls. Dressed stone (ashlar) had to be quarried elsewhere and brought to the site by wagon or boat.

Limestone from Caen in Normandy was very popular in northern France and England. Such dressed stone was often used for corners, windows, and other areas where carving was required. Brick was increasingly seen in the later Middle Ages, especially in low-lying areas where there was plenty of clay.

above: A hoist raises building materials to the top of a tower in an illustration from Conrad Lycothenes's *Prodigiorum ac ostentorum chronicon*, Basel, 1557.

The bonding agent was made from sand, lime, and water, the lime sometimes prepared on-site by burning limestone. Iron was needed for nails and tools, some of which were of steel. Plaster was used for interiors, as occasionally was window glass.

Often the outer and inner skin of a wall was of fine blocks, the middle filled with rubble and mortar. Some ashlar blocks have mason's marks cut into them. Particularly in the 11th century, walls were built around a framework of poles.

Workmen's tools differed little from those in use today. A block-and-tackle or a treadmill-driven windlass hoisted stone and timber. Timber piles were driven into the ground with a ram, or a raft of timbers was constructed on soft ground.

A large castle could take between two and ten years to build, and often was extended over the centuries. Costs varied; some programs, such as that of Edward I in Wales, cost nearly £100,000, when his most successful tax was rated at £116,000.

left: Forms of timber scaffolding used by castle builders. Horizontal beams were inserted into putlog holes, which can still be seen in many castles. The spiral (helicoidal) scaffolding shown bottom center was introduced into Wales and England from Savoy in the reign of Edward I (1272–1307).

France

The First Castles

The death of Charlemagne and disagreements of his heirs threw France into disarray. Vulnerable to attack, command was given to lords and their knights, who gathered their forces in *castella*—the first castles.

this page: View of a typical motte-and-bailey castle.

In AD 800 Charlemagne, king of the Franks, was crowned Emperor by the Pope. His domain stretched across much of western and central Europe and down into northern Italy. After Charlemagne died in 814, his sons and grandsons squabbled over their inheritances and the government began to splinter. The great lords, dukes, counts, bishops, and abbots could not control their large estates. Into this chaos came Hungarians and Saracens from the east and south, and Vikings from Scandinavia.

Faced with Viking ships that were rowed up rivers in hit-and-run raids, the people in northwest France found it pointless to appeal to their governor or king for aid. By the time he could even be located, the enemy was long gone. Local government and defense therefore devolved to local lords, themselves companions, vassals, or relatives of the great men, bound by ties of loyalty and land. These seigneurs gathered bodies of warriors, some of whom received land (fiefs) for service, or lived with their master at his expense-the first knights.

The lord's home, his *castellanie*, where local government and justice was carried out and where many of his troopers lived, was defended by earthworks and timber palisades: *castella*, the first castles. Already in 864 Charles the Bald, king of the West Franks, banned castle construction without his permission and ordered the destruction of *castella* and *firmitates* (fortifications).

Gradually castles spread, as lords sought to protect themselves and their people; peasants were important, since their labors in the fields brought food to the military table. This structure of society, bound by ties of land and loyalty, with the castle and mounted knight a prominent part of it, is known as feudalism.

The Motte-and-Bailey

From northwest France, the notion of the castle spread, its level of success dependent on conditions of government and terrain. The number of castles caused a real headache for the king, whose true authority was confined to the Ile-de-France until the 12th century.

800–1100	800	814	864	1000–1100	c.1200	1305–77	1316
Timber structures and earthworks are gradually replaced by castles	Frankish king Charlemagne is crowned Roman Emperor by the Pope	Death of Charlemagne and division of his empire among his descendants	Charles the Bald bans castle construction in the West Frankish lands	Ascendancy of the Normans greatly increases castle construction	Castles begin to be designed for residential comfort as well as for defensive purposes	The papacy and its monastic orders take refuge in Avignon	Construction of the fortress at Avignon is begun by Pope John XXII

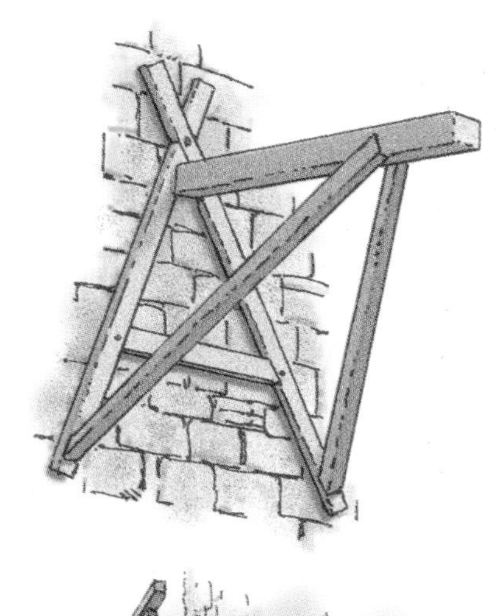

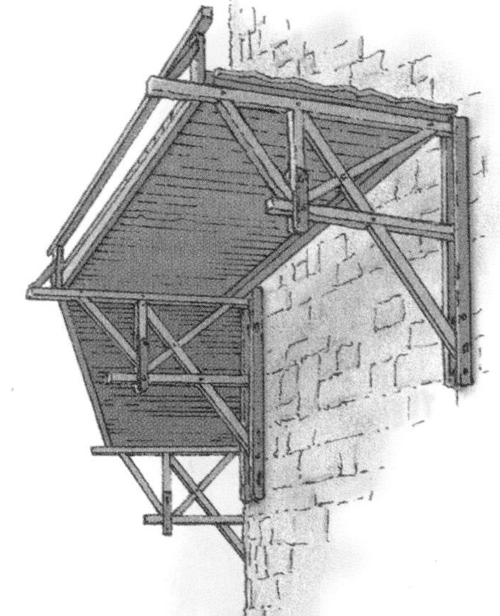

800 Frankish king Charlemagne is crowned Roman Emperor by the Pope

814 Death of Charlemagne and division of his empire among his descendants

864 Charles the Bald bans castle construction in the West Frankish lands

1000–1100 Ascendancy of the Normans greatly increases castle construction

c.1200 Castles begin to be designed for residential comfort as well as for defensive purposes

1305–77 The papacy and its monastic orders take refuge in Avignon

1316 Construction of the fortress at Avignon is begun by Pope John XXII

These first castles usually consisted of an area enclosed by a ditch, the earth from which was thrown up on the inner side to form a steep-sided bank, thus increasing the height an attacker had to climb. Along the top of the bank ran a timber palisade, made from large tree trunks rammed into the earth and fixed together. A wooden platform ran along inside to provide a wall-walk, and the space below was sometimes filled with earth to thicken the base of the palisade.

This enclosure, now known as a ring-work, was filled with the buildings a force of men required: a hall, kitchen, barns, stores, stables, animal pens, workshops for carpenters and smiths, a chapel, and a well. Most men slept on palliasses in the hall, since trestle tables and benches were cleared away at night. Even the lord might sleep with his companions; privacy was lacking and is one thing the modern visitor would notice.

At some time in the 11th century a new form of castle appeared: the motte-and-bailey. The motte—now corrupted into "moat" in English—was a mound to one side of the courtyard, though a few were inside it, as at "La Tusque" at Sainte-Eulalie d'Ambarès (Gironde). The courtyard was called the bailey (also known as the court or ward). In its elevated position, the flattened top of the motte held a watchtower, but the larger ones were probably soon used as the lord's living quarters; towers became clearly-seen symbols of lordship.

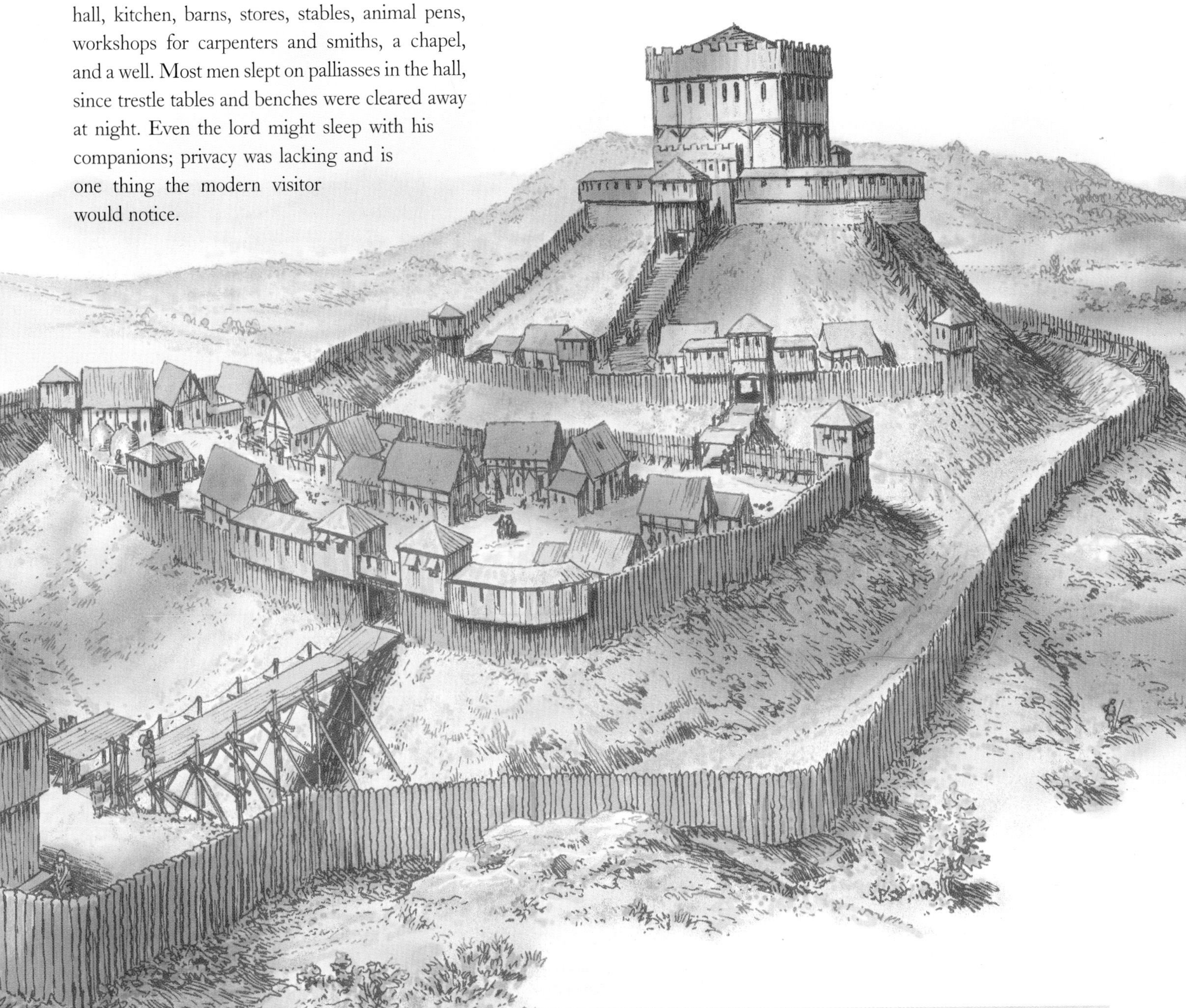

1334–52
The fortress at Avignon is extended and further fortified by successive Popes

1337
Hundred Years War breaks out between England and France

1346
Edward III defeats French at Crécy; first recorded use of cannon in battle

1348
The Black Death

1356
The Black Prince wins Battle of Poitiers

1429
Siege of Orleans by English

1431
Joan of Arc burned at Rouen

1453
Battle of Castillon. French recapture Bordeaux; Hundred Years War ends

Materials and Design

Motte-and-bailey castles became common in France. Their mounds were formed from the earth from the castle's ditch, which was rammed into layers. The motte was as much as 230 feet around the base and 49 feet around the flattened summit. Usually the lip of the summit was defended by a palisade, with a flying bridge to connect with the ground.

Earth and timber castles could be built quite readily and within a matter of months, if necessary, using timber from nearby woods or forests. However, timber could be burned. Already in the 10th century some castles contained a stone tower; surviving examples are rare, and it must be supposed that few were erected around this early date.

Stone towers took more money and time to construct; stone and a mason's skills had to be found and paid for. Few were built on a motte; an artificial mound could rarely take the great weight without settling for many years first, unless the keep's basement lay at ground level within the motte. These towers are now known as keeps, a word only used from the 17th century. Such a structure was called a "great tower" or *donjon*, a word now corrupted in English to "dungeon."

below: The top of the motte at Gisors, with the octagonal donjon rising inside the shell wall.

Doué-la-Fontaine

This stone tower, known as "La Motte," is 20 miles south of Angers. It is the earliest known stone donjon, probably the work of Theobald, Count of Blois. It was built in about AD 950 and was discovered within a later motte in excavations between 1967 and 1970.

The building original-

above: Two walls of the very early donjon at Langeais survive.

ly consisted of a ground-floor stone hall erected in about 900. When this was damaged by fire, it was converted into the surviving donjon. An upper story was added, together with a forebuilding to protect the entrance; both additions have since been lost.

The ground floor was converted into a basement and its entrances blocked off, so the castle was entered via a new first-floor entrance, a design which is essentially the forerunner of later donjons. Doué-la-Fontaine was captured in about 1025 by Fulk Nerra (the Black), Count of Anjou.

Langeais

This early tower overlooks the Loire Valley, between Tours and Saumur in Touraine (Indre-sur-Loire). The castle was built by Fulk Nerra, one of about 27 fortresses he erected. A 10th-century charter mentions a siege before the castle of Langeais.

Two walls of this rectangular tower survive, constructed typically of small stone blocks, with its first-floor entrance and evidence of residential

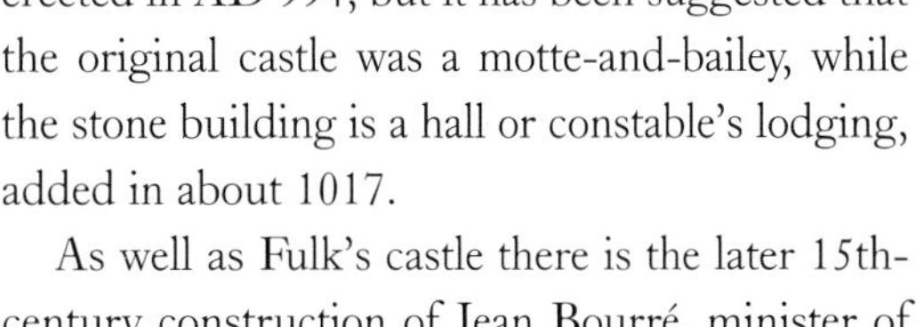

accommodation within. The tower may have been erected in AD 994, but it has been suggested that the original castle was a motte-and-bailey, while the stone building is a hall or constable's lodging, added in about 1017.

As well as Fulk's castle there is the later 15th-century construction of Jean Bourré, minister of Louis XI. This has an upper story set back from the wall-walk. Charles VIII married Anne of Brittany at Langeais in 1491.

Gisors

This, the capital of the Norman Vexin, is some 19 miles southwest of Beauvais. The Vexin was disputed territory between the Norman dukes and French Capetian kings. Gisors was founded in the 11th century, the motte built in 1096 by William Rufus, King of England and Duke of Normandy.

It was later given an elliptical shell wall, within which is an early example of an octagonal donjon, built either by Rufus's brother, Henry I (1100-35), or more probably Henry II (1154-89).

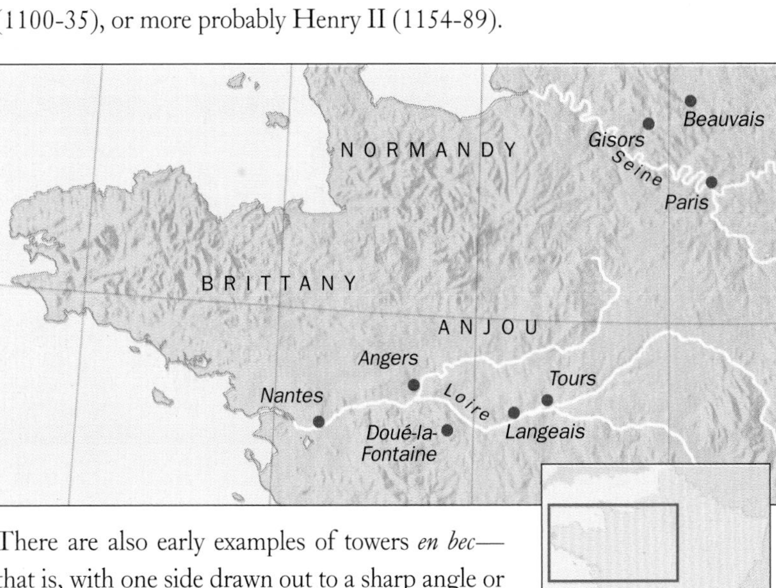

There are also early examples of towers *en bec*—that is, with one side drawn out to a sharp angle or beak. After King Philip Augustus of France took the castle in 1193 he added the great cylindrical donjon, the "Prisoners' Tower."

The Donjon, Stone Tower, or Keep

below: Plan of the donjon at Loches, seen below, rising beyond the later 12th-century walls.

In the later 11th and 12th centuries, more donjons were built in France, many by the Norman and Angevin kings of England. Their impressive size gave authority to the owner, a mark of lordship even greater that the timber castle.

They were usually constructed on flat ground and consisted of several stories, often with a vaulted basement but with timber floors above. The entrance was at first-floor level for safety and presentation, sometimes shielded by a forebuilding. The only access between floors was by spiral or straight stair in a corner turret, or sometimes by ladder.

Though some donjons were used as residences and as a last line of defense, they were equally a statement of power, used for receptions and state occasions.

Falaise

The castle at Falaise in Normandy is some 22 miles south of Caen, and was often used by the early dukes. It was here that Robert the Magnificent was said to have spied Arlette, a tanner's daughter, in the valley of the Ante, at the foot of the cliff on which the castle stands. The result of this union was William, later known as the Conqueror, born in the castle in 1027 or 1028.

One of William's sons, Henry I, built a rectangular donjon in the 1120s; the donjon at Norwich, England, is of similar but more decorated plan. After the English kings lost Normandy in 1204, Philip Augustus of France erected a cylindrical donjon next to Henry I's. Now known as the Talbot Tower, it was named after the English lord who repaired it during the Hundred Years War.

The surrounding walls date to the 13th century. Despite heavy fighting in this area, the Falaise Gap, in 1944, and a shell through the fabric of Talbot Tower, the castle has escaped major damage.

Loches

Loches, 22 miles southeast of Tours, was referred to as a fortress by Gregory of Tours in the early Middle Ages. Fulk Nerra made it a base against Blois, and the early rectangular donjon was probably begun at this time.

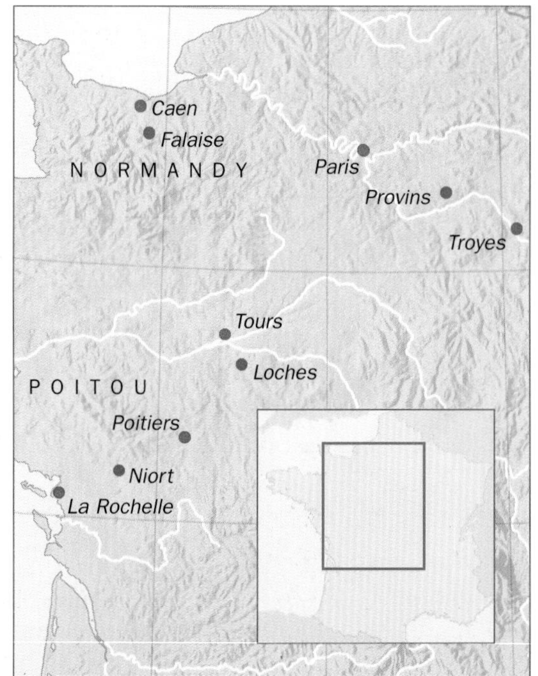

The donjon was rebuilt in the late 11th or early 12th century; it has no cross-wall but has a fore-building to guard the entrance and semi-circular external buttresses. Philip Augustus added the towers *en bec* along the curtain wall, their beaks or prows facing the field.

In the 15th century Loches became a prison. It also contains the white marble tomb of Agnès Sorel, mistress of Charles VII.

Niort

Niort stands on the River Sèvre Niortaise, between Poitiers and La Rochelle. Henry II of England built the castle in the late 12th century.

The twin towers of the double donjon were originally separate but in the 15th century a building was constructed to link them together. The southern donjon carries machicolations, in which the battlements are pushed forward beyond the wall to rest on corbels (brackets), leavings gaps through which offensive materials could be dropped on enemy soldiers at the wall face below. 18th-century drawings show that the bailey wall originally had 16 round towers.

A French force finally took the castle in 1436; in 1588, during the Wars of Religion, it was badly damaged by Protestants, despite Niort supporting the Huguenots. The northern donjon was reconstructed in the 18th century.

Provins

Provins lies between Paris and Troyes, where the Rivers Voulzie and Durteint meet. The donjon—the so-called Tower of Caesar—was built in the 12th century by Theobald, Count of Champagne. Unusually, it begins as a rectangle and rises to an octagon, as the builders sought to eliminate blind corners and lessen the weakness of right-angled corners to the enemy miner's pickaxe.

Philip IV of France (1285–1314) took the castle but it was recaptured in the 15th century during the Hundred Years War. The English destroyed neighboring houses and built the surrounding wall, known as the Pâté aux Anglais.

above: The rectangular donjon of Henry I or Henry II at Falaise stands next to the cylindrical donjon of Philip Augustus.
below: The Tower of Caesar, the donjon at Provins, with its octagonal upper section.

Curtain Walls and Mural Towers

In about 1200, French military architecture began to change direction. The demands of increasing comfort perhaps find their greatest expression in France, and gradually the residential aspect of the castle grew in importance. Finally it resulted in open castles, where the defensive element was a token consideration, while purely military fortresses appeared as an alternative.

The donjon lost its importance as a final line of defense, which was now placed on strong curtain walls that hopefully wouldn't be breached. The wall was divided into (usually straight) sections by mural towers. These jutted beyond the walls to allow archers to shoot along the wall face at enemies that got too close.

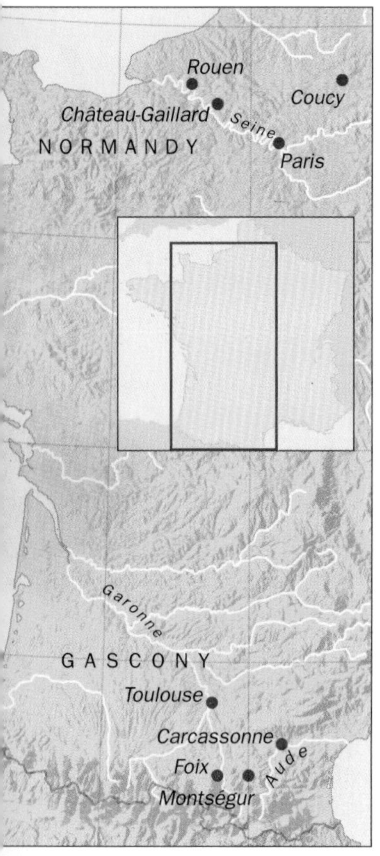

Château-Gaillard

Situated on a ridge overlooking the River Seine at the village of Les Andelys, 22 miles southeast of Rouen, Château-Gaillard (literally "Saucy Castle") was built between 1196 and 1198 by Richard I (Lionheart), to defend Normandy after losing Gisors castle to Philip Augustus of France. Richard is said to have remarked that he would hold it if it were made of butter.

The steep hillsides mean there is one main line of advance, which is cut off by a ditch. There are three courtyards, defended by curtain walls and towers, the latter being among the first circular towers in France.

Gaillard has a donjon within the third courtyard, one side drawn out to a sharp angle (*en bec*). The sides of the donjon are strengthened by thick buttresses designed to carry the battlements out from the walls to command the wall base. Each of the courtyards can help support the others with defensive fire and provide additional obstacles, making Gaillard a proto-concentric castle.

When John succeeded Richard, Philip Augustus attacked Château-Gaillard in 1203-4. As food ran short, the "useless mouths"—the old, sick, or very young—were thrown out and spent the winter in the ditches, since the French refused to let them through. Most perished.

Eventually, French soldiers entered the castle by climbing the chute of a privy, but the defenders refused to give up until forced back to the donjon. The fortress was dismantled in 1603 by order of Henry IV of France.

Montségur

Perched majestically on a crag in the Pyrenees, 20 miles east of Foix stands Montségur. Built in 1204, it consists of a donjon and a thick pentagonal curtain wall that hugs the mountain top. There are, however, two large unfortified gates

right: The concentric curtain walls of Carcassonne.

and windows, rather than arrow loops.

In 1243 a crusader army under Simon de Montfort—whose son fostered notions of parliament in England—besieged 300 Cathar heretics who had fled to Montségur, center of their faith, as their final refuge. The garrison, under Ramón de Perella, was betrayed after two months and submitted. The following year, over 200 Albigensian heretics who refused to recant were burnt at the foot of the mountain, and Montségur was dismantled.

above: The ruins of Château-Gaillard perch on the cliff above the Seine.

left: A reconstruction of Coucy, destroyed in 1917, with its great tower placed along the curtain walls.

Carcassonne

The Visigoths extended the Roman defenses around the town of Carcassonne in the fifth century. In the 13th century these were taken into consideration when a new defensive structure was put in place. A curtain wall was built, supported by round flanking towers—at this date still quite rare—but lacking the machicolated galleries that later became typical.

The gateway was defended by a turret on either side, while the Narbonne Gate has sharp projections to cover dead ground. The quadrilateral citadel was probably built between 1130 and 1150. The gatehouse has two portcullises, winched from different floors to protect from treachery. The arrow loops are placed in a pattern of five to prevent weakening of the wall.

A large semicircular barbican was later erected to guard the gate, and an outer wall added to make a perfect concentric defense. The Black Prince burnt the bourg in 1355 but left the walled city alone. The walls were heavily restored in the 19th century by Viollet-le-Duc.

Castles with Style

The 14th and 15th centuries were a time of much upheaval in France. For much of this period the Hundred Years War raged, yet both nobles and lesser lords spent large sums in building or improving their castles with a desire for comfort. Castles that were built to look attractive to the eye, proclaimed the wealth and importance of an owner who could afford to spend money on elaborate tracery and expensive gilding.

Saumur

The castle of Saumur is one such castle, set between Nantes and Tours. The original castle dates from the 10th century, in the time of Fulk Nerra, but several building programs overlie this. In the late 14th century the Duke of Berry carried out the most important works.

The castle was decorated with particular attention to the upper areas, which were covered with Gothic tracery, flying turrets, and golden weathercocks. We are fortunate that a book of hours belonging to the duke, the *Trés Riches Heures*, still survives, which illustrates Saumur on the page for September. The castle can be seem as it might originally have looked, one of the most luxurious examples in France.

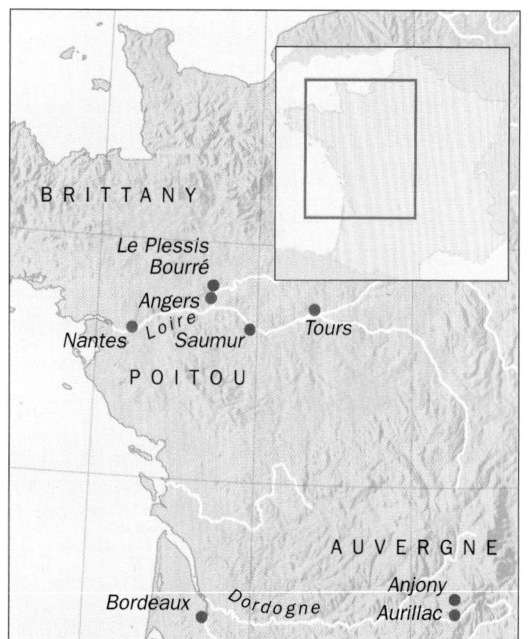

above: Saumur stills retains much of its elegant 14th century architecture.

The golden weathercocks and fleurs-de-lys atop the merlons are now gone but the illustration allows us to see the castle as it was intended to look—like something out of a fairytale. The windows were filled with clear and stained glass, chambers paneled and hung with tapestries, or else painted with devices.

Saumur was abandoned in the 17th century when the west wing collapsed, after which it became a prison followed by a barracks. Today it houses a museum containing tapestries and ceramics.

Anjony

Another type of castle appeared during the 14th century, with high walls, four closely set corner towers, and, occasionally, another carrying the stair. They could be built on a massive scale, and represented a nobleman's version of the many fortified dwellings of the time.

Anjony, near the little town of Tournemire in the Auvergne, is one of the best examples of this type. It was built on a promontory between 1435 and 1439 for Louis II of Anjony, companion in arms of Joan of Arc, though a 14th-century date has also been proposed.

The rectangular tower with cylindrical corner towers has a basement with gun loops and a chapel on the ground floor at the southwest corner. The second, principal floor, is a vaulted great hall, and machicolated battlements border a *chemin de ronde* (covered way). In about 1525, Louis III of Anjony added a work at the front of the castle, the platform of which probably carried artillery.

Le Plessis-Bourré

With the end of the Hundred Years War in 1453 there was an increase in the provision of luxurious living accommodation. There were still numerous towers, often with machicolations and strong walls. Indeed, some castles, such as Le Plessis-Bourré, were equipped with provisions for state-of-the-art artillery.

Situated at Ecuillé, 12 miles north of Angers, Le Plessis-Bourré was acquired by Jean Bourré, minister to Louis XI in 1462. Bourré was interested in the development of artillery and sought to provide his castles with up-to-date defenses.

The castle is very uniform, occupying a platform set in a very wide moat, and is designed to accommodate artillery. The battlements are not machicolated, this feature considered obsolete by now. Instead, a low terrace was provided on the inner bank of the moat to allow cannons to be positioned on it.

Inside, however, the castle is fitted for comfort and luxurious living, decorated in a way that foreshadows the later Renaissance chateaux. The decoration is enhanced by an early 16th century decorated ceiling.

above: The high walls and close-set towers at Anjony

below: Le Plessis-Bourré has a more utilitarian appearance and was built to take artillery that could keep attackers well back from the wide moat.

French Palaces

Royal fortresses became increasingly comfortable as the Middle Ages wore on. The separation of residential and defensive elements became more noticeable in those castles held from the king.

Vincennes

The royal palace of Vincennes lies in the Ile-de-France, 1.25 miles east of the Porte de Vincennes, Paris. The first buildings belonged to a royal hunting lodge; the construction of the castle was begun by Philip VI in the early 14th century. King John of France was followed in the 1360s by Charles V, who spent a great deal of time and effort to turn the castle into a comfortable home.

The six-story donjon has a massive battered plinth and four round corner turrets, being divided internally into four equal vaulted rooms, with wood paneling even to the vaults. There are two tiers of battlements and a turret for the privies.

It is set within a *chemise* with a splayed base, sitting in a moat astride a break in the line of a curtain wall that runs with mathematical precision around an enormous rectangular courtyard, 1,096 by 604 feet . The latter is set with nine rectangular mural towers and large square corner towers, which have been likened to donjons. Of these, only the Tour de Village, the main entrance, remains to its full height. It has two drawbridges, one for carts and one for foot traffic.

Plan of Vincennes

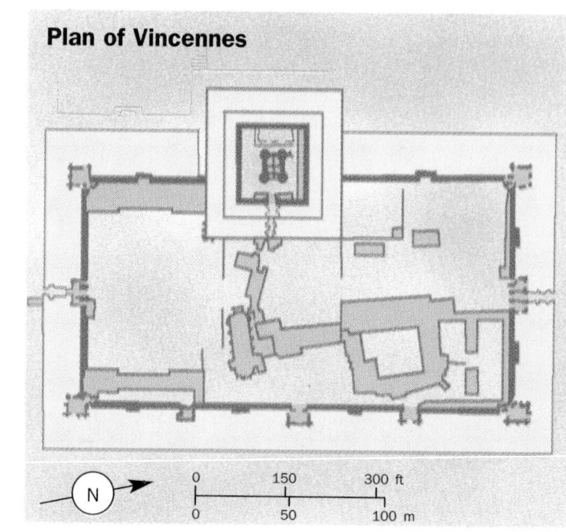

There are no flanking towers on the donjon side, to prevent an enemy who has seized a tower from using it to attack the donjon itself. However, the square moat in which it sits is a weak spot, and was seen as such by Jacques de Chabanne when he recaptured it from the English in 1432. The donjon appears to have been a private residence for the king; its gatehouse housed his library, while the ample courtyard space is for his following, or even a small army.

Vincennes appears in the *Très Riches Heures* book owned by John, Duc de Berry. Several royal personages, including Louis X, Charles IV, and Charles IX of France, died here, as did Henry V of England after contracting dysentery at the siege of Meaux. Mazarin also died within its walls. It was later used as a prison for such persons as Bonnie Prince Charlie and Diderot.

Ambois

Ambois is situated on a rocky plateau on the Loire, between Tours and Blois. The first fortress was built here by the Franks, but the castle as it survives today was constructed by Charles VIII of France, who rebuilt it before his death in 1498.

This castle is designed much more as a residence than as a fortress. In 1560 King Francis II sheltered at Ambois against a vain Huguenot attempt to capture him. Like a number of castles, Ambois became a prison, latterly becoming the residence of the Compte (controller) de Paris.

Avignon

Avignon was created during the period of "Babylonian imprisonment" (1305-77), when the papacy took refuge in southern France and surrounded itself with the cardinals' residences, monastic orders, and the university. It is one of the most important fortresses of the period.

Begun by Pope John XXII in 1316, it was extended by Benedict XII (1334-42) and again by Clement VI (1342-52). The first group of buildings comprises a square of domestic rooms, including several large halls, around a court of Italian style. Benedict built a huge rectangular tower on the south side of the complex as a private residence, while rectangular towers set into the walls guard the palace. Pointed-arch machicolations are used, the buttresses of the battlements reaching the ground, while the arches localize any undermining of the fabric.

Clement's new palace involved a larger courtyard to the southeastern side surrounded by buildings, of which the large audience hall and chapel are the most notable. Two towers have some of the earliest stone machicolation in France.

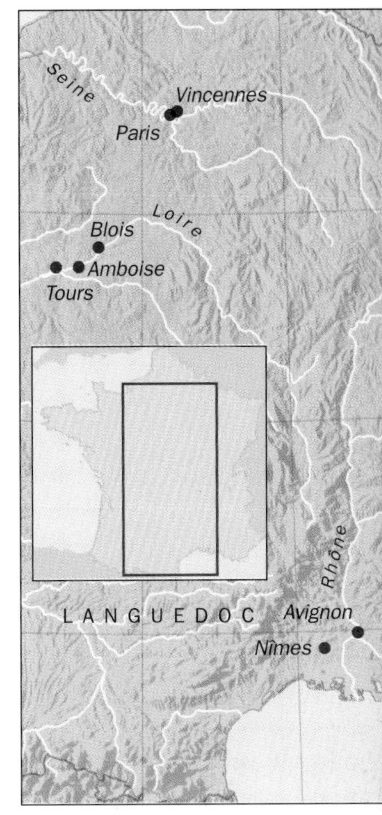

facing: View and plan of the royal palace of Vincennes.

left: The extended fortress of Avignon, and above, a plan of the Papal Palace.

Raising the Walls

From the end of the 14th century perhaps the greatest change in the construction of French castles was in the height of the curtain walls. They began to equal that of the mural towers—over 30 feet—probably as a counter-measure against ladders and artillery.

Because this meant that battlements were now on a similar level to towers, wall-walks were usually roofed and extended all the way around the castle, facilitating swift movement of the defenders. Machicolations sometimes ran right around the castle, being more common in French military architecture than elsewhere. Outworks and outer walls were no longer popular.

The raising of the walls made it easier to add stories to residential buildings within the walls. Square or rectangular great towers (as opposed to cylindrical) again found favor, as the convenience of comfortable living began to take precedence over defense. Walls were pierced with windows for light and air, and spiral stairs became common, but it was becoming increasingly difficult to balance the elements of defense and dwelling.

below: A 19th-century painting by Paul Huet shows Pierrefonds as it might have been.

Pierrefonds

This large castle in the Oise region was built between 1390 and 1407 for Louis of Orléans, brother of Charles VI of France, which, together with his other castles, allowed him to threaten Paris from the east and northeast and acted as a breakwater against any Burgundian threat. Jean Lenoir undertook the work.

Sited in a marshy area to hamper attackers, in

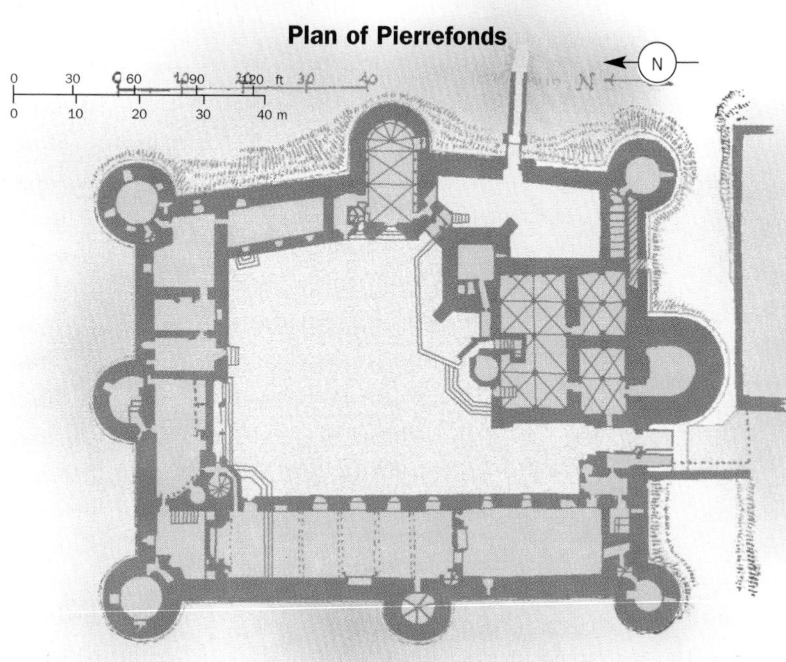

plan Pierrefonds is almost rectangular; the curtain wall has angle-towers and further towers along the other walls. Nearly all the towers are round, with sculpted decoration to relieve their heaviness. As walls match the height of the towers, a machicolated covered gallery projects from the curtain wall slightly below the covered wall-walk, with similar galleries on the towers, forming a continuous line around the castle walls. In this way Pierrefonds' firepower capability was noticeably increased.

As at Vincennes and Tarascon, the residential rooms are separated from the defenses. There are narrow living areas on three sides, while on the entrance side a large house jutted out, which included the duke's private residence. The castle was much restored in the 19th century for Napoleon III (a castle lover who also reconstructed trebuchets) by Viollet-le-Duc, who produced a spectacular result, if something of a medieval fantasy in design.

Tarascon

Situated on the rocks on the River Rhône below Avignon in Bouches-du-Rhône, Tarascon as it survives today was begun in the late 14th century by Louis II of Anjou, Count of Provence. King René of Anjou made additions early in the following century.

Tarascon's design was influenced by the Bastille in Paris, improved with a wider roof platform to give greater mobility to troops. The curtain wall was raised to that of the flanking towers, and so provided a continuous wall-walk. Most of the towers are rectangular and the walls received machicolations, which have been restored.

Inside, the rooms were designed for comfortable living; however, the larger windows that resulted would always be a weakness, despite the iron grilles secured through the 10-foot thick walls. The frontage pierced with windows looks out onto the river, and a postern leads to the bank. Unlike in the palace of Vincennes, the separation of the living quarters from the rest of the castle does not weaken the outer defenses.

Across the river stands the strange triangular 12th-century donjon of Beaucare, modernized later in the Middle Ages. The castle of Tarascon passed to the king in 1481, and was later used as a prison (until 1926). It has since been restored.

below: Tarascon, showing the high walls and reconstructed machicolations.

Artillery Comes of Age

At first, the advent of gunpowder in the first half of the 14th century did little to alter the design of castles. Early manuscript illustrations show vase-shaped cannons that fired four-sided arrows rather than balls. This could only have been of use against men venturing out of a gate or sortie passage. Within a century cannon had improved rapidly and were a force to be reckoned with.

Kings and powerful lords, like the Duke of Burgundy, had numerous pieces in their artillery train, including massive siege weapons called bombards, some of which could hurl stone shot weighing 330lb or more. French architects responded quickly to counter this threat, but obvious changes in style did not appear until the 15th century. The easiest response was to add gunports low down in castle walls, but gradually new forms of fortress evolved to counter flying cannonballs.

Bonaguil

Situated 15 miles west of Cahors, Bonaguil stands on a rocky outcrop overlooking two valleys. Begun in the 13th century by the de la Tour family, it has a narrow pentagonal donjon built on a slim spur of stonework, further reinforcing its base; the sharp angle juts out on the north side. The thick curtain wall was provided with round corner towers.

The Hundred Years War left the first castle in ruins. In 1483 it passed to Bérenger de Roquefeuil, who began to restore it to provide a home worthy of his position, and to bring the defenses up to date. These included new towers, with gun loops set low down to enable small cannons to blast the ground in front. A great round tower 90 feet high competes with the donjon. A *caponiere* (stone pillbox) was built in the moat, to sweep it of attackers. An impressive buttressed artillery terrace was added to the north side and a long vaulted casemated passage to the south side, in which 104 loopholes survive.

Ironically, much of this modernization was unnecessary, since there was little chance of

left: The 15th-century great tower on the left replaced the pentagonal donjon at Bonaguil, while low casemates extend to the right.

below: Crouching in its ditches, the low walls of Salses attest to the response to artillery siege trains.

Bonaguil being attacked. Nonetheless, it was a forerunner of the great artillery strongholds of Vauban in the 17th century.

Comfort is evident from the molded decoration on fireplaces and mullioned windows, but the castle gradually fell into ruin, until bought and restored by Marguerite de Fumel in 1761. A huge esplanade to the west was built with stone obtained by lowering the outer ramparts. After her death, the walls were lowered by government decree; the ruin was bought by the town of Fumel in 1860 and restored two years later.

Salses

Salses (or Salces), near Perpignan, was built by a Spanish engineer, Ramirez, for Ferdinand II of Aragon, who in 1497 set out to defend the rights of his countrymen to Rossillon. In a siege in 1503, French artillery destroyed all the upper parts of the defenses, but before they could complete their victory a Spanish relief force arrived. During a truce the Spanish repaired the castle in the form it still retains.

This was a new design for castles, a low thick wall flanked by wide, low bastions enabling cannons to be mounted. They were connected to the main building by vaulted underground galleries. The lower walls presented less of a target to artillery pieces, while their thickness was designed to absorb enemy cannon fire. Lower walls also meant that their guns were sited at a more practical level for firing at an enemy position or raking enemy troops. The whole castle appears almost half sunk into the ground, as if hiding in its ditch.

Chapter Three: Gazetteer—England

The Castle Comes to England

England's landscape was transformed by the arrival of William the Conqueror, who planted a series of castles across the country to secure dominance. Civil wars and threats from over the borders and across the sea prompted further developments.

below: The mid-13th-century gatehouse leading into the castle within the Roman fort at Pevensey.

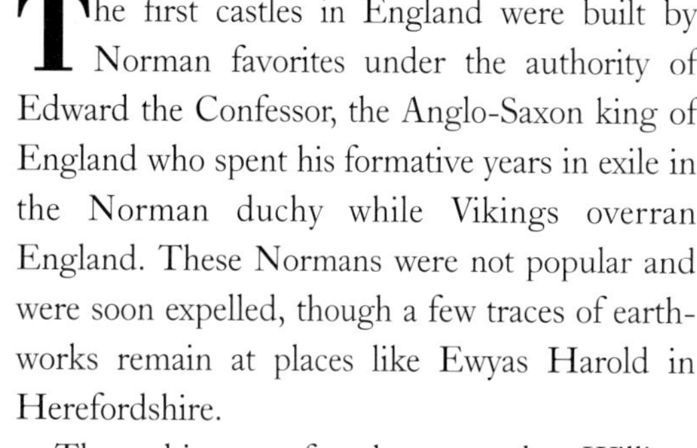

The first castles in England were built by Norman favorites under the authority of Edward the Confessor, the Anglo-Saxon king of England who spent his formative years in exile in the Norman duchy while Vikings overran England. These Normans were not popular and were soon expelled, though a few traces of earthworks remain at places like Ewyas Harold in Herefordshire.

The real impact of castles came when William the Conqueror staked his claim to the crown on the death of Edward and accession of Harold II in 1066. One of William's first acts upon landing was to place a castle—brought over in prefabricated parts, according to a 12th-century chronicler—in the Roman ruins at Pevensey.

A second castle was built at Hastings, though whether the present mound was part of William's castle is unknown; a motte is certainly depicted on the Bayeux Tapestry, which William's half-brother, Bishop Odo, commissioned within 20 years of the Battle of Hastings. As William moved around the country, putting down revolts, he sited castles. Towns such as Warwick, Nottingham, and Stafford were given a castle. York, which revolted three times in three years, received two castles.

1066	1078	1085	1087	1135–54	1154–89	1215	1282–84
Williams the Conqueror constructs first English Norman castle at Pevensey	Construction of the Tower of London begins	Construction of Ludlow castle on border with Wales, the "Welsh Marches"	The Domesday Book compiled, the first census in medieval Europe	Period of civil war in England; many unlicensed castles constructed	Henry II founds Plantaganet dynasty and controls most of France and England	King John signs the Magna Carta	Edward I conquers Wales and adopts Welsh longbow as key English weapon

The earth and timber fortifications were quick to build, utilizing local labor. Soon enclosures (ringworks) and motte-and-bailey castles sprang up in quantity. During the civil wars of Stephen's reign (1135–54) many unlicensed castles were built—many of which were pulled down when Henry II succeeded to the throne.

At the same time, a few stone towers, such as those at the Tower of London and Colchester in Essex, began to be erected within a bailey, as much symbols of the new order as defensive buildings. Under the Norman and Angevin kings, notably Henry I (1100–35) and Henry II (1154–89), such towers became much more common, although sometimes replacing the palisades around an existing motte with stone sufficed. Few were placed on such artificial mounds for fear of subsidence; Clifford's Tower, placed on one of the mottes at York in the mid-13th century, has cracked.

Luxury defeats castles

The Angevin Empire of Henry II stretched from Scotland to the Pyrenees, but by 1204 Normandy was lost. The barons struggled against King John and again in the civil wars of Henry III and Simon de Montfort mid-century, an incentive to build or improve castles. Henry's son, Edward I, was a great castle-builder and directed much of his energy to Wales. Many of the aristocracy found themselves in armies marching in wars against the Welsh and Scots.

Thereafter England suffered relatively little unrest. Dynastic problems were few and the main threats came from Scotland, Wales, and France. Many men were embroiled in the Hundred Years War (1337–1453) in France, during which more comfortable castles were built, such as Bolton, with its rectangular plan and numerous rooms.

After the English lost their French possessions, the struggles of the houses of York and Lancaster erupted in the Wars of the Roses, which only effectively ended with the victory of the Tudor Henry VII over Richard III at Bosworth in 1485, and which gave new incentive for security. However, by this date many men of property preferred to live in relative comfort than to invest heavily in defense. With the Tudors still wary of baronial revolt, any hint of treachery was stamped on mercilessly.

By this date castles were becoming an anachronism over much of England, but they had a role in the north and west, where raiding could occur. In the south, Henry VIII planted forts along the coast, filled with cannons to face any threat from France or Spain.

below: The 13th-century quatrefoil tower on the Norman motte at Clifford's Tower, York.

1290
Jews are expelled from England

1330
Edward III leads a party of nobles against his mother, Queen Isabella

1330–76
Lifetime of Edward, Prince of Wales (the Black Prince)

1337–1453
English monarchy tries to keep French domains in Hundred Years' War

1381
Peasants' Revolt ends with killing of its leader, Wat Tyler

1455
Wars of the Roses breaks out between rival Lancaster and York dynasties

1485
Battle of Bosworth ends Wars of the Roses; start of Tudor dynasty

1534
Act of Supremacy is passed, making Henry VIII head of English Church

Earthwork Castles

Earth and timber castles were erected all over England after the Norman Conquest and even into the 13th century. Some were simple ringworks but many were of the motte-and-bailey style. Only a few have been thoroughly excavated, but they allow a reconstruction which reveals that the bailey was often crowded with buildings, a very different picture to how such castles have been depicted in the past.

Pleshey

Situated near High Easter in Essex, Pleshey has a large, kidney-shaped bailey with a motte at one side. It was built for Geoffrey de Mandeville after the Norman Conquest as the center (caput) of his honor or lordship. "Pleshey" comes from the French "le pleissie," meaning an enclosure, the fortified town having grown up with the new castle beside it.

The motte is made from rammed layers of earth and 49 feet high; the bailey has a rampart 39 feet high, possibly refortified in the 12th century. A 15th-century brick bridge still connects the motte and bailey, as a timber example would have done earlier. There may have been another bailey to the north, perhaps an earlier feature.

right: The barbican leading to the original gate tower at Restormel.

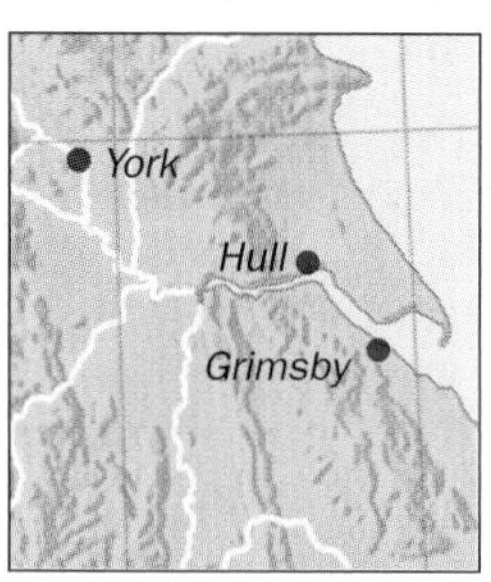

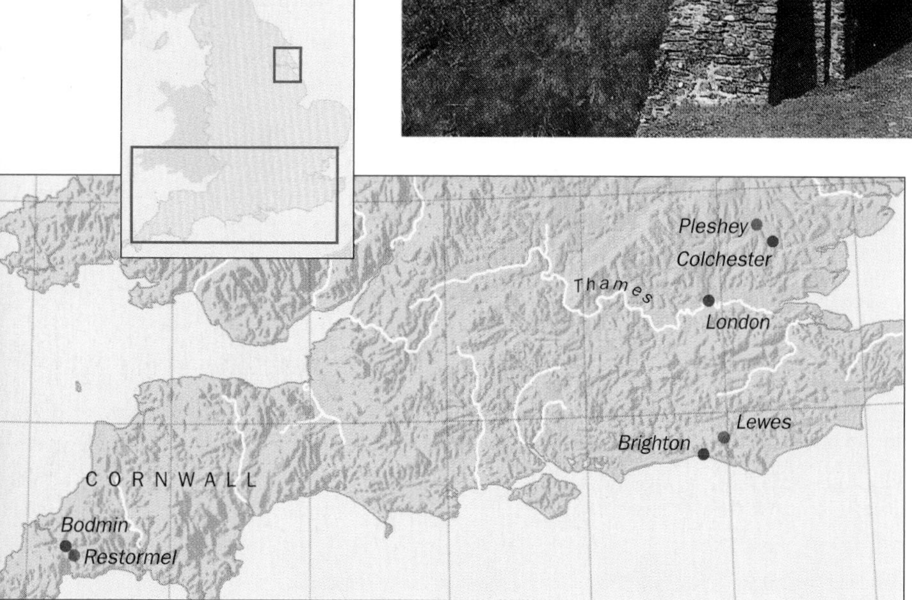

The castle remained in use until the end of the Middle Ages, having first been taken over by the Bohuns, Earls of Hereford, then Thomas of Woodstock, Duke of Gloucester and uncle of Richard II, and finally by the duchy of Lancaster.

Lewes

On the south coast of Sussex, Lewes castle was built within the old English burh, or communal fortification, by the new Norman lord, William of

Warenne, later Earl of Surrey. Lewes is unusual in having two mottes, to the south and north. Only Lincoln has a similar arrangement in England. The second motte may well be the result of dual lordship, in this case that of William's wife, the lady Gundreda.

The northern motte (Brack Mount) is in poor condition but still bears traces of a shell keep on the summit. The southern motte is much better preserved, with a late 11th- or early 12th-century shell keep, complete with herring-bone stonework. Two semi-octagonal towers were added later and there is evidence for residential apartments around the inner face of the keep walls. A gatehouse (probably 11th century) survives with a machicolated barbican in front, erected by John of Warenne before his death in 1347. The castle passed to the fitzAlans, but gradually declined, to be partially dismantled in the 17th century.

York

A castle was raised at York by William I in 1068 and, after a revolt in 1069, a second on the other side of the River Ouse, now overgrown but still visible. Both were burned in the revolt of 1069, and William only rebuilt one. In 1190 it was consumed by fire, together with the Jews of York, who were sheltering in it. The rare quatrefoil tower now visible on the motte was built c.1250 and became a headquarters in the early 14th-century Scottish wars. The danger of building on an artificial mound is visible in the cracked walls.

In 1322 Roger de Clifford and other rebels were hung from the walls in chains by Edward II, and latterly the structure became known as Clifford's Tower. York castle was battered by cannons in the English civil wars and burned in 1684, after which it slowly fell into decay.

Restormel

Restormel lies on a spur above the River Fowey in Cornwall. It was built soon after the Norman Conquest and held by Turstin, the Sheriff of Robert, Count of Mortain, half-brother to William the Conqueror.

The bailey had an inner circular ringwork with high banks above the ditch. A gate tower of about 1100 is joined by a ringwall, perhaps late 12th-century, around the top of the circular bank. In the late 13th century a projecting barbican was added, together with the rooms inside the enclosure: kitchen with buttery and pantry, hall, solar, chapel and ante-chapel, and two chamber blocks—residential areas for lord and family.

The castle fell into decay soon after 1362 and, despite attempts to utilize it during the English Civil War, Parliamentary forces decided that it was not worth demolishing.

below: Lewes castle has two mottes, one with a surviving shell keep and 13th-century towers, plus a 14th-century barbican.

Hall Keeps and Tower Keeps

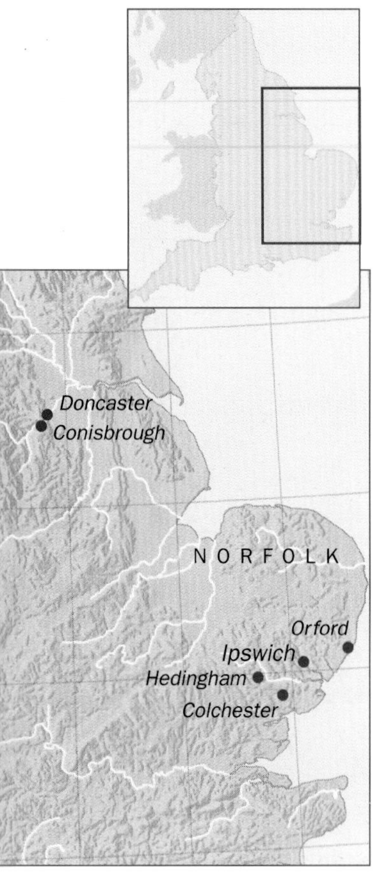

Stone towers or donjons were first seen in England after the Norman Conquest but were relatively rare in this period. The first towers usually had a large floor area compared to their height and have been called hall keeps. Most had cross-walls dividing the interior into two unequal halves, to alleviate the problem of spanning a large area with a single wooden ceiling or roof beam. This created two rooms on each floor, usually identified as a hall with adjoining chamber.

Later towers were taller in relation to their area and many had no cross-wall. Such buildings are known as tower keeps, which are often modest in size. It is probable that a number of these donjons were for appearance only; some tower keeps are too small for practical use. Others may have been private suites for lords.

Colchester

This early hall keep in Essex was built on the foundations of a Roman temple to their emperor, Claudius, the temple itself built within a British stronghold. It is one of the largest keeps, being about 170 by 145 feet, yet only two stories survive and it may never have possessed more. Many Roman bricks were reused by the workmen, and the keep is very like the White Tower in the Tower of London, possibly built by the same master mason.

below: The early Norman donjon at Colchester is one of the largest and is similar to that in the Tower of London in many respects

It was begun in about 1080, probably for Odo, half-brother to the Conqueror. The entrance has been moved to the ground floor. The castle was fought over during the civil wars of King John's reign (1199–1216). Inside, the keep is subdivided by a cross-wall into two very unequal rooms, with further, small rooms formed by thick walls on the south side, near the basement of the chapel.

Hedingham

This tower keep in Essex, standing within earthworks, is all that remains of a castle built c.1140 for Aubrey de Vere, first Earl of Oxford, apart from a bridge across the ditch, constructed in 1496. There is a storage basement reached only by a spiral stair and two residential floors above. The entrance passes through a now-ruined forebuilding to the first floor.

On each floor the cross-wall is replaced by a magnificent arch, 28 feet across; the second floor has a mural gallery built into the walls. The uppermost set of windows used to be associated

Cross section of Hedingham's keep

with a top floor, but it has now been realized that this was the roof-space and the windows were added for appearance only. This keep was built to impress, and was probably used solely for special occasions, such as feasts; there are no obvious wall chambers.

Orford

Orford, near the south coast of Suffolk, was built in 1165–7 for Henry II to constrain Earl Bigod of nearby Framlingham. A curtain wall and towers were soon added, but are now missing.

Orford is of an experimental design, externally polygonal, in an effort to remove sharp angles—a weakness against besiegers' pickaxes—and to remove blind spots for archers at corner battlements. Three large turrets are integral to the design.

Inside it forms a comfortable self-contained living space for the king, with chapel, kitchen sinks, drains on two floors, and even a urinal outside a mural chamber. It remained a royal castle until Edward III gave it to Robert de Ufford in 1336.

Conisbrough

This keep in south Yorkshire was built in about 1180 by Hamelin Plantagenet, half-brother of Henry II. It stands within a semi-circular bailey, with stone towers and splayed walls for a thicker base.

Conisbrough is one of the first circular keeps erected in Britain, and is unusual in having six buttresses jutting out. Only the one that partly contains the chapel is not solid. Though now partly ruined, there were originally four floors above a vaulted basement, with a first-floor entrance.

qbove: The polygonal tower at Orford has three additional turrets and a forebuilding to protect the entrance.

left: The circular donjon at Conisbrough is notable for its large buttresses.

The Curtain Wall

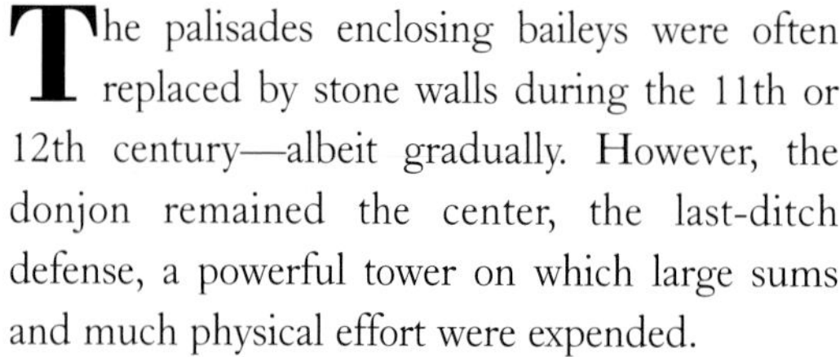

right: Framlingham lacks a donjon but has high walls set with early open-backed mural towers—and later ornate Tudor chimneys.

The palisades enclosing baileys were often replaced by stone walls during the 11th or 12th century—albeit gradually. However, the donjon remained the center, the last-ditch defense, a powerful tower on which large sums and much physical effort were expended.

By the late 12th century, however, a few castles were built without a keep. They were a continuation of the ring-work, and made up for the lack of a great tower by making the single ring of defensive curtain wall as impressive as possible. The walls were interspersed with strong mural towers that jutted out, allowing archers inside to shoot along the wall face at attackers.

above: The donjon (one of the first stone-built Norman keeps in England) formed from the early gatehouse on the early curtain walls surrounding the inner bailey of Ludlow.

Ludlow

Ludlow castle stands beside the River Teme in Shropshire, near the Welsh border. It was begun around 1085 by Roger de Lacy. The inner bailey is separated by a rock-cut ditch and protected by a curtain wall built around 1100 in straight lengths, with a sloping plinth. There are four square mural towers, three of them open-backed.

Originally, a T-shaped early gatehouse, with a barrel-vaulted passage running through it, jutted out a little from the curtain wall, but this was modified into a larger square donjon, perhaps after the wars of 1143–8. The beautiful circular nave of the Norman chapel stands within the inner bailey. The square outer bailey also has a curtain wall and an open-backed square mural tower. The round towers and many domestic buildings, such as the hall and great chamber, were added in the late 13th and 14th centuries.

below: Ludlow's circular Norman chapel sits within the walls.

Henry VIII's elder brother, Prince Arthur, died at Ludlow in 1507, traditionally in Arthur's Tower. Renovated, Ludlow castle was used by the Lord's President of the Council of Wales. A north gatehouse was added in 1581.

Framlingham

Framlingham castle in Suffolk was built for Roger Bigod, Earl of Norfolk, in the late 12th century. It has no donjon, the enclosure instead protected by high curtain walls, themselves guarded by a series of tall towers projecting forward from the wall face. These towers, complete with later ornate Tudor chimneys, are open-backed and may have had timber backings that could be removed in times of war, should an enemy gain a tower. Wooden platforms originally spanned the gap between the wall-walk and tower doorways; removing them obstructed any attacker trying to enter a tower from a wall.

King John besieged and took Framlingham in 1216. The Bigods lost their lands to the crown in Edward I's reign, and Framlingham passed to the Mowbrays, then the Howard family, as Earls of Norfolk. In 1553, on one of several occasions when the castle was in crown hands, Princess Mary was resident when she became queen. In

1636 the castle was bequeathed to Pembroke College, Oxford, on the proviso a poorhouse was built; however, all the domestic buildings were pulled down.

Goodrich

Goodrich, above the River Wye near Ross, was first documented in 1101–2. Owned by Godric, the rock-cut ditch may follow the early defenses. In the mid-12th century a modest three-story donjon was built, and some traces of the 13th-century square enclosure wall survive on the east side.

In 1246 the castle was granted to the de Valence family and in about 1300 it was rebuilt. The donjon was swamped by the great curtain walls that form a roughly rectangular layout, round angle-towers grounded to the rock by deep spurs. On the east side the gate is protected by a well-preserved semi-circular 14th-century barbican, the walls extending to form an outer enclosure along the more vulnerable north and west sides, since the earlier layout and terrain prevented it being made into a concentric castle.

In the 14th century the Talbots took over until 1616 when Goodrich passed to the Earls of Kent. In 1643 it was garrisoned by the Parliamentarian Earl of Stafford, who withdrew when powerful royalist forces arrived. Sir Henry Lingen held it for Charles I, even after the latter's surrender. Lington was forced to capitulate after the water supplies were cut, and the castle was slighted.

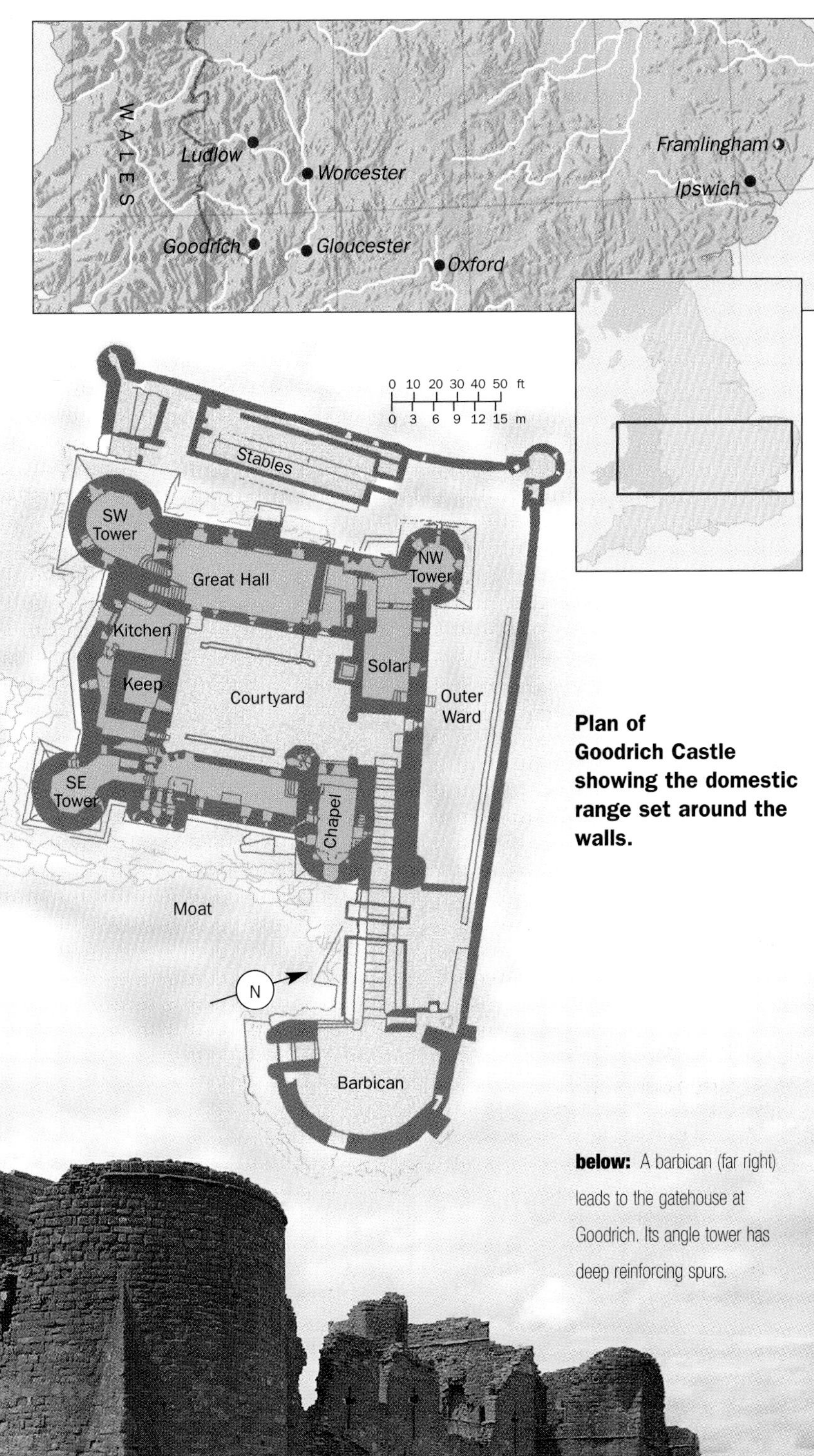

Plan of Goodrich Castle showing the domestic range set around the walls.

below: A barbican (far right) leads to the gatehouse at Goodrich. Its angle tower has deep reinforcing spurs.

The Concentric Castle

The idea of two sets of walls mutually protecting one another was occasionally seen in England. Several royal castles were gradually extended to become great concentric works, but the sheer cost of such modifications would have taxed the purse of even a great lord. By the time concentric designs became noticed, the crown had too strong a hold to allow barons to enlarge their castles without royal consent.

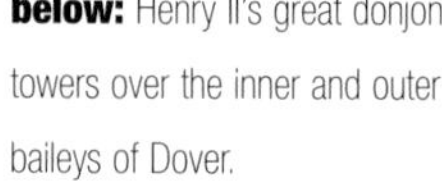

below: Henry II's great donjon towers over the inner and outer baileys of Dover.

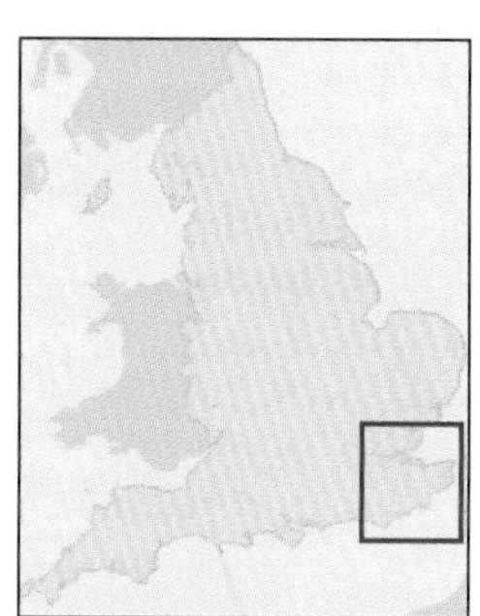

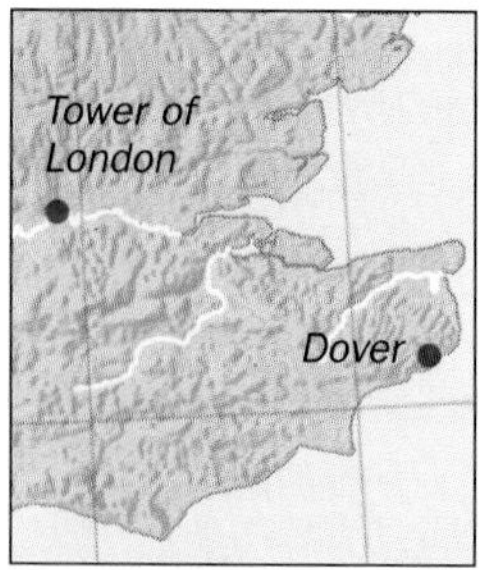

Dover

Dover castle, on the cliffs of Kent overlooking the English Channel, is one of the oldest fortified sites in England. When Duke William arrived at the site after the Battle of Hastings, he found an Iron Age fortification which may have been utilized by one of Edward the Confessor's Norman favorites before the Conquest, a Roman lighthouse or pharos, and a 10th- or 11th-century Saxon church. William spent eight days strengthening the stronghold, but no certain trace remains.

Henry II erected an imposing rectangular donjon in the 1180s, with walls 21 feet thick at the base; it was obsolete in design but provided the necessary chambers and private access to a chapel as was fit for a king. The donjon was set within a high curtain-walled inner bailey and early examples of open-backed flanking towers—14, including gate towers—thrust forward to cover the wall faces. The bailey now has 18th-century barrack buildings in place of medieval domestic ranges.

Henry also began building an outer bailey, also with flanking towers, still visible on the eastern side of the castle. Dover castle was not only expensive—about £6,000 when the annual royal revenue for England alone was about £20,000—but also futuristic in outlook.

With its three lines of defense, the castle had a proto-concentric design. The outer walls were incomplete when Henry died, but son John continued work along the north side. He added D-shaped towers, instead of rectangular ones, and built a wall to enclose the church and pharos.

above: The 11th-century White Tower, with later enlarged windows, is the center of this royal fortress.

In 1216, while John fought civil wars, barons invited Prince Louis, son of the king of France, to take the throne. Louis besieged Dover, held by Hubert de Burgh, and seized the barbican protecting the northern gate. A mine driven under the gate brought down the eastern gate-tower but Hubert plugged the gap with timbers and fought off the enemy until news of John's death made Louis withdraw. The infant Henry III was crowned.

The adult Henry spent vast sums on Dover, partly to extend the walls down to the cliff edge, so around 1256 the castle reached its full extent. It fell into slow decay until the 18th and early-19th centuries, when the castle was modernized during the Napoleonic wars. Bomb-proof arches were fitted in the donjon, outer towers were cut down for artillery platforms, and a tunnel gave access to a northern spur work. Bastions and musketry galleries were constructed; further batteries were added in the mid-19th century and modified as late as the Second World War.

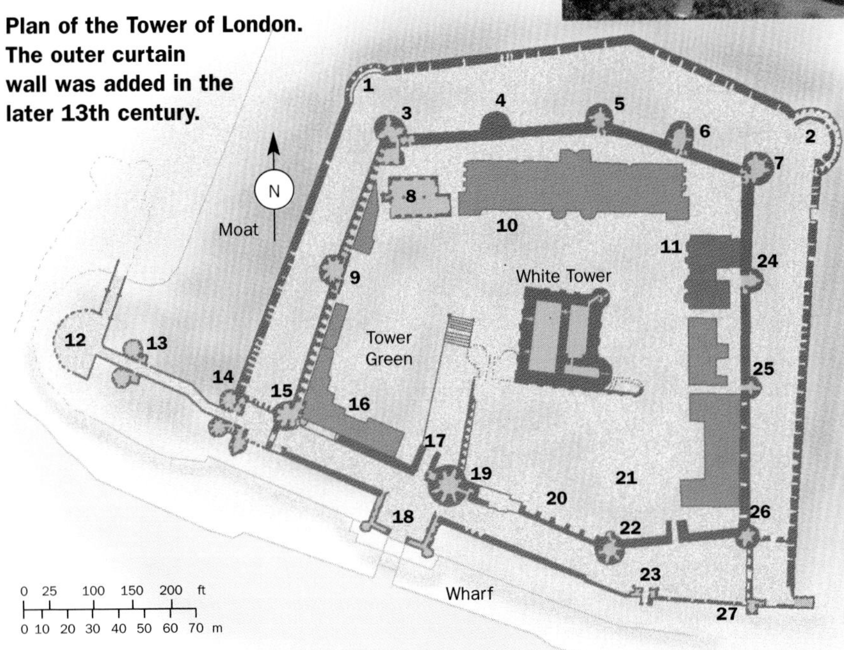

Plan of the Tower of London. The outer curtain wall was added in the later 13th century.

1 Legge's Mount
2 Brass mount
3 Devereux Tower
4 Flint Tower
5 Bowyer Tower
6 Brick Tower
7 Martin Tower
8 Chapel of St. Peter ad Vincula
9 Beauchamp Tower
10 Waterloo Barracks
11 Museum
12 Lion Tower
13 Middle Tower
14 Byward Tower
15 Bell Tower
16 Queen's House
17 Bloody Tpwer
18 St. Thomas's Tower
19 Wakefield Tower
20 site of Great Hall
21 Roman town wall
22 Lanthorn Tower
23 Cradle Tower
24 Constable Tower
25 Broad Arrow Tower
26 Salt Tower
27 Well Tower

The Tower of London

The Tower was begun in 1066 by William the Conqueror in the southeast corner of the city, by cutting off the angle of the old Roman city walls by the River Thames. Within ten years work began on a huge donjon, known in Henry III's reign as the White Tower, from the whitewash it received to protect it from weather.

In the late 12th century the castle walls were pushed westward, while in Henry III's reign they extended north and beyond the Roman wall on the east, and received new D-shaped and round mural towers. It was Henry's son, Edward I, who added a new moat, 160 feet wide, and an outer circuit of walls between 1275 and 1285 to produce one of the most powerful castles in the country.

At first quite low, the outer wall was raised c.1300. Edward even reclaimed land from the river for the southern wall and added a new water gate, St. Thomas' Tower, with Traitor's Gate. A new entrance comprised a barbican and two gatehouses.

The Tower largely lost its function as a royal palace by the 16th century, and though home to the Royal Mint, record office, and zoo until the 19th century, it was largely used as an arsenal under the Board of Ordnance. The Board was abolished in 1855, following a disastrous fire in 1841 and the Crimean War, and the Tower increasingly became a tourist attraction.

The Lord's Residence

facing top: Warwick castle boasts several mighty towers and an impressive domestic range.

facing bottom: The 14th-century castle of Bodiam, set within its moat, has become a picturesque ruin.

below: John of Gaunt's ruined domestic range stands to the left of the Norman donjon at Kenilworth.

Comfort was not always lacking in castles. Though some Norman castles would feel sparse by modern standards, the balance between residence and fortress increasingly tipped in favor of the former, especially during peacetime.

Kenilworth

Kenilworth in Warwickshire owes part of its fame to Walter Scott's 19th-century novel of the same name. The red sandstone castle was built in the 12th century by Geoffrey de Clinton and taken for the crown by Henry II, who built the large rectangular donjon. King John built the outer walls in about 1205; Henry III besieged it in 1266.

In the 1370s Kenilworth castle was remodeled by John of Gaunt, son of Edward III, who lavished money on creating a fine residence fit for a prince, down to ornamented timber in the stable block. Despite their ruinous condition, the lost grandeur of the rooms, including the hall with its decorated oriel windows, can be appreciated. In the 16th century Robert Dudley, Earl of Leicester, added his own buildings and in 1575 entertained Elizabeth I with 19 days of festivities.

Warwick

This imposing castle stands on a sandstone ridge above the River Avon in Warwickshire. The Anglo-Saxons erected a fortification against the Danes here in the 10th century, but the first castle was built by the Normans in 1068, the motte of which survives, with fragments of a slightly later octagonal shell keep on top

In the 14th century Warwick castle was largely rebuilt into its present form, with the safer south side, overlooking the river, given extensive residential rooms. The north curtain has a machicolated gatehouse, barbican, and two impressive towers, in the French style. Caesar's Tower (no connection with Romans) has five stories above a basement, a thick plinth at its base, and two-tiered battlements.

In 1604 James I granted the castle to Sir Fulke Greville, who spent the vast sum of £20,000 on refurbishment and the castle grounds. His family held this now-fine residence until 1978.

Bolton

This castle in Wensleydale, North Yorkshire, was built for Richard le Scrope around 1379. The rectangular courtyard is surrounded by rooms backing onto the curtain walls, which have rectangular corner towers and turrets halfway along two sides. A passage protected by portcullises at each end guarded the entrance, and only four doors, each with a portcullis, led from the courtyard to the rooms. Stables and stores were on the ground floors, halls, kitchens, and chambers on the first

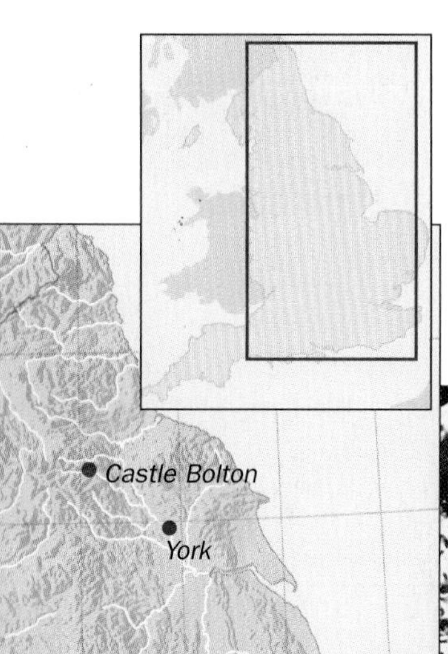

and second. The southeast corner could be shut off to form a self-sufficient unit.

From 1568–9 Bolton castle was used to incarcerate Mary, Queen of Scots. It was slighted during the English civil wars.

Bodiam

The epitome of a fairy-tale castle, Bodiam was erected in 1385 for Sir John Dalyngrigge to counter threatened French attacks. Sitting in a huge moat, it is near Robertsbridge in East Sussex, by the River Rother.

Bodiam's symmetrical walls surround a square courtyard, with round towers at the corners, a square tower at the middle of each side wall, and a gatehouse at front and rear. The front gatehouse is larger, rather like a donjon brought to the front; it has three portcullises, the rearmost cutting the gate off from the courtyard. Along the lower part of the walls are early keyhole loops for the new cannon, but that is the only concession to gunpowder.

Domestic rooms are set against the inner side of the walls, those on the west of higher quality. Dalyngrigge's first-floor suite was connected to his private pew in the chapel and included a presence chamber, and inner chamber with two adjoining bedrooms. Beneath this suite was another for an important official.

When completed Bodiam castle was already virtually redundant, since English ships regained control of the Channel in 1388. It fell into decay until restored in 1917 by Lord Curzon.

The floors of Castle Bolton

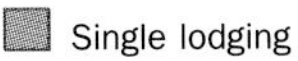

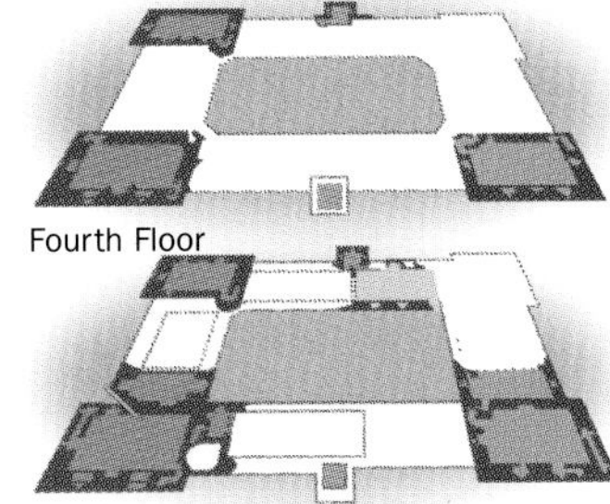

Fourth Floor

Third Floor

Chapel

Second Floor

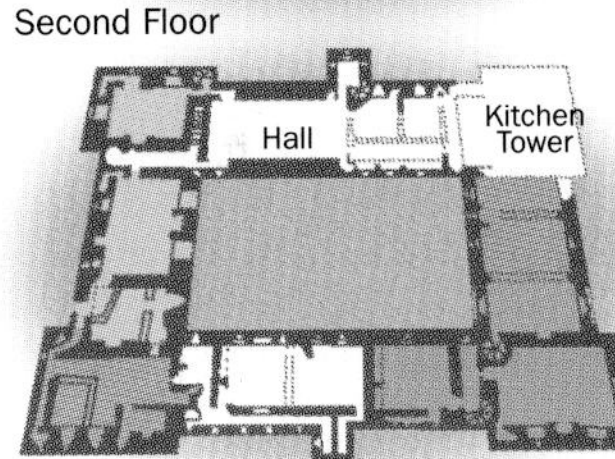

First Floor

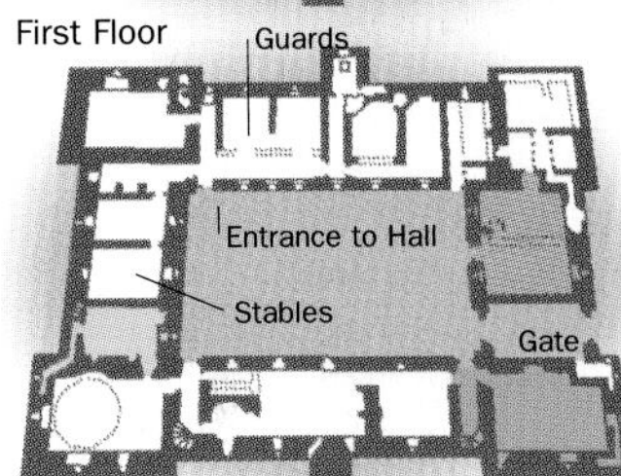

Ground Floor

Tower Houses

The tower house was a private tower for the lord and his immediate family or friends. It was the successor to the donjon in that it was primarily for the lord's use, but unlike many donjons tower houses were designed for family life. In this respect it is related to the 13th-century chamber tower. It required a ground-floor storage area, usually vaulted to prevent fire, a hall or great chamber on the next floor, and a chamber above. These towers were separate buildings within small castles.

Tower houses became popular in the early 15th century, especially in areas likely to suffer raids or riots, such as at borders, where their strong walls were useful protection, though inadequate to withstand a determined siege.

Warkworth

Warkworth is situated on the River Coquet in Northumberland, where a Saxon stronghold probably once stood. In the 12th century the shape of the castle was established. By the time King John stayed at Warkworth in 1214, the walled enclosure had a hall complex on the west side and a chapel next to the gatehouse on the south.

The Percy family bought it in 1332 and began creating a luxurious stronghold, which includes the tower known as the "Grey Mare's Tail." The donjon on the old motte to the north was turned into a tower house c.1390, the corners cut off and projecting bays fitted to the

middle of each side. A huge heraldic lion was carved on the wall facing the town below. Inside were hall, kitchen, chapel, chambers, and cellars. The solid outward show is betrayed by the large windows at first-floor level and the numerous cupboards, closets, and stairs that weaken the wall.

Learning of a conspiracy by the third Lord Percy and his son, Harry "Hotspur" Percy, Henry IV besieged and took Warkworth in 1405. Although the Percys were restored in 1416, Sir Thomas Percy was beheaded in 1572 for his part in the "Rising of the North" against Elizabeth I, and the castle fell into disrepair.

Tattershall

Tattershall in Lincolnshire is still referred to as a donjon in contemporary records. Virtually nothing remains of the castle built in 1231. The surviving feature is the brick-built tower house erected in 1450 by Ralph Cromwell, Lord Treasurer of England. Much of the castle was sold to speculators; only the timely intervention of Lord Curzon in 1911 saved the remains for posterity.

Cromwell's new tower was connected to the old hall by a first-floor passage. Despite a moat, it demonstrates little pretence to serious defense. The main front is pierced by large windows, excellent for light but hardly protective against missiles. The doors are at ground-floor level rather than raised. There is a pointless but decorative roof gallery, and while the machicolations along the wall tops are functional, those on the turrets are false.

Inside were state rooms; each floor had a single room, with smaller chambers and passages in the turrets. The castle finally fell into decay in the late 17th century.

left: Tattershall demonstrates how domestic comfort outweighed defense requirements.

Ashby-de-la-Zouch

The 12th-century stone hall and solar of the Zouch family at Ashby in Leicestershire were reconstructed in the 14th century, from which date much of the domestic building belongs. Lord Ormonde was executed in 1461 and William, Lord Hastings, obtained a license to crenellate the manor house in 1474.

To the south of the domestic buildings he placed a huge rectangular tower-house, four stories and 90 feet tall, with a seven-story square east wing. A high curtain wall surrounded all. Unlike Tattershall, it was strongly fortified, with its own well, though its entrance is at ground floor level. An overhanging turret or bartizan projects at one corner.

Richard III had Hastings beheaded while at the Tower of London in 1483. Colonel Henry Hastings defended Ashby in the English civil wars, but it was taken and blown up, destroying half of the tower.

facing: The late 14th-century tower-house at Warkworth sits on a Norman mound.

below: Slighted by gunpowder in 1649, the 15th-century tower-house at Ashby-de-la-Zouche remains as a ruin.

Chapter Four:
Gazetteer—Wales

Welsh and English Castles

Largely ignored by the Anglo-Saxons, the first Welsh castles only arose when the Normans invaded. A colony was established in the southwest by Henry II and English and Welsh struggled for possession... until Edward I made a show of power.

Wales, a land with a mountainous center, lay on what has been called the "Celtic fringe" of Britain, where the Anglo-Saxon invaders did not settle. There was often friction between the two peoples, but sometimes alliances. However, after the Norman Conquest castles were raised along the Welsh border and soon afterward adventurous lords began to push along the south and north coasts, building castles as they went.

These castles were first of earth and timber, quick to assemble in a hostile country. Under Henry II, however, there was a more concerted movement once Norman and Angevin warlords began to assemble defenses deep in Wales. Henry brought English and Flemish settlers to colonize Pembrokeshire (Dyfed) on the southwest tip of Wales, which became known as "little England beyond Wales." Fortresses such as Pembroke were built to safeguard the new colony.

Other impressive castles were begun in this early phase, such as Manorbier a little way eastward along the coast, perhaps best known as the birthplace and home of 12th-century chronicler Gerald of Wales (or de Barry). Gerald wrote *A*

below: The curtain walls of Manorbier were erected in the 13th century, though some 12th-century work survives in the castle.

left: Carreg Cennen broods over the Welsh landscape.

Journey through Wales, a book that provides an intriguing glimpse of the country during his time.

Welsh chieftains and kings were subject to influences from their English neighbors. Castles were often built in hilly or mountainous regions that acted as bases for revolt, and some were captured alternately by English and Welsh lords.

Edward's Towering Message

One of the most impressive is Carreg Cennan (Dyfed), on a crag above the River Cennan by the Black Mountains. It may have been built by Rhys ap Gruffydd in the 12th century, and changed hands a number of times during continuous struggles with the English invaders. Edward I took the castle when he invaded in 1277 and the new Giffard lords added much of the present stonework. However, the castle again fell to the Welsh in 1403–4, when it was seized by Owen Glendower.

By contrast, the original 11th-century castle at Carew (Dyfed), now much altered by later building, was erected by Rhys ap Tudor, the prince ruling South Wales. It was given as a marriage gift when his daughter, Nest, married the English lord of Pembroke, Gerald de Windsor. Henry I encouraged the wedding—he already had an illegitimate son by Nest.

This castle-building program by Welsh and English kings and lords continued in a country that constantly threatened stability in western England, and further works were added to existing buildings. However, it was Edward I who left an indelible stamp on Wales, with a vigorous program along the north coast and down the west side of the country. These castles are justly famous as some of the best examples of military architecture in Britain. They were often huge, straining the resources of the kingdom, but there is no doubt of their message. They impressed that the king was determined to subdue the country by force, and even today their towering walls loom over the approaching visitor.

During the 15th century, Welsh insurrections lessened. In 1485 the last Lancastrian claimant to the English crown, Henry Tudor, crossed from France and landed in Wales. Henry was Welsh through his father, but had a tenuous link to the Lancastrian royal house via his mother. Having killed the Yorkist King Richard III in battle at Bosworth, he was proclaimed king and the reign of the Tudor dynasty began in England.

above: Raglan boasts well-preserved machicolated parapets.

below: The original work at Carew was much altered after 1480 and again by the Elizabethans to produce comfortable domestic ranges.

1158–65	1277–95	1284	1330–76	1359–1416	1405	1409	1536
Henry II gradually conquers Wales	Edward I's Welsh wars spark frenetic castle-building	Edward I succeeds in conquering Wales	Lifetime of Edward, Prince of Wales (the Black Prince)	Lifetime of Welsh leader Owen Glendower	French forces land in Wales to support Owen Glendower's rebellion, but leave in a year	Henry IV finally suppresses the Welsh rebellion; Owen Glendower flees stronghold at Harlech	Wales is united with England

Castles of the Invaders

The Normans were an aggressive race; it is hardly surprising that they began to encroach on Welsh territory. Before the Conquest in 1066, Norman friends of the Anglo-Saxon king, Edward the Confessor, had built a few earth and timber castles, mainly in the west of England near the borders, at a time when no other castles existed in Britain. The number of strongholds gradually increased as the borderlands were secured and the foreign knights pressed into Wales.

Chepstow

An impressive fortress perched along a narrow cliff overlooking the River Wye in Gwent, Chepstow was begun in about 1067 by William FitzOsbern, Earl of Hereford and close friend of William the Conqueror. It effectively guarded the river crossing, while providing a base for armed incursions into Wales.

FitzOsbern built one of the earliest donjons to survive in Britain, completed before his death in 1071, a two-story structure connected by a narrow passage between walled baileys, the whole extending along the ridge like a ribbon. In 1115 the castle passed to the Clares and received attention from William Marshall, who married the heiress to the Clares in 1189. Their sons added a lower bailey with a twin-towered gatehouse to the south side, and a barbican to the upper bailey. The donjon was partially heightened by adding a further story at one end, and the passageway was given a cover to form a gallery.

On the death of Anselm Marshall in 1245,

right: Deep spurs on a tower at Chepstow.

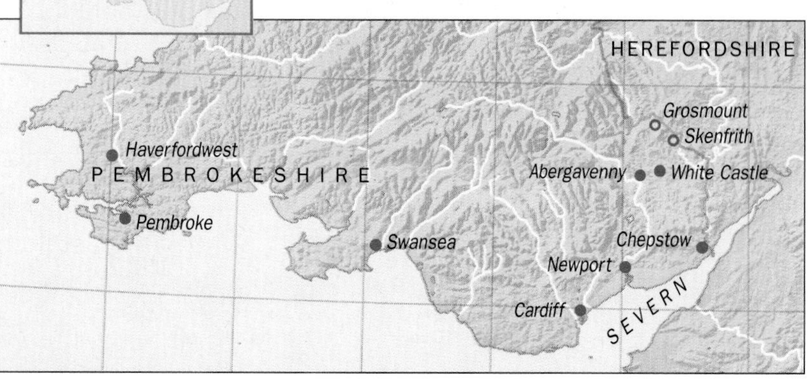

Chepstow castle eventually passed to the Bigod family. Roger Bigod III extended the donjon's additional story, added a hall range of domestic buildings to the lower bailey, and in 1285–93 built a strong D-shaped tower with spurs to thicken the base. Designed as a residential suite, it later imprisoned Henry Marten, one of the men who signed the death warrant of Charles I. Chepstow was twice besieged during the English civil wars, but unlike many others was not slighted.

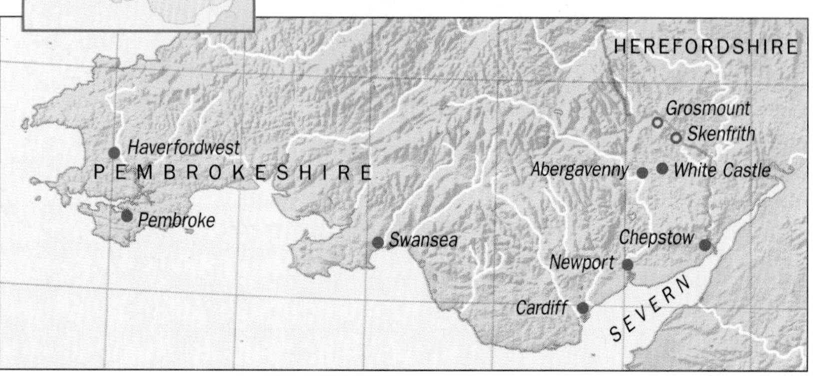

left: The castle of Pembroke, protected by and dominating the river.

Pembroke

Pembroke castle juts out on a rocky promontory into a loop of the Pembroke river, with cliffs on three sides and the town behind. The first castle of earth and timber was erected in 1093 by Arnulph of Montgomery, but in the late 12th century William Marshall, Earl of Pembroke, replaced the first defenses with walls to form a roughly triangular enclosure, inside which he built a huge cylindrical donjon 80 feet high and 20 feet thick at the base.

In about 1250 the landward area was extended to create a second bailey, with a powerful gatehouse and barbican opposite the town. In 1648 the castle was attacked by Oliver Cromwell after John Poyer, who held Pembroke, changed sides. After six weeks the castle fell and was slighted by the Parliamentarians.

White Castle

White Castle, near Abergavenny, Gwent, is the best preserved of the "Three Castles" that also includes Grosmont and Skenfrith, which form a mutually supportive triangle. It was first known as Llantilio castle, but by the 13th century received a covering of white plaster.

In the mid-12th century a donjon and a surrounding wall were built; a wet moat connected them to a new timber outer bailey to the south. It was given to Hubert de Burgh in 1201; he did not alter the castle much, but during the later 13th century Welsh unrest prompted large-scale rebuilding. The donjon was demolished and four round towers added to the curtain wall. A twin-towered gatehouse was created, access controlled from a new outer bailey on the north side, which had its own dry moat and curtain wall with four towers.

Despite all this impressive work, the threat was reduced by Edward I's actions in Wales and White Castle lost much of its role. By the 16th century it had been abandoned.

below: White Castle relies on strong towers and curtain walls for defense, the donjon having been demolished.

Castles of Edward I

Edward I was a great castle builder, initiating a major construction program during his Welsh Wars of 1277, 1282–3, and 1294–5. In addition to strengthening many existing castles in Wales and the Borders region, Edward built ten new castles (two of them in the south) and four new strongholds for his marcher lords—Hawarden, Denbigh, Holt, and Chirk. Five of the new castles—Aberystwyth, Flint, Rhuddlan, Caernarfon, and Conwy—were created with a fortified town beside them.

below: The large tower at Flint stands in center foreground.

Flint

Flint castle was begun by master mason James of St. George in 1277, during Edward's campaign against the Welsh prince, Llywelyn ap Gruffydd. It was set on "the Flint," a rocky outcrop on the estuary of the River Dee in Clywd.

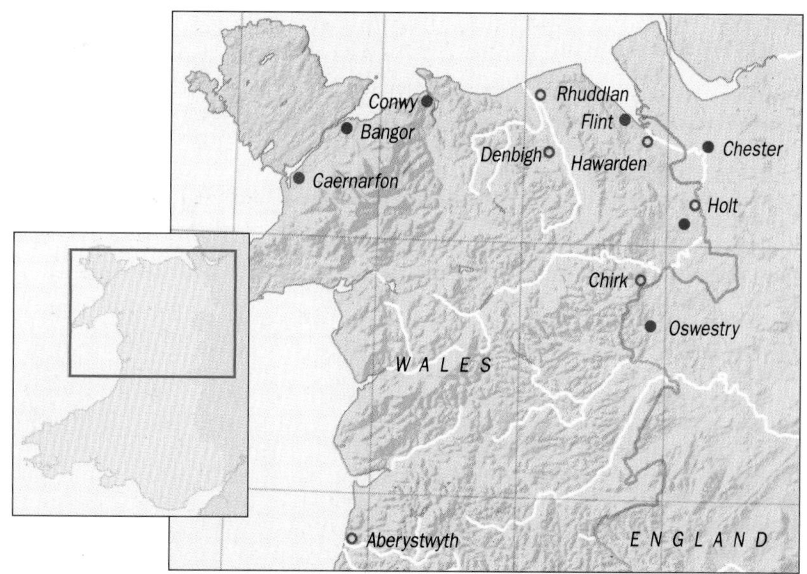

Flint consists of two baileys and a huge round tower, its walls 23 feet thick and inner diameter a similar measurement. The outer bailey is now mostly gone; the square inner bailey has a curtain wall set with round towers at three corners. The fourth corner has a much larger tower surrounded by its own moat and accessed via the bailey. This tower is almost like a donjon in that it did not represent current military thinking.

Despite its strength, part of the castle was captured by Llywelyn in 1282, although the revolt was eventually put down. Legend says that the deposed Richard II met opponent and successor Henry Bolingbroke here.

Conwy

Another of the fortresses by James of St. George, this magnificent castle stands on a rock by the River Conwy in Gwynedd, made more impressive by the fact that the town walls also still stand, complete with 21 mural towers along their length.

Conwy was built between 1283 and 1288, a major feat for a castle of this size. Its long oval shape encloses the rock, and high walls and round mural towers retain their full height. There is no gatehouse but the entrance, from the town, is guarded by two of its wall towers.

The interior is divided into two baileys by a cross-wall, although the domestic ranges are ruinous. The four towers of the inner bailey held the royal apartments, private access given by a back gate and barbican. This great period did not last long and the castle began to decline.

During the English civil wars it was easily captured by Cromwellian troops. In 1817 Thomas Telford constructed an impressive river bridge near the castle; Stephenson built a second bridge next to it in 1848.

Caernarfon

Caernarfon castle stands at the southern end of the Menai Strait in Gwynedd. The site was first used by the Normans for a motte-and-bailey castle, but the present massive structure was the work of Edward I's master mason, James of St.

George, who started work in 1283 after the northern Welsh castles were taken.

This castle is shaped like an hour-glass, with a cross-wall at the narrowest part forming two baileys; the old motte is in the eastern bailey. Caernarfon is protected by very strong curtain walls and 13 multi-angular mural towers. Their shape, and the red stone lines running horizontally along the walls, is deliberately reminiscent of the old walls at Constantinople, capital of the Eastern Roman Empire, and must have alluded to Edward I being a type of emperor.

Like Conwy, there is no donjon, but the Eagle Tower is designed as a three-story residential tower—almost an early tower house—with a basement giving access to the river. Moreover, there are numerous defensive tricks, such as shooting galleries within the wall thickness, twin-towered gates, and "murder holes." Walls from the castle enclosed the town, a rare British example of a bastide. Edward used Caernarfon as his administrative center for Wales, since the place had been so used by the Romans and Welsh, and would continue to be until the mid-16th century

above: View from the lower ward into the upper ward at Caernarfon.

left and reconstruction above: The powerful walls and towers at Conwy were built to impress as much as to defend the town.

The Great Concentric Castles

Some of the finest concentric castles are in Wales. Here, men at the inner wall fire over the heads of their friends on the outer wall, directing twice the firepower onto an enemy. Similarly, if the outer wall is taken, attackers find themselves under fire from those on the inner wall.

Unlike castles with several baileys, where mutual defense only takes place when one bailey's wall is close enough to another, concentric defense ensures that the inner is always near the outer. The outer bailey therefore becomes a strip running between the two sets of walls.

below: Harlech's monumental inner baily wall with its round corner towers overlooks the very low outer wall.

Caerphilly

Caerphilly castle in Mid Glamorgan is the largest in Wales. Gilbert de Clare, Earl of Gloucester, built the castle largely between 1268 and 1271, with additions mainly in the late 1270s and 1280s, so Caerphilly predates the great concentric castles of Edward I. The rectangular space has two lines of curtain walls with strong twin-towered gates, the inner wall also having round corner towers and one along the south curtain.

Beyond are huge water defenses, achieved by shaping a gravel spit of land between two streams to form an island with a huge western outer bailey. The eastern dam itself has a stone wall 1,000 feet (305m) long set with platforms, crenellations, towers, and gatehouses. It is thought that Gilbert had the idea for lakes after seeing that at Kenilworth during the siege of 1266. Some additions were made in the late 13th century and in 1326. Edward's efforts reduced the Welsh threat but it was besieged twice in the 14th century during the struggles with Edward II, and occupied for a time by Owen Glendower in the early 15th century.

The ruinous state of Caerphilly castle is blamed on gunpowder used to slight the castle in the English civil wars. There is no documentary evidence and it may be that the removal of stone in 1583, together with neglect of the sluicegates and resultant drying out of the fabric, were the real culprits.

Harlech

Harlech sits on a rocky cliff overlooking Tremadoc Bay in Gwynedd. It was built in the 1280s by Master James of St. George for Edward I.

The inner walls of the rectangular enclosure have huge round corner towers but the very low outer wall has none. An outer bailey wall to north and west drops down to the sea, but the other two sides were given extra protection from a ditch cut into the rock. There is an impressive gatehouse to the landward side, originally with a drawbridge either end of the moat, and a barbican.

In the Wars of the Roses Harlech castle was besieged by Yorkist troops for seven years before finally surrendering, remembered in the song *Men of Harlech*. The last royalist stronghold in Wales after the civil wars, it gradually fell into ruin.

Beaumaris

Perhaps the most perfect example of a concentric castle, Beaumaris was never completed. Set on the Isle of Anglesey, Gwynedd, it was begun by Edward I in the early 14th century, the last of his great building projects and another of the works of Master James. The flat ground permitted an almost symmetrical plan. The outer wall has 16 towers—the higher inner wall has them at the corners—and two fine gatehouses. The wet moat is fed from the Menai strait.

It took over 35 years to build the castle to its present state; the rear of the southern gatehouse was never completed, since the Welsh threat was dissipating and money was running out. Both gatehouses contained suites of rooms for royalty, and other domestic buildings stood along the inner walls. Within 20 years the timber was rotting and walls deteriorating. One gatehouse has now been lost.

above: For additional defense and display, Caerphilly sits within a huge lake.

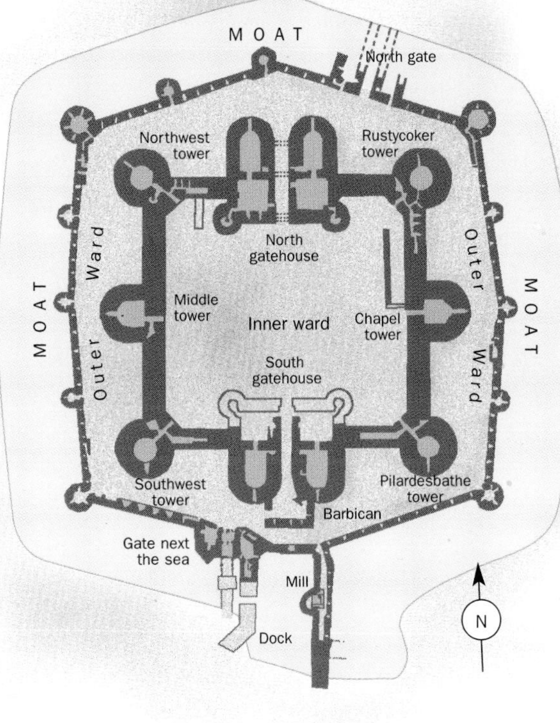

Plan of Beaumaris, a perfect concentric design.

left: Beaumaris from the air, and **below**, Beaumaris castle was never completed. The moat is fed from the Menai strait.

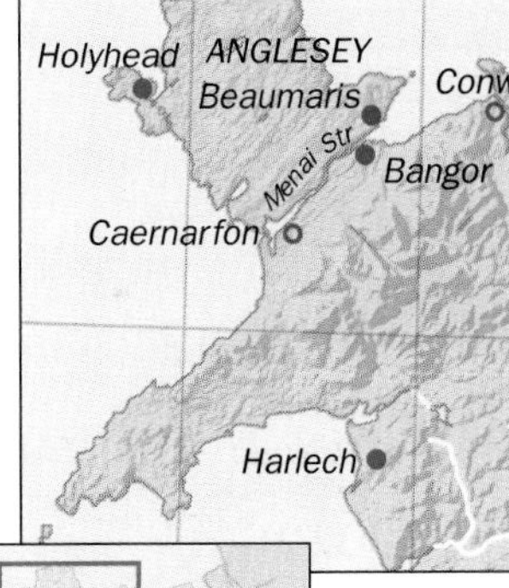

Chapter Five:
Gazetteer—Scotland

Outsider Influence

Castles arrived in Scotland with the Normans in the 12th century, who also brought their feudal ways wit them. The lords lived in motte-and-baileys, and stone castles remained a rare luxury in Scotland for almost 200 years.

below: The rocky outcrop at Urquhart was the ideal site for a castle to control the area around Loch Ness.

below right: Of this reconstruction of Dirlton in the 13th century, only the great donjon now survives to any notable extent.

It was about 1113, when David, son of Malcolm III and St. Margaret, became ruler of southern Scotland while his brother, Alexander I, was king, that the first foreigners began settling in Scotland. The process continued until about 1214, with the death of William the Lion, David's grandson. The Conmore kings helped the new continental lords and their new ideas.

As in England, it was realized that motte-and-bailey castles were quick to build in a potentially hostile environment, and were often used as administrative centers. Some of the mottes in Scotland were the work of Scottish nobles, such as Earl Duncan of Fife, who is probably responsible for the late 12th-century motte at Huntly castle. Others were natural mounds, such as the site of Urquhart castle above Loch Ness. A number of castles may have been in ring-work form, a banked and ditched enclosure as seen in Norman England.

By contrast with England, stone castles were rare until the 13th century, and then only in the Lowlands at first. However, the earliest datable Scottish stone castle may be Cobbie's Row Castle, on the Isle of Wyre in the Orkney Islands (part of Norway until 1468). Within an oval enclosure with ditch and bank stands a rectangular tower; a ruinous square building is attached to the north corner of the east wall. This stronghold was built in about 1145 by Norse chieftain Kolbein Hruga, from which the castle derives its modern name. It was mentioned in the *Orkneyinga Saga*, a work that

1010	1018	1072	1138	1297	1305	1314	1329
Scotland is united after King Malcolm II defeats the Danes	Malcolm II invades Northumbria; Tweed becomes Scotland's southern border	Anglo-Norman forces invade Scotland and establish control	Scotland's David I is defeated by English forces	William Wallace leads an uprising against English rule	Wallace is captured and executed by the English	Robert the Bruce defeats England's Edward II at Bannockburn	Under the Peace of Northampton the English recognise Scotland's independence

detailed the lives of the earldom of Orkney from around 900 to the late 12th century.

By this date the Norsemen in Scandinavia had also adopted the stone castle and could use Norman masons who had come north to build castles and cathedrals such as Kirkwall. Perhaps the earliest surviving stone castle similar to a Norman donjon is on the southeast shore of Loch Sween, 7 miles southwest of Achanamara. Sween castle consists of a rectangular tower with pilaster and angle buttresses; a large oblong tower house and a round tower were added later.

French Influence

There was relative peace with England for much of the 13th century, and some impressive castles were built in southern Scotland to proclaim lordship through stone. French influence is evident: a large cylindrical tower, almost a donjon, is set in the main curtain walls of Dirleton (East Lothian) and Bothwell by the Clyde, as at Coucy in France.

In the north the powerful Comyn lords built strongholds such as Balvenie in Glen Fiddich. In the west, kings of Scotland and Norway rubbed shoulders with the kings of Man and the sons of Somerled. Such uneasy conditions led Walter the Stewart, for example, to build a large shell keep at Rothesay on Bute (broken into by the Norse in 1230). The sons of Somerled, themselves of Irish blood, built a number of stone castles on the Isles.

It should be remembered that stone castles were very costly and many lords of Norman descent to the east were still living in earth and timber castles. By the later 13th century, however, castle design had reached a par with that of England and France.

In 1296 Edward I appeared in force at Berwick, and for the first half of the 14th century Scotland suffered the turmoil of two Wars of Independence. During this period more castles were dismantled or destroyed than were built. The return of David II brought some relief but insecurity blighted Scottish life into the 17th century.

James I and those who followed him slowly took a grip on the country. When James II of Scotland toppled the Douglas family in 1455, there was a major redistribution of land. The royal cannons had shown their power and exerted more influence on castle architecture. In 1587 James VI took control of Scotland and gradually peace broke out. He was crowned King of England in 1603.

above: In the 16th century John Stewart built a new residence at Balvenie outside the old defenses, in the form of a horizontal palace.

below: Reconstruction of Bothwell. The large donjon is reminiscent of that at Coucy in France.

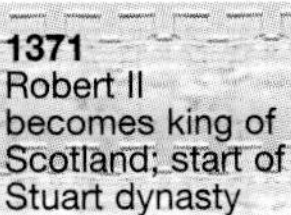

1371	1482	1542–87	1547	1550	1640	1640–92	1644
Robert II becomes king of Scotland; start of Stuart dynasty	English forces take Berwick and Edinburgh, but are later forced out of Scotland	Lifetime of Mary, Queen of Scots	After decisive Battle of Pinkie, English troops occupy Edinburgh	Aided by French troops, Scottish forces retake English-occupied areas	Scottish forces invade Northumberland	Lifetime of Hugh Mackay, Scottish general	Scottish forces fight on the Parliamentary side in the English Civil War

Castles of the English and Scots

The Normans first came to Scotland at the invitation of the Scottish ruling house. Mottes were rare in the eastern Lowlands, but more common in the west, especially by Galloway. This was the beginning not only of the rise of French families like the Bruce, but of increased tension with England, which led ruthless Edward I—"Hammer of the Scots"—to march north and stamp his authority on Scotland.

Duffus

Duffus castle is 5 miles northwest of Elgin. It is said to have been built by Freskin the Fleming in 1151 for David I. In 1130 David had dispossessed landowners in Moray who revolted over his continental policies.

Duffus is a motte-and-bailey castle, with an ovoid outer ditch. The timber palisades were replaced by a curtain wall in the 14th century. A stone donjon was erected on the motte itself but, as was always possible when stone towers were placed on manmade mounds, the earth subsided under the enormous weight and the donjon split in two. The hall in the bailey was reconstructed in the 15th century. Duffus was also the seat of the Moravia or Murray family, now represented by the dukes of Atholl and Sutherland.

Kildrummy

Kildrummy in Grampian, 30 miles west of Aberdeen, was built in the 13th century to the design of St. Gilbert de Moravia, royal treasurer to the North 1223–45. Kildrummy stands next to a ravine that guards one side. An *enceinte* castle, it consists of a semicircular courtyard enclosed by curtain walls set with five round mural towers. The largest, now known as the Snow Tower, served as a donjon.

In 1305 there was an attempt to place Robert the Bruce on the Scottish throne. When this failed at Methuen, he fled to the Western Isles but sent his queen and her ladies to Kildrummy. The following year Edward I ordered his son, Prince Edward (later Edward II), to besiege the castle. Under the Bruce's younger brother, Sir Nigel Bruce, it held out for weeks; by the time it was captured, the queen had escaped.

It has been told that the treachery of the castle's blacksmith allowed it to be taken. The English promised he could have as much gold as he could carry; his reward was to have the molten metal poured down his throat.

When Edward I took over the castle he added a great gatehouse with twin towers. Kildrummy

right: Reconstruction of Caerlaverock, protected by an inner and outer moat.

left: The ruins of Kildrummy stand above two ravines.

below: The semi-circular walls and strong towers at Kildrummy can be seen in this reconstruction.

then featured in Scottish history from the Wars of Independence to 1715, when the Earl of Mar supported the Jacobite rising and the castle was slighted.

Caerlaverock

Caerlaverock is 7 miles south of Dumfries. The first castle was a rectangular edifice built around 1230 and now resides several hundred yards away in a wood. The triangular castle—the only one in Britain—was built c.1280 and sits in a wet moat, beyond which are earthen banks with another moat and ramparts. A twin-towered gatehouse sits at the apex and there are drum towers at the other two angles.

Edward I besieged and captured Caerlaverock castle during his Scottish campaign in 1300. The siege became the subject of a contemporary poem, in which the coats-of-arms of numerous lords are lovingly recalled, to the delight of modern genealogists and historians of heraldry. Thirteen years after the capture of Caerlaverock, Sir Eustace Maxwell sided with Robert the Bruce rather than Edward II, and dismantled the castle to render it useless to the English.

In the 15th century the gatehouse was altered internally to make a comfortable living area. Gunports were added in the late 16th century. In the 1630s Lord Nithsdale, who held the castle for the king, added a three-story guesthouse range with a classical Renaissance façade. However, Covenanters captured the castle in 1640, despite a three-month resistance by Nithsdale. Further dismantling followed, but much original stonework survives.

below: Caerlaverock, showing the gables of the Nithdale apartments.

Castles on Crags

As in most places, designers in Scotland were eager to construct castles at the most secure sites. Thanks to rugged terrain in many parts of Scotland, a number of excellent examples of such strongholds were constructed and have survived.

Edinburgh

The famous castle of Edinburgh looms nearly 300 feet above the Scottish capital city. The first stronghold seems to have been erected by Edwin, King of Northumbria (the northern kingdom of England) during the early seventh century, hence the name: Edwin's burgh. The castle, built on the same site, was fought over by the Scots and English. When it fell to Robert the Bruce's nephew in 1313 the buildings were pulled down; the only surviving early structure is the charming 11th-century chapel of St. Margaret. By 1341 Edinburgh castle had reverted to the English and been re-fortified. An open space was left in front of the main gatehouse so approaching enemies had no cover.

In 1573 a sturdy bastion, the Half-Moon Battery, was built on the remains of a tower built in about 1370 by King David II, son of the Bruce. To the south lies the 16th-century banqueting hall, whose wall carries upwards from the sheer rock face; to the east is the palace, mainly rebuilt in the early 17th century.

Oliver Cromwell received Edinburgh castle's surrender after a 12-day siege during the English civil wars.

Stirling

Stirling castle, perched on its narrow basalt outcrop in Stirlingshire, is an imposing sight. It controlled the main ford across the River Forth linking the Highlands and the Lowlands, for which it has been called the "Key to Scotland." It has changed hands more times than any other. The Scots held it from 1299 to 1304, when Edward I took it after a great siege. The Battle of Bannockburn (1314) was fought nearby to decide who should hold the castle. The victorious Robert the Bruce dismantled it, for fear of the English seizing it again.

This first castle, which possibly originated in the early 12th-century, appears to have been an earth-and-timber construction, but nothing remains. The earliest surviving work dates from the 15th century.

The Great Hall, one of the first Renaissance buildings anywhere in Britain, was built for James III (1460–88); the central turreted gatehouse, with flanking towers and curtain wall, probably

below: The famous castle perched on its crag overlooks the city of Edinburgh.

date from the same period. The palace was built by James IV (1488–1513) and his son. James VI (acceded 1567) and his son, Frederick Henry, were baptized in the Chapel Royal and rebuilt it in 1594.

The court moved to England after 1603 and Stirling castle lost its royal glamour. However, it was considered enough of a threat to be besieged by General Monke in 1651 during the occupation of Scotland by Cromwell's troops, and again in 1745 by Bonnie Prince Charlie.

Tantallon

On the cliffs above the sea opposite Bass Rock, 2½ miles east of North Berwick in East Lothian, is the castle of Tantallon. It was built by the Douglas family some time before 1374.

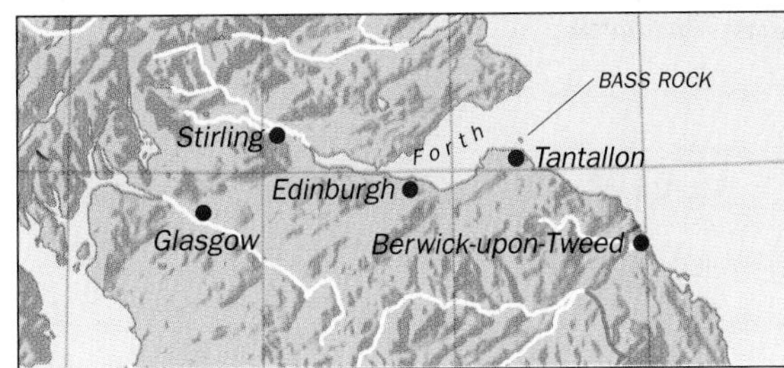

The sea protects the site on two sides, while ditches guard the other two sides. A massive curtain wall covers the promontory from one end to the other, each end guarded by a huge cylindrical tower. In the middle of the wall stands a gatehouse and residential quarters for the lord. There is an upper hall for the lord and a lower hall for use by the garrison.

Tantallon was witness to several sieges, since the Red Douglases were a fiery family. The fifth Earl, Archibald "Bell the Cat" Douglas, held out against royal troops for a year, and the following year was made Chancellor of Scotland. His grandson, the Earl of Angus, was also besieged in 1528.

From 1639 Tantallon was garrisoned by Covenanters. It was dismantled in 1651 after being badly damaged by General Monke's artillery, yet remains a rugged and romantic fortress.

left: The remains of Tantallon, with Bass Rock standing from the North Sea iin the background.

below: Stirling castle sits above the battlefield of Bannockburn.

Tower Houses

right: A great machicolated wall was added to the tower house at Craigmillar in the 15th century.

By the end of the 14th century, following the Wars of Independence, castle building was increasing once more. However, new castles tended to be of rather simple form—the rectangular tower house was coming into prominence. The uncomplicated design was relatively cheap to build; single rooms were piled one on top of the other, instead of next to each other like an old hall-house. It served for baron or laird and the security afforded was necessary in a still unstable environment.

Threave

Threave stands on an island in the River Dee 18 miles southwest of Dumfries in Kirkudbrightshire. It was built for Archibald the Grim, third Earl of Douglas, c.1360–70, and consists of a four-story tower next to a hall. The tower was protected by an outer barmkin wall, sloping on the exterior to lessen the force of enemy cannon fire and set with round towers pierced by gunloops, that separated the hall from the tower.

This wall may date from 1455, after James II besieged it. James Douglas, the ninth Earl, had accused the king of murdering his brother and went into revolt. James II besieged Douglas's castles, finally arriving at Threave with his huge bombard, Mons Meg. The castle was lost following a bombardment, which may have prompted the rebuilding of the walls.

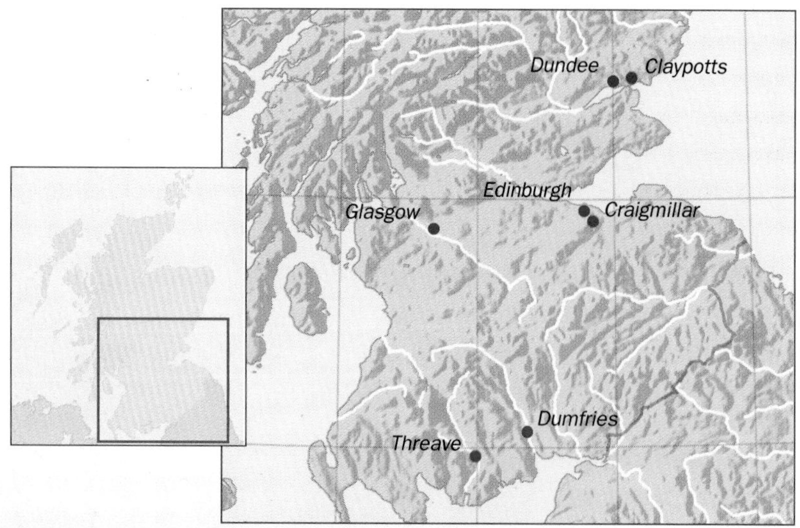

right: The tower house at Threave is guarded by a barmkin wall, its towers pierced with gun-loops.

Threave Castle elevation looking west

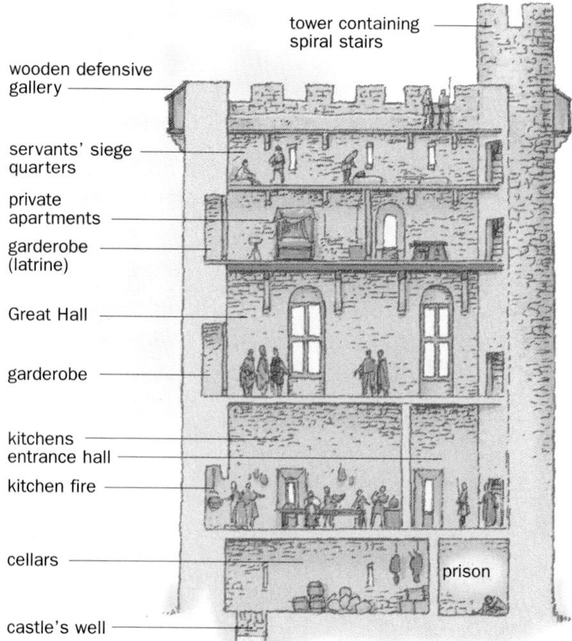

Threave castle was dismantled after being captured by the Covenanters in 1640, and held French prisoners during the Napoleonic Wars.

Craigmillar

Craigmillar stands on a ridge just outside Edinburgh and, not surprisingly, became a popular retreat for Scottish kings and queens. The castle was begun in 1374 by Sir Simon Preston of Gorton, and his family held the castle as hosts to the royal family of Scotland for nearly 300 years.

The main part of the castle is an L-shaped tower house. The main block was four stories high and a five-story wing included a kitchen conveniently close to the hall and Sir Simon's chamber above. The wing also allowed the vertical stair to be removed from the main block. The entrance vestibule had a removable timber ceiling to facilitate the repelling of intruders or for the delivery of goods.

In the 15th century, 30-foot curtain walls were added to enclose the tower house, complete with round corner towers and gun emplacements. It is interesting to note that no gun loops were made in the tower house itself. Machicolations run continuously around the walls and mural towers. This strengthening of the defenses and enlargement of the space for domestic buildings was increased the following century by the addition of an outer walled and moated enclosure.

In 1544 the Earl of Hertford led an expedition that burned Craigmillar castle. The eastern range of surviving buildings was probably built after this incident. The western range was built in 1661 in the outer enclosure by Sir John Gilmour. Mary, Queen of Scots often stayed at Craigmillar.

Claypotts

Near Dundee in Tayside stands Claypotts castle. This was begun in the 1570s by John Strachan after the family bought the land from the Abbey of Lindores in 1560.

Claypotts is an early example of a Z-plan Scottish tower house. A three-story oblong central block forms the core, with round towers built into the northeast and southwest corners. Each tower has an additional story and the cylindrical shape cleverly culminates in a flattened gable-ended watch-chamber with corbelled corners, carved with the construction dates of 1569 and 1588, hence why they are not symmetrical.

The central block has a garret, and a slender semi-circular tower is squeezed between the central block and southwest tower. The round corner towers are rectangular internally, making it easier to fit furnishings! Both residence and stronghold, Claypotts castle has a parapet walk and loops for firearms, even in the kitchen. The military precautions proved unnecessary, although one of the owners was Claverhouse, "Bonnie Dundee"—a Jacobite leader.

below: The 16th-century cylindrical towers at Claypotts terminate in a flattened gable-ended watch-chamber.

Chapter Six:
Gazetteer—Ireland

Holding Ireland

When King Henry II invaded Ireland in 1169, the Norman adventurers found no castles. Fortifications were lost to the past, but the traditional motte-and-bailey became part of the troubled Irish landscape held by the English.

below: Stark against the sky, the ruined castle at Ferns.

The Irish had defended themselves with fortifications, chieftains protecting their halls with earthen rings (a *dun*, *lis*, or *rath*) or much larger earthworks that enclosed houses, streets, and churches, like English burhs. The family and community were more important than stone walls. Gerald of Wales noted that the Irish preferred to use forests or bogs to assist them in warfare, and when they were besieged in a walled town it was one whose defenses were built by the Danes.

Once again, motte-and-bailey castles used by the Norman invaders were common at first, a type that would be seen well into the 13th century. Their speed and ease of construction proved their worth. Rectangular and cylindrical donjons also appeared; some rectangular ones, like that at Ferns in Co. Wexford, had round corner turrets of a type peculiar to the Leinster area in the early 13th century.

Dermot McMurrough, King of Leinster, abducted the wife of a rival prince, driving the latter into alliance with the high-king, Rory O'Conor. McMurrough was subsequently driven out and gave fealty to Henry II of England.

In 1169, Anglo-Norman adventurers captured Wexford, to be followed by Richard Clare, known as Strongbow. Henry's papal-backed invasion on McMurrough's behalf set out in 1171 and seized Waterford. Dublin fell in 1171 and Henry built a palace there, which would become the capital of the Anglo-Irish settlement. Limerick was temporarily captured in 1175.

Recognition by Irish princes meant little in reality, and those who married Irish wives or took up Irish customs became another source of unrest. John de Courcy conquered Ulster largely in 1177. Through marriage to Strongbow's daughter, William Marshall, Earl of Pembroke, inherited Leinster and gave it good law and order.

795
Vikings make their first raids on Ireland

797
Donnchadh Midi Mac Domnaill, Ireland's high king dies

c.800
Book of Kells begun in Iona and completed at Kells in Ireland

left: Dun Aengus, a Celtic fort poised on the edge of the known world on Inishmore, westernmost of the three Aran islands.

In 1210 King John visited Ireland and a strong stone castle was completed in Dublin by 1215. By this time the two-thirds of Ireland ruled by the English was at peace, as the barons there supported John. By 1235 Richard de Burgh had almost conquered Connaught.

Adopting the English

After King John left in 1210, no English king came to Ireland until the reign of Richard II (1377–99). The English therefore relied on their castles to prevent themselves from being overrun. Gerald of Wales congratulated Hugh de Lacy for his work in planting castles in Leinster and Meath. The governor had little control beyond the boundary around Dublin, and the settlers began to consider themselves as Irish.

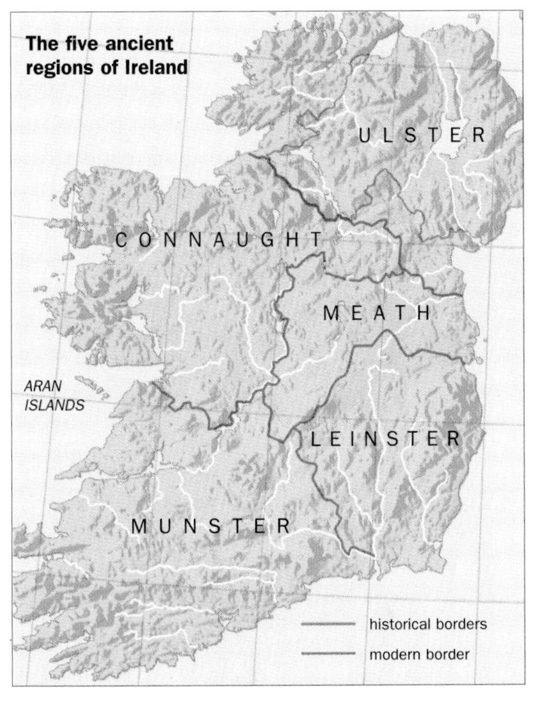

Castles were sometimes built in towns, or near earlier monasteries, a focus for settlers. Some were placed more to facilitate the lord's mercantile interests than for military needs. By 1225 only 20 stone castles had been built in Ireland, but the Irish could be successful against earth-and-timber fortifications, which were less of an obstacle.

The threat became more acute when Edward Bruce, brother to Robert, landed from Scotland in 1315 to ally with the Irish. Carrickfergus was besieged and captured after holding out for a year. Robert the Bruce then arrived and in 1317 the allies threatened Dublin. However, the plan did not hold and the Scots left.

During the remainder of the 14th and 15th centuries the English lords were preoccupied with France, despite an expedition to Ireland in 1394. English lords still occasionally campaigned, but during the 15th century some Irish lords began to live in castles and study siege warfare as part of a conscious desire to copy English methods. Not until the late 16th century did Queen Elizabeth I's ministers turn again to Ireland, in the face of a perceived threat to Protestantism.

above: Dublin castle's circular tower is almost lost amid later buildings.

832 First Viking forays into interior of Ireland

918 Vikings defeat Niall Glúndubh Mac Aeda, Ireland's high king, near Dublin

919 Irish king Niall Glundub is killed in attempt to take Viking-held Dublin

920 Vikings capture Limerick

1002 Brian Boru becomes Ireland's high king

1014 Brian Boru dies while successfully fighting off the Danes

1103 Viking leader Magnus III campaigns and is killed in Ireland

1169–71 Henry II's Norman knights, led by Richard of Clare, take Ireland

Earthworks and Stone Towers

above: The cylindrical donjon of Nenagh, heightened later in the 13th century.

Norman settlers erected the first castles in Ireland, as they had in England. Mottes are sparse in the south, where the invaders presumably found little opposition, but noticeable in Ulster and the eastern midlands.

Castletown Geoghegan

Seven miles north of Kilbeggan in Co. Westmeath, Castletown Geoghegan was built in the 13th century by the MacEoghagins who ruled the county, hence the name of the village. Geoghegan castle is a good example of a motte-and-bailey earthwork, now lacking its timber defenses.

Carrickfergus

The castle is 8 miles northeast of Belfast on a narrow, rocky peninsular in Belfast Lough. It was built between 1180 and 1205, by John de Coucy or Hugh de Lacy the younger, his successor, and is one of the largest Irish castles to survive.

A basalt rubble curtain wall runs around the peninsular, the entrance flanked by round towers. There had also been an intermediate curtain wall with small square towers. The inner bailey at the south tip of the peninsular is trapezoidal.

After the seaward curtain was finished, a square donjon was built over the north angle. It has red sandstone dressings, exchanged for yellow sandstone higher up, and the entrance was reached by a stair along the east wall. The donjon has four floors; the lower floor is a basement of two chambers, each with a groined vault. Here too was the all-important well. However, the great hall and chapel are not contained in the donjon—it seems to be a private residential tower.

King John stayed here when he visited Ireland in 1210. In 1690 William III first set foot on Irish soil here when he landed at the quay below the western wall of the castle, before the Battle of the Boyne.

Trim

The largest castle in Ireland, Trim in Co. Meath is 27 miles northwest of Dublin on the banks of the River Boyne. The Song of Dermot tells how the first Hugh de Lacy built the castle in 1173, and how, the following year, the *meysun* (donjon) was burned in his absence and the motte leveled. The latter, together with the ditched and fortified house, was restored and then rebuilt in 1220, though the donjon and north curtain may be slightly earlier. The flattened motte survives within the triangular bailey of the castle, which is surrounded by a curtain wall with mural towers: square, semi-circular and open-backed, and cylindrical.

The early form of gatehouse is a rectangular

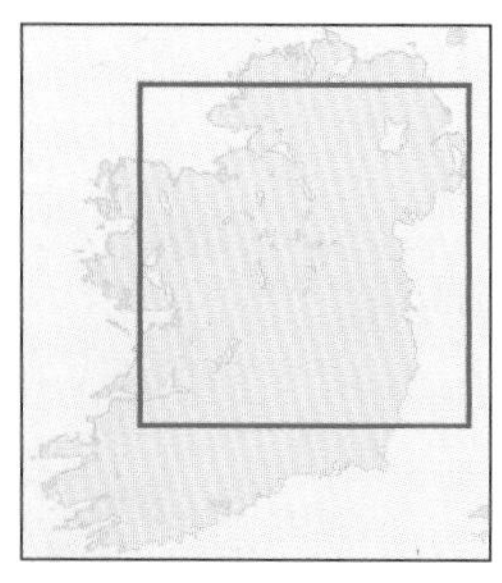

right: The square projections on the donjon at Trim give it an unusual shape.

tower pierced by a passageway. Most of the walls on the river frontage have now gone. The square donjon is unusual in that it has a square projection from each side, although the north projection is now almost gone. The eastern projection held the chapel, reached from a stair leading to the lord's great chamber on the third floor. Two stairs link some rooms as suites.

An internal cross-wall rises only to the first floor of the donjon; creases in the wall at this height indicate that the roof was originally at this level. The donjon was later raised to its present height, though externally the squared blocks of masonry were no longer used; instead, the top half was built from flat slabs.

Prince Hal, later Henry V, stayed in the large southern cylindrical gate-tower when he was left at Trim by Richard II in 1399. Since Trim lay on the edge of English territory, it was involved in many of the struggles that took place over the centuries.

Nenagh

Nenagh in Co. Tipperary is 25 miles northeast of Limerick in County Tipperary. The castle was probably built by Theobald Walter, King John's butler and head of the Butler of Ormond family, who died in 1206. It consists of a small pentagonal bailey surrounded by a curtain wall with round angle towers, the southern pair forming the front gatehouse. A three-story cylindrical donjon is set into its northern apex, separate from the great hall to provide comfortable privacy. It was heightened later in the 13th century.

left: The donjon at Carrickfergus, set in the narrow castle enceinte.

Irish Enceintes and Tower Houses

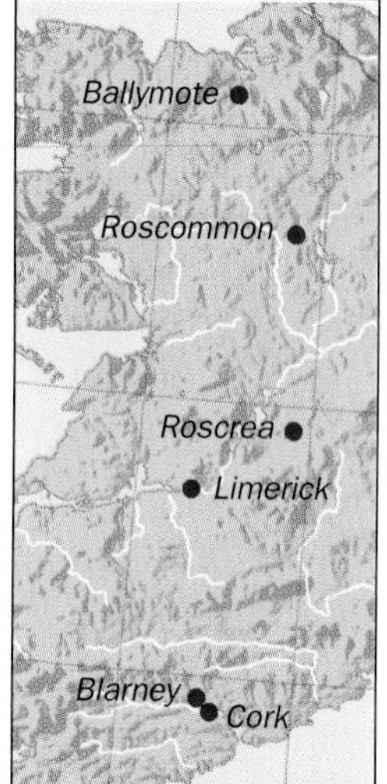

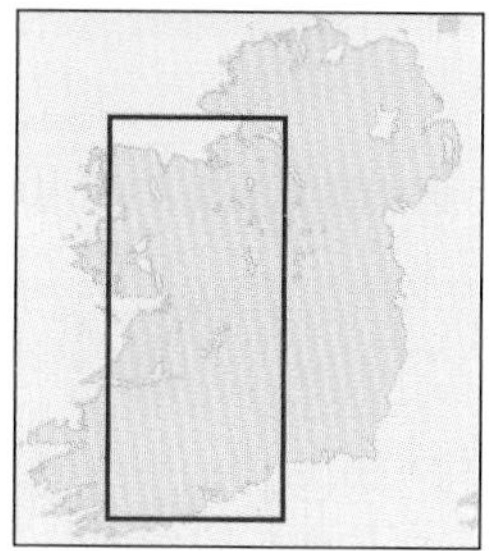

Motte-and-bailey castles and donjons lasted longer in Ireland than in England, partly because of the costs of erecting stone castles. However, as in the rest of Britain and the Continent, new castles sometimes concentrated on a powerful gatehouse or strong mural towers, excluding donjons from the plan.

Roscommon

This royal castle is situated in Co. Roscommon. It was built or restored by Robert de Ufford the Justiciary c.1280, since work he began in 1269 seems to be among that destroyed by the rival O'Connor family. Entrance to the almost rectangular bailey with angle towers is via a twin-towered gatehouse.

Ironically, around 1300 the O'Connors built an extremely similar edifice—though with a very small gatehouse—at Ballintubber, only ten miles northwest of Roscommon. It was rebuilt as a country house in the 16th century.

Roscrea

Roscrea lies 25 miles southwest of Port Laoise in Co. Tipperary. There appears to have been a motte-and-bailey, together with a *bretasche,* built during King John's reign, destroyed during a complete rebuilding in the time of Edward I.

below: The gatehouse at Roscommon defends a rectangular enceinte.

The new castle was set a short way from the first, and no donjon was constructed, the builders concentrating on a more modern design. Instead, it consists of a bailey shaped like an irregular polygon, with a rectangular gatehouse-tower of the 13th century. This castle cost the not insubstantial amount of $1,000 in the sixth and seventh years of Edward I's reign, according to the official records of the Irish Pipe Rolls.

Ballymote

Ballymote in Co. Sligo is the best example of a late 13th-century castle in Ireland. Built by Richard de Burgh, second Earl of Ulster, to protect his newly won lands, the rectangular *enceinte* is set with towers at the angles and in the centers of the east and west curtain walls. There is a twin-towered gatehouse in the center of the north wall, and passages run through the walls, giving access to the towers.

A postern in the south wall is incomplete, perhaps as a result of the castle being lost to the O'Connors in 1317. They lost the castle to the Macdiarmada in 1347 and it changed hands several times until Richard Bingham, governor of Conaught, took it in 1584. Four years later it was burned down; Ballymote castle was still in need of repair when it was handed to the English in 1602. Captain Terrance MacDonagh nevertheless held it for James II in 1690 until forced to surrender to the cannon of Lord Granard.

Blarney

This famous castle lies 6 miles northwest of Cork City, County Cork. The site was occupied by a hunting lodge in the 10th century, and the first stone castle was built in 1210. The present structure is the work of Dermot McCarthy, who built a tower house on the limestone mound in 1446.

Little is left of the castle except for the ruins of the tower house. The family lost the castle to Oliver Cromwell in 1646 but in 1660 Charles II regained the throne and the McCarthys were reinstated, only to lose it again after the Battle of the Boyne in 1690; the castle was sold to the

left: The tall tower house at Blarney. The famous stone is located in the slim machicolated parapet.

Governor of Cork in 1703.

High on the tower's machicolated parapets is the famous Blarney Stone. This is supposedly half of the Stone of Scone on which Scottish kings were crowned, given to Cormac McCarthy by Robert the Bruce for support at the Battle of Bannockburn in 1314. Having climbed one of the spiral stairs to the wall-walk, those wishing to kiss the Blarney Stone and receive the gift of eloquence must lay on their back and lean out to the inside face of the jutting parapet. The story dates from the time of Elizabeth I, who wanted Irish nobles to hold land by swearing allegiance. Cormac Teige McCarthy, Lord of Blarney, talked so much without agreeing to anything that the queen called it "a lot of Blarney."

below: The ruins of Ballymote.

Chapter Seven: Gazetteer—Germany

The 10,000 German Castles

In medieval Germany, feudalism was adopted much more slowly than in Western Europe, largely because powerful lords held territories as a buffer against Slav tribes to the east. Emperor Henry I (918–36) had tried to introduce fortresses (largely communal) and fortified towns against Slav and Hungarian attacks, many being of earth and timber.

right: Map showing the Germanic states under the Holy Roman Empire (bold type) and their modern equivalents.

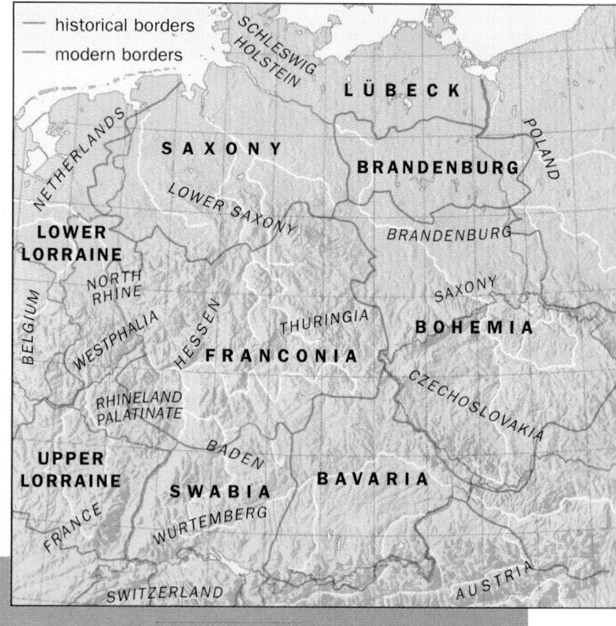

From the tenth century, Germany was unique in producing a form of unfree knight, the ministeriales, one of whose main duties was to hold castles, either their own or their master's. It was during the Investiture Wars, which began in 1075, that castle building started in earnest.

The greatest growth came at the time of the Hohenstaufen Emperors, especially Frederick I Barbarossa (1152–90), who was responsible for about 350 castles and residences. This program had waned by the mid-13th century, during the struggles of the Interregnum (1254–73), as small territories emerged and the cohesion of imperial fortresses was lost.

1030	1038	1041	1077–1106	1138	1156–73	1166–68	1241
Hungary defeats incursions by German Emperor Conrad II	Emperor Conrad II adds Burgundy to the Holy Roman Empire	Henry III of Germany defeats Bratislav I of Bohemia	Under Henry IV Germany is wracked by civil war	Conrad III becomes Holy Roman Emperor and establishes Hohenstauffen dynasty	Under Frederick I Barbarossa, Germans campaign widely in Central and Eastern Europe	Germans hold Rome until disease forces them to leave the city	Conflicts between Frederick II and the Pope lead to German troops pillaging Italy

Increasingly, fortresses were the property of powerful lords or came into the hands of the lesser nobility, often being designed as, or converted to, private residences. So the areas that now constitute modern Germany became thickly sown with castles of various sizes. It has been estimated that there were some 10,000 castles in the German-speaking lands.

German castles demonstrate perhaps a greater variety in design than anywhere else in Europe. Several factors contribute to this: the nature of the terrain; characteristics of the small states; the use of occupied sites; and the relationship of a castle within a settlement. The motte-and-bailey castle never became popular, though some existed, such as the Husterknupp, a ninth-century Carolingian fortified farm, which was gradually enlarged and then given a motte in the 12th century.

In Lower Saxony, fortresses consisting of a single small tower surrounded by buildings were erected. These turret fortresses were also popular in western Germany, where the tower (or *bergfried*) varied in size, and this form spread to the North Rhine

Schildmaier/Randhausburgen

In some areas a *schildmaier*, or strong wall, was used to protect the approach side, and increasingly took over from the *bergfried*, as at Schönburg on the Rhine. Such mantle-walls waned in the 14th century, to be revived when firearms became popular. A number of early castles had a strong surrounding wall as the main defense, and if a tower was included it was usually subordinate. From the 11th century, this distinction was frequently lost.

Imposing sites helped cut down the need for expensive defenses, popular especially among the lesser nobility, and domestic buildings could be incorporated closer to the outer walls than might be prudent elsewhere. This style of castle sited on a crag was increasingly seen in the later Middle Ages—a wall enclosing the living space, and a moat or ditch to cut off the most accessible side.

Where all-around protection was needed, despite being set on a prominence, either a wall with a central tower was used, as before, or else strong buildings surrounded the court, such castles being known as *randhausburgen*.

Castles with regular plans tend to occur only in western areas, such as Gudenau in the Rhineland. Flanking towers were slower to make an appearance than in the west. Later in the Middle Ages, many older fortresses were improved by adding a surrounding wall with flanking turrets.

In Thuringia and Hesse, old castles were extended but few new ones were built in the later Middle Ages, while Saxony cannot compare with the large numbers of castles seen in the Rhineland. Many German castles have small rooms and, often, only the women's quarters had fireplaces.

The variety of German castles—**facing below:** Veste castle, high above the town of Coburg in northern Bavaria; **top right:** Godesburg in Bad Godesberg near Bonn; **below:** Castle Klopp in Bingen, Rhineland-Palatinate.

1321	1367	1372	1376	1394	1433	1471	1515
Cities in southern Germany establish the Swabian League	Civil war breaks out between the Swabian League and the German Emperor	Swabian League is defeated	Swabian League is revived by city of Ulm	The Swiss attain independence from Holy Roman Empire	King Sigismund becomes Holy Roman Emperor	Right to feud is formally abolished in attempt to stem lawlessness	Germany obtains Bohemia and Hungary from Poland in exchange for Prussia

Bergfried Castles

Many castles in Germany have one tower that is higher than those around it. This is called a *bergfried* and is, perhaps, derived from the Roman frontier watchtower. Many of these towers are not particularly spacious, and probably served as observation posts and places for last-ditch defense, rather than being used for domestic purposes by the lord. However, many are vented with flues for fireplaces, which means that heat was readily available without resorting to portable braziers. As with Anglo-Norman keeps, the entrance was on the first floor.

Cochem

The imperial fortress of Cochem is situated on the River Moselle, 25 miles southwest of Koblenz. The town was founded in AD 866 and later developed around the castle, which was built c.1020. It was given to the archbishops of Trier in 1294 and was enlarged by Bishop Baldwin in the first half of the 14th century. It was used as a toll station on the Moselle and controlled traffic by stretching a chain across the river.

Cochem castle was destroyed by the French in 1689 but the impressive *bergfried* survives, as does parts of the main gate, the Hexenturm building, and a vaulted undercroft. The castle was restored in neo-gothic style between 1868 and 1878. Nearby is the ruined castle of Winneburg, built in the 13th century by the Metternich family.

Münzenberg

Münzenberg castle straddles a long basalt outcrop overlooking the town in the Wetterau district of Hessen, 25 miles north of Frankfurt. It was largely begun in about 1174 by Kuno von Hagen, perhaps the most famous of the imperial ministeriales of Frederick Barbarossa, and is an excellent example of its time. The emperor had been trying to build territorial lands from Swabia to Thuringia, between those of the powerful German princes, and founded Münzenberg town.

Like many castles at this time, Münzenberg has two *bergfrieden*, both circular and each protecting a different area of approach. Von Hagen built the eastern tower. The castle is elliptical in plan and follows the contours of the hilltop.

Set along the north and south walls are all the domestic arrangements that a prosperous lord would require: a three-story palace, the first floor originally reached by external wooden stairs, hall, private quarters, toilets, and chapel over the gate. An outer curtain wall is set with round towers.

Münzenberg is a *ganerbenburg*, a castle under

right: The largely original bergfried at once-Imperial Cochem dominates castle, which was restored in neo-gothic style in the 19th century.

the joint ownership of different members of a family, and eventually passed through the hands of 48 heirs. In 1286, much of this castle came under the Falkenstein family, who strengthened it and added the palace on the south side of the courtyard.

Drachenfels

On a crag above the town of Königswinter, 6 miles south of Bonn, Drachenfels broods over the right bank of the Rhine. It was built in the first half of the 12th century by the archbishops of Cologne. In 1147, it was granted to the Cassius monastery at Boon, which gave it to the counts of Drachenfels as a form of enfeoffment (the process of investing with an estate held in fee).

The *bergfried*, now in ruins, survives from the 12th century. The castle itself was enlarged in the 15th century, from which time the curtain wall with round towers survives on the east side. During the Thirty Years War (1618–48) Drachenfels was abandoned, and much of the fabric on the river side was taken during the 19th century.

The romantic ruin features in Byron's *Childe Harold*; in a cave nearby, the Teutonic hero Siegfried was said to have killed the dragon guarding the treasure hoard of the Nibelungs and then bathed in its blood.

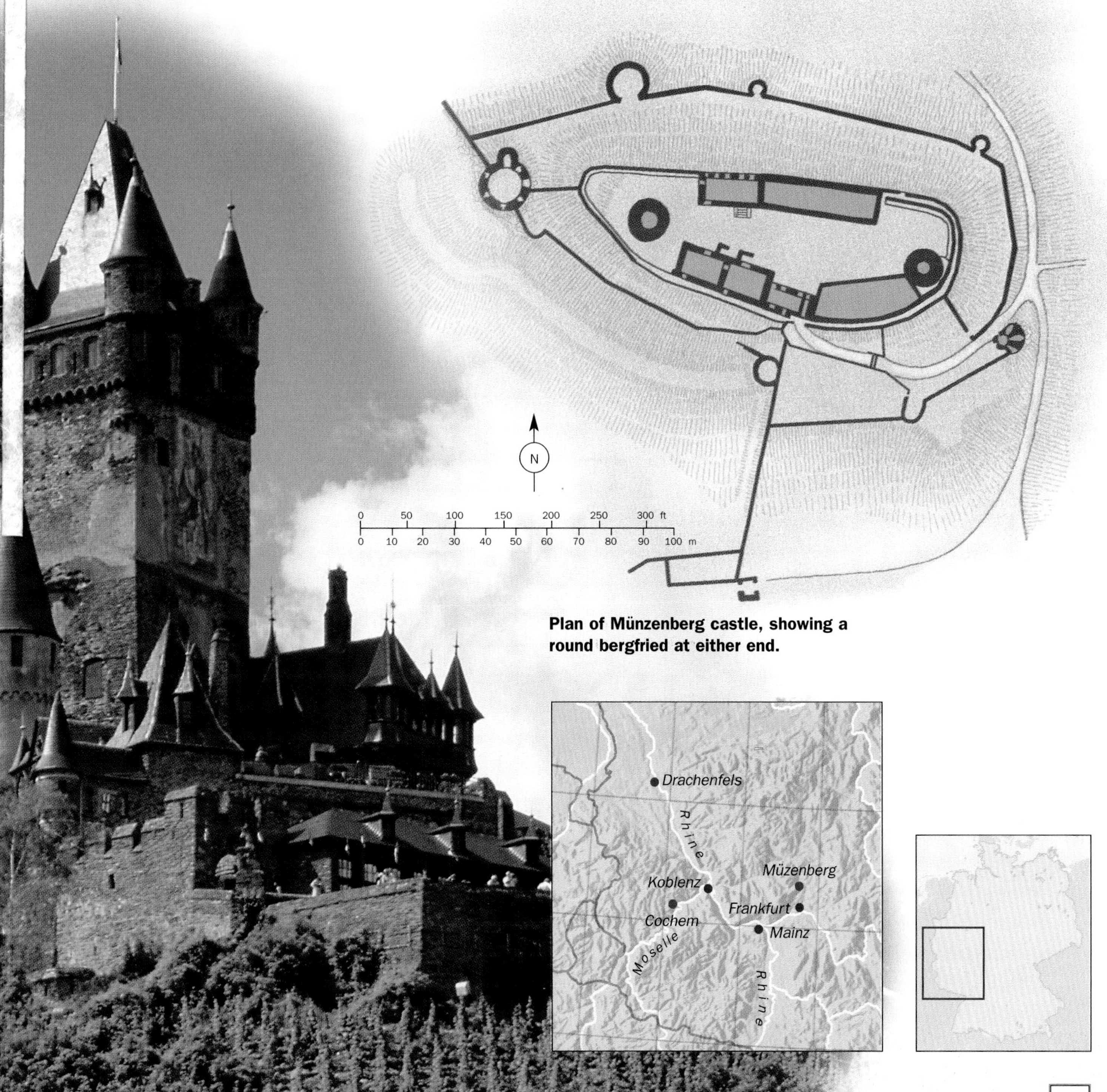

Plan of Münzenberg castle, showing a round bergfried at either end.

Palace Castles

As western emperor, Barbarossa saw himself as heir to the old Roman Empire and that of Charlemagne in AD 800. He made conscious efforts to copy the open effect of the Carolingian palaces like Aachen, and restored those at Ingelheim and Nijmegen. His palaces, or *pfalzen*, contrasted with imperial castles (*kaiserburgen*), which controlled and protected trade routes but were effectively centers of administration.

The palaces were more attractive and largely belonged to the emperor. Goslar in the Harz Mountains is perhaps the most famous imperial palace, but is almost wholly a 19th-century reconstruction. The open plan of these palaces reflects the confidence of imperial power at this time, when defense was secondary to luxury, although at Gelnhausen in Hesse there is a strong wall and a *bergfried*.

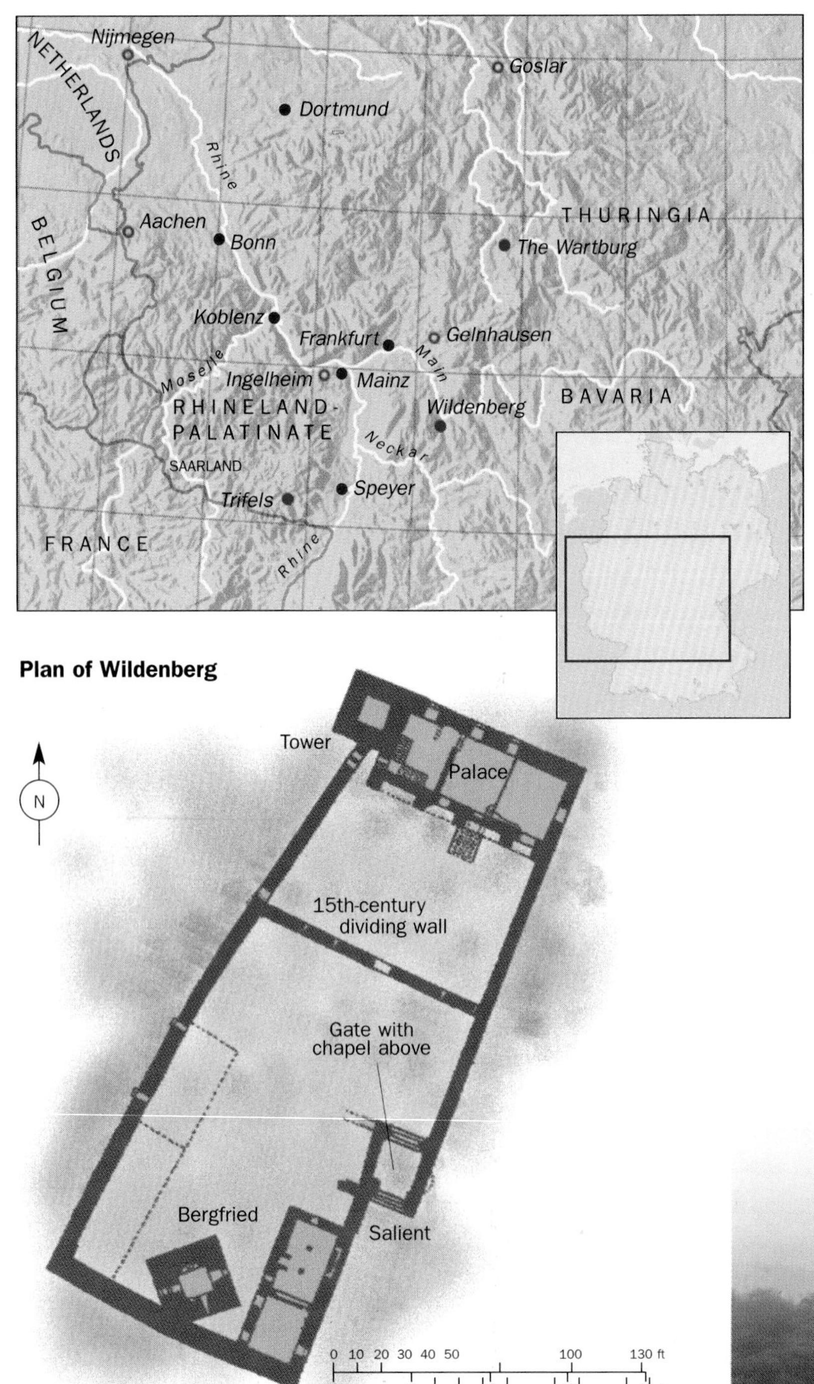

Wildenberg

Wildenberg lies in wooded country in Odenwald in Bavaria (Franconia), 31 miles northeast of Heidelberg. The castle was begun by Rupert von Dürn soon after 1168. Konrad von Dürn continued its growth in the 13th century, adding the upper floor of the palace, which boasts early Gothic two-light windows. The enclosure wall forms a rectangle with a salient for the gate. Above the latter is a chapel. At the western end is a square *bergfried* in rusticated masonry, while a palace and tower are set against the east side. Such castles, with limited access, could be divided into sectors with ditches. In the 15th century, the courtyard was split in half by a dividing wall.

Unfortunately, a fire damaged the castle in 1525. The Bavarian knightly *minnesinger* (poet and singer), Wolfram von Eschenbach (died c.1220), mentions Wildenberg when speaking of lords that he apparently served in the area.

The Wartburg

This famous castle rises on a steep cliff above the south side of Eisenach in the Erfurt region. Ludwig von der Schauenburg first built it in the mid-11th century as a timber structure, with two

above: Reconstruction of Trifels, which commanded an important trade route.

timber towers by 1080. In the 12th century the castle was rebuilt by one of Frederick Barbarossa's followers, Hermann I, Landgrave of Thuringia, in the hope of counterbalancing the powerful princes; it is one of the few examples not built for Barbarossa himself.

The impregnable terrain allowed domestic comfort to take precedence, for example in the impressive sanitary arrangements and large external palace windows. Even so, a stout wall surrounds the site. The window arcades on the courtyard side open into loggias (galleries). The Romanesque palace of the Thuringian Landgraves has survived, though the castle has undergone much restoration, largely faithful to the original design.

Hermann's court was visited by the *minnesingers*, Walter von der Vogelweide and Wolfram von Eschenbach, and was remembered a few generations later in the poem "Sängerkrieg," on which Wagner based his opera *Tannhäuser*. The Wartburg became a symbol of strength for Luther when placed here for his safety by the Elector Frederick III of Saxony, between May 1521 and March 1522.

Trifels

Unlike the palaces, Trifels, perched on a mountain near Annweiler, is a *kaiserburg*, an imperial fortress. Like some other *kaiserburgen*, the emperor appropriated the site from its owners. Trifels similarly lies close to an important trade route, that from Speyer to the Saar, which connected the middle Rhine lands to France. Together with Anebos and Schnarfenberg it forms one of the "Trinity of Fortresses." Barbarossa enlarged the site in 1153.

Trifels castle is now a ruin, although the triangular layout is clearly visible. The large staircase, usually in front of the palace building, here leads to the square tower, inside which is the palace entrance. The semi-circular apse (usually at the east end of a church or chapel, often with a domed roof) here juts out on the floor above, an early example of this feature.

below: The watchtower is one of the earliest remaining parts of Wartburg castle.

Castles on the Rhine

facing: Most powerful of all the Rhine castles, Rheinfells resisted several attempts at its investment, only to be reduced by the need for building materials at the end of the 18th century.

A castle built near a river was ensured a swift means of transport and a source of fresh water. More importantly, it could enforce tolls on traffic passing down the river. With a waterway such as the Rhine, this could be an extremely profitable—it is not surprising that its whole length is dotted with castles.

Most acted as toll stations at some time, but it is a myth that these castles were the haunt of thieves; only a few were held by robber knights, from 1250 to 1273, after the death of Emperor Frederick II. Some acted as secure sites for money-collected for powerful princes.

When Strasbourg was annexed to France in 1681, Louis XIV had no intention of allowing the tolls to bleed his coffers and, in 1689, ordered the destruction of the castles, though tolls were not completely stopped until France seized the whole left bank in 1797.

Marksburg

The Marksburg sits on a hill above the Rhine at Braubach, about 7½ miles south of Koblenz, and is one of the best preserved of the Rhine castles. The site of a nobleman's residence in about 1100, it soon passed to the Palatine Counts on the Rhine. The castle is first recorded in 1231, having probably been built in the early 13th century by Count Eberhard II von Eppstein. A Rhine toll was set up in the mid-13th century and, just before the toll was abolished, the Bavarians handed the castle over to the counts of Katzenelnbogen. The Landgraves of Hesse obtained it in 1479 and it remained with them until 1866.

There are three ranges of buildings, surrounding a triangular courtyard where stands a square *bergfried*. Within this complex are the remains of a palace with Romanesque windows and blind arcading on the north side, with a chapel-tower to the south. In the 14th century another palace was built on the east side of the courtyard and a line of outer defenses added. Another curtain wall with round towers was built in the 15th century, and bastions added to the east side in the 17th century.

Rheinfels

The ruins of Rheinfels, once the strongest castle on the Rhine, crown a spur above the river near St. Goar, approximately 15 miles south of Koblenz. The Taunus counts of Katzenelnbogen set up a toll castle on the shore at St. Goar and with the proceeds built Rheinfels on the hill.

It was begun by Count Diether von Katzenelnbogen in 1245, a roughly rectangular

right: Three ranges of buildings and a bergfried form the inner core of Marksburg castle.

layout with a *bergfried*, but only the foundations of the original building work remain. Wilhem II von Katzenelnbogen (1332–85) reinforced Rheinfels with a huge screen wall to the south side, each end defended by square towers. He also built a palace with round corner towers on the north side of the castle. After 1479 the Landgraves of Hesse-Kassel rebuilt it as a more comfortable residence, although some impressive outworks were also added. In 1692 it was shelled by the French in vain, but in 1797 it was blown up for building materials, leaving only a third of the castle intact.

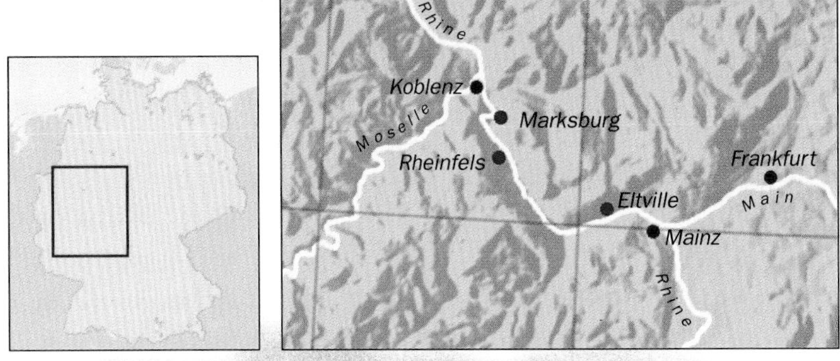

Eltville

From the early Middle Ages a fortification existed at Eltville, 9 miles west of Mainz. In 1330–32 Archbishop Baldwin of Trier began to build a castle above the old one. Completed about 15 years later, the archbishops used it as a residence until the second half of the 15th century.

At the corner of a quadrangular enclosure stands an imposing residential tower with polygonal corner turrets at the summit, and an octagonal stair turret. Inside are painted wall decorations of the 14th–15th centuries. The remains of the palace lie to the west of the tower. Eltville castle was destroyed by the Swedes in 1635 but was restored later in the century.

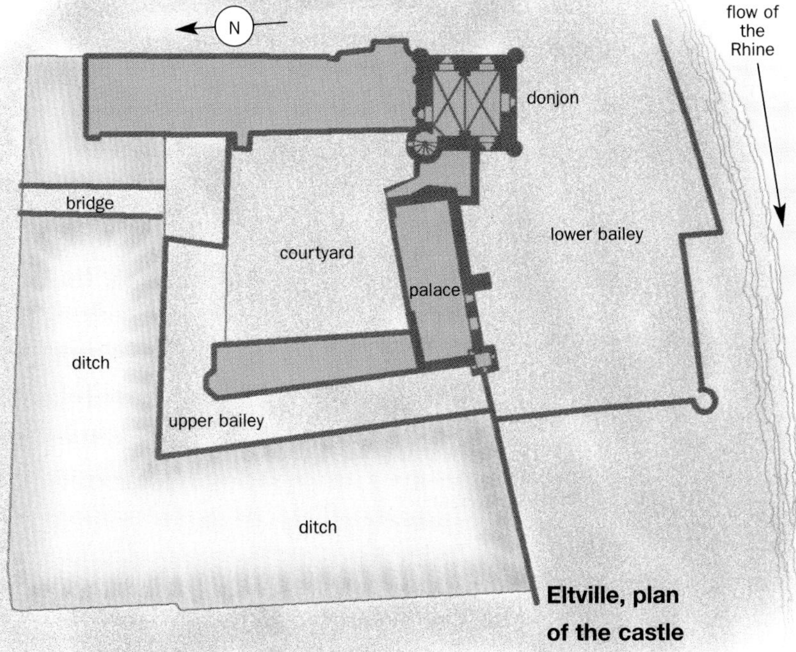

Eltville, plan of the castle

Divided Castles

The German practice of partible inheritance meant that a number of castles were designed so that they could be divided up into sections or units, each belonging to a different branch of the family who owned it. Such castles are called *ganerbenburgen*. This form of castle was also seen in the Midi of France, either shared by brothers or different families.

center: The courtyard at Burg Eltz is hidden by surrounding buildings.

Burg Eltz

This grand pile, with its thrusting pinnacles, is perched on a crag above a bend in the River Eltz, a tributary of the Mosel, near Wierschem, Rhineland-Pfalz. First mentioned in 1157, the counts of Eltz, who owned the castle, had split into several branches by 1268, and the various groups moved into the six *häuser* (buildings) that surrounded the courtyard. Little survives from this period, since most were rebuilt from the late 15th century. However, the 14th-century chapel survives and, at the western end of the courtyard, the Platt-Eltz tower has earlier fabric surviving. Four dwellings open onto the inner courtyard.

below right: The approach at Schönburg is guarded by a ditch and a strong wall or *schildmauer*, seen on the left.

The large number of castles in Germany often resulted in existing castles being rebuilt, instead of new ones being created. The cramped building at Eltz means that the often half-timbered domestic units have large windows for light as they rise higher toward the sun, and bartizans (projecting turrets) jut out from upper stories, rather as in the narrow streets of a medieval town. Inside, the rooms are small but provided some luxury for the nobles, and lively, colorful decoration survives to brighten them. The altar end of an oratory pushes out into a bartizan.

Salzburg

Salzburg lies at Bad Neustadt an der Saale (Bavaria, Franconia), about 44 miles north of Würzburg. One of the best examples of a *ganerbenburg* in Germany and first recorded in 1162, it was built by the bishops of Würzburg but soon came into the possession of the Voite family.

Situated on a spur, the curtain walls follow the contours of the sides. The weakest spot, the eastern approach, is cut off by a ditch and wall set with four square towers. The gate-tower, which dates to about 1200, has rusticated masonry.

Salzburg castle was divided up into six sectors, those to the south and west being the best preserved. The mid-13th century Munze palace survives, and has stepped gable ends and Gothic windows. After the 16th century the castle fell into decay.

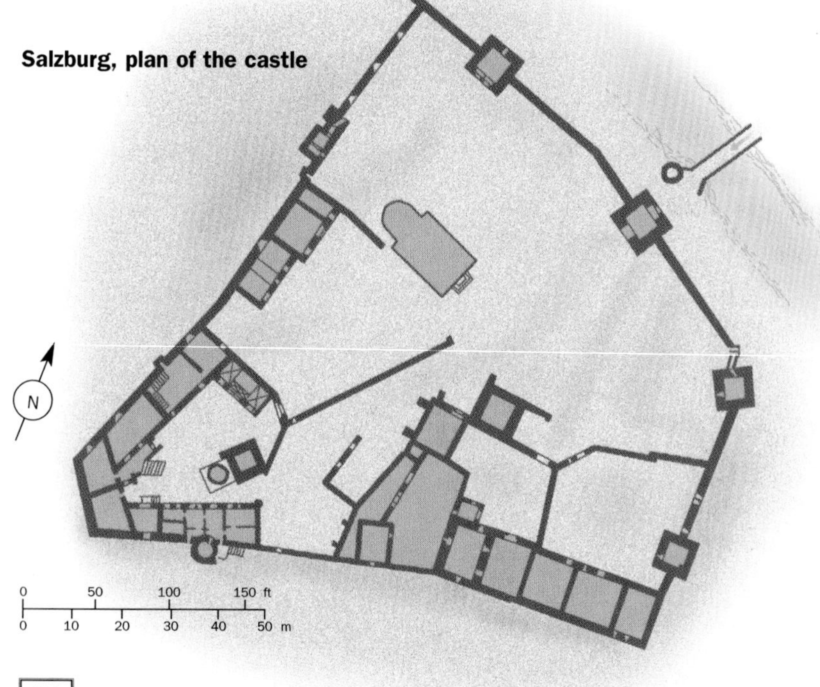

Salzburg, plan of the castle

Romanesque chapel and a round tower. The square *bergfried* is probably of 14th-century date, but the surrounding buildings were rebuilt in the 15th and 16th centuries. The better preserved southern end also has a *bergfried* and adjoining half-timbered domestic buildings.

Schönburg

This castle at Oberwesel in the Rhineland-Pfalz stands on a terraced hill above Schönburg town on the River Rhine, about 29 miles south of Koblenz. First mentioned in 1149, the castle was largely owned by the archbishops of Magdeburg until the 14th century, by which time it had become a *ganerbenburg* of the Counts of Schönburg. It was divided to accommodate members of the family's three branches.

The castle plan is irregular and access from the south is blocked by a rock-cut ditch and a machicolated *schildmauer* (high wall), probably dating from the 14th century. Each family owned a *bergfried* and palace buildings within Schönburg castle; both a square and a round *bergfried* survive, and a small gothic chapel sits in the courtyard. The castle was sacked by the French in 1689

above: Use as a *ganerbenburg* has resulted in an irregular layout at Lichtenstein.

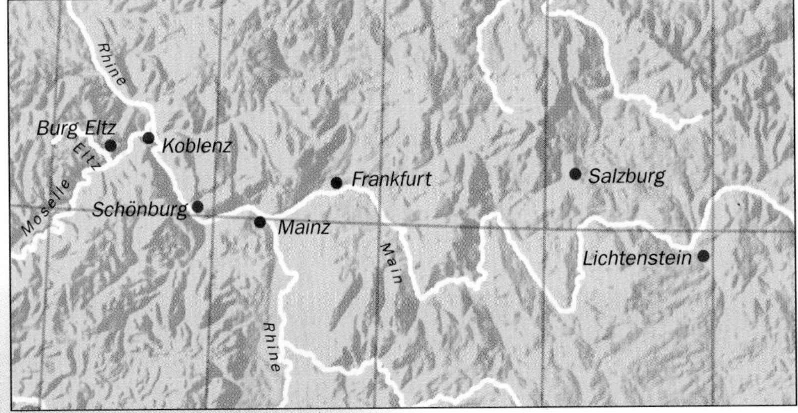

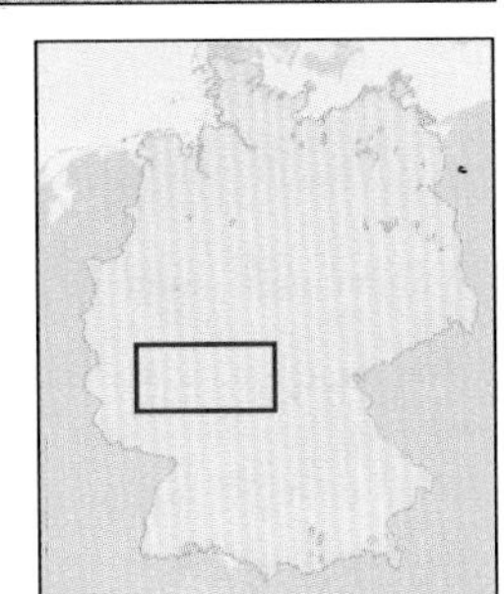

Lichtenstein

Lichtenstein is situated to the north of Bamberg, in Bavaria, Franconia. The castle was first mentioned in 1232 and was divided between three branches of the family of the lords of Lichtenstein, which accounts for its unruly plan.

The northern part of Lichtenstein castle is in a much more ruinous condition than its southern section. The north has a 13th-century curtain wall in rusticated masonry, within which is a

Regular Designs

facing top: Kaub is distinguished by having two castles. Guntenfels stands on a hilly promontory, while Pfalz guards the Rhine. The toll castle's tower dates from before 1330. while the curtain wall was built shortly after 1340.

Castles built on a regular plan did not become common in Germany until the 15th and 16th centuries. One of the most striking examples is the Pfalzgrafenstein at Kaub, a hexagonal castle sitting on an island in the Rhine.

Herzogkasten/Neues Schloss

The Herzogkasten is at Ingolstadt in Nieder Bavaria, about 50 miles north of Munich. The original, 13th-century castle has now largely gone, except for the Herzogkasten, a large, three-story building with stepped gables and a high saddle roof.

As the town expanded, the Neue Schloss was built on the site in the early 15th century. This is a rectangular courtyard with a large warehouse, a round tower on the north side, and the Hauptbau on the east side. The latter is a rectangular palace building with Gothic vaulted rooms and a square and a pentagonal tower. It suffered damage during the Second World War and has been restored.

Glücksburg

Glücksburg in Schleswig-Holstein is 8 miles northeast of Flensburg. The castle was built by N. Karies for the Duke of Holstein-Hadersleben between 1582 and 1587, near the site of a former Cistercian monastery. It is typical of a late 15th - and 16th-century castle of regular plan, being a square castle with octagonal towers at the angles.

It sits on an island and is a good example of a *wasserburg*, or water castle, a type found in flat, low-lying areas. There are three buildings within the walls, with vaulted interiors. They include decoration and furnishings of the 17th to 19th centuries.

Schloss Heidelberg

This castle crowns a spur above the town in Baden-Württenberg. The stronghold known on this site from 1255 was the seat of the Palatine Counts of the Rhine. In 1303 a second fortress was mentioned on Molkenkur, destroyed by lightning in 1537.

Schloss Heidelberg is a huge fortress with a roughly quadrilateral plan, the corners protected by massive towers. Much of the medieval work has been lost, although the Ruprecht Building at the southwest corner of the courtyard, built by Elector Ruprecht III, and the three cylindrical towers on the east side, date from the 15th century. The northernmost of these, the Bell Tower, was heightened in stages to produce a slim octagonal

below: Schloss Heidelberg, with the façade of the Friedrich building flanked by the Bell Tower (left) and Thick Tower (right), and rampart and Great Battery below.

tower in 1525. A rampart was built in front of it to guard the arsenal, and from there the Great Battery extends to the Thick Tower at the northwest corner, the whole formidable obstacle facing the town.

The buildings surrounding the court are largely post-medieval, the first erected in 1508 on the south side; others followed later that century and early in the next. The Ottoheinrich Building of 1556 (on the east) has a beautiful Renaissance façade to the courtyard and is perhaps the most famous part of the castle. The Friedrich Building on the north side, erected by Friedrich IV between 1601 and 1607, became the palace of the Electors; it has a particularly fine façade, with copies of statues of the Wittelsbach family (the original statues were kept under cover inside).

In 1689 and again in 1693 Schloss Heidelberg was destroyed by French troops; in the latter attempt they tried to blow up the southeastern medieval tower, the Krautturm ("Powder Tower"), since it held gunpowder in the lower floor. They only succeeded in splitting it in half, the outer portion sliding into the ditch. It is now sometimes called the "Exploded Tower." The Friedrich Building was restored between 1897 and 1900.

Guntenfels and Pfalz

Gutenfels and Pfalz comprises two castles, the former on a hill above Kaub (22 miles south of Koblenz), the latter on an island in the river. Gutenfels was probably constructed in the first half of the 13th century by the knights of Falkenstein. The heart of the castle survives from this date, a residential block with a rectangular courtyard flanked by wings. A square *bergfried* is attached on the east side. There are several outer curtain walls enclosing courtyards, added later as was common in German lands. The Pfalz (Pfalzgrafenstein) was built as a pentagonal tower by King Ludwig of Bavaria in 1327 to be used as a toll station. Between c.1338–42 the hexagonal enclosure was added around it. Finally a bastion was joined to the southern end in 1607. Because of the swift currents in this part of the river the Pfalz was never taken.

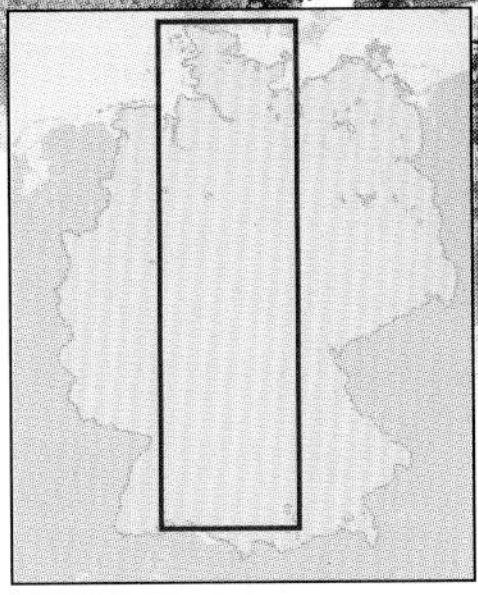

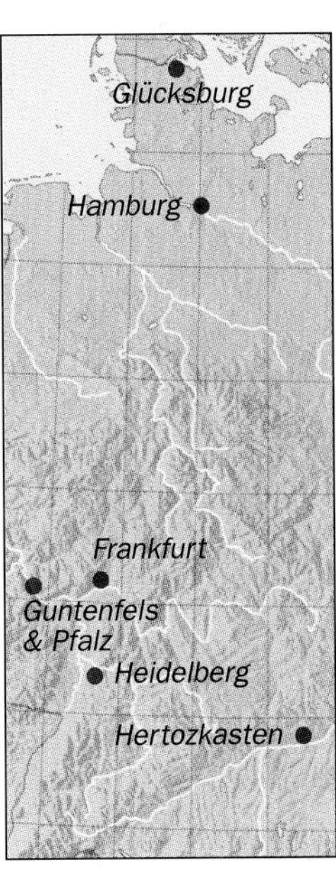

Chapter Eight:
Gazetteer—The Low Countries

In the Wake of Charlemagne

When Charlemagne died and his empire split, the feudal system took hold of the Low Counties. Castles were needed not just as centers of administration but also to stand against threats from Germany and France.

When Charlemagne's empire broke up in the ninth century following his death, most of the Low Countries eventually came under his grandson, Lothar, who ruled a long middle strip of Europe running from the English Channel to northern Italy, with the kingdom of an envious brother on each side. However, the middle kingdom was finally divided up. Gradually, as in France, feudal dynasties grew up as a stabilizing force in the Low Countries and dukes and counts established themselves. Civil unrest and the threat from French and German states in particular meant that many castles were built in these areas.

below: The exterior of the Burcht at Leiden.

Perhaps not surprisingly, the architecture of castles in the Low Countries was greatly influenced by the design of French and German castles. However, they also display many unique features, which are evident from quite an early date. This is particularly noticeable in Holland. One of the oldest Dutch castles is the Burcht at Leyden, built in about 1150, where a hill has been crowned with a circular wall to form an enclosure. A shell tower was also built but the walls are not as high as most examples in England. The wall is set with arches supporting a gallery, a feature that would become characteristic of Holland and the Lower Rhine.

The flat terrain in Holland favored the simple ring-work and this was popular. The Burcht was copied at Teylingen and Oostvoorne. Here, however, additions were later built at Teylingen in the form of a main block, while an almost square tower was placed within the center of the motte at Oostvoorne, and similar structures at Kessel and Wouw.

In the 13th century the square or rectangular castle plan appears in Holland, with towers at angles. Muiden, with its circular angle-towers, is

1297	1302	1305	1340s	1479	1499	1530s	1567
French king Philip IV invades Flanders	Flanders defeats France at the Battle of the Spurs at Courtrai	Flanders submits to French rule	Wind-driven pumps are used to drain marshland in Holland to reclaim land	French troops invade the Netherlands but are defeated by Hapsburg troops	Hapsburg emperor Maximilian I puts down a rebellion in the Netherlands	Renaissance brings new styles of architecture to the Low Countries	Dutch war of independence against the Spanish begins

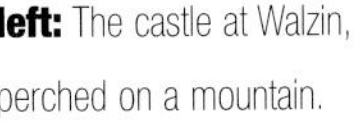

left: The castle at Walzin, perched on a mountain.

the best example of this type. Others of this form were built, notably Helmond, raised in the early 15th century and latterly used as a town hall. The circular angle-towers reflect French influence but there is still a Dutch feel to the work. The round towers at Sluis are a good example of strong French influence, for which a French designer was employed in 1384. The castle was later destroyed.

Comfort versus defence

Another form of early design in Holland was the turreted castle, which was to become an important form in Flanders. It first appears in the Romanesque period, though examples of such defenses have been largely destroyed or have fallen into decay. However, a small number of the fortified houses erected by nobles from the 13th century have survived. It often began as a tower, usually cubical and built in brick. To this was added a wing, creating an L-shaped house similar to those seen in Scotland. A wall was often built to connect the corners, so creating a small defended courtyard. Other domestic buildings were protected by an outwork, usually added in the later Middle Ages. As elsewhere, as the centuries passed defensive needs gradually gave way to a desire for comfort.

Although Belgian castles are similar in many ways to those in Holland, there is more evidence of French influence. The suspended flanking towers on the curtain walls at Gravensteen in Ghent are a case in point. Composite structures for defense and comfort became usual in Flanders; the polygon with flanking towers, successor to the ring-fort, would be built until the end of the Middle Ages. Latterly such structures were modified, such as Gaasbeck, or else rebuilt.

Already in the late medieval period castles were displaying the elegant designs reminiscent of those seen in manuscript illustration, again in a similar vein to some French fortresses. Walzin demonstrates this on the side of the fortress overlooking a mountain side. The merchant classes copied these defenses by placing pinnacles and small towers on their town halls and cloth halls.

left: Reconstruction of Oostvoorne, showing the central tower.

left and below: The ruins of Oostvoorne's central tower.

Belgium and Luxemburg

The earliest castles in Belgium appear to date from the 11th century. The flat nature of much of the area means that often castles are of the *wasserburg* type, set in a wet moat.

Gravensteen

This unique castle is in Ghent in Oost-Vlaanderen, Belgium, at the confluence of the Lieve and the Lys rivers. A timber erection was the first fortress to be built on the site (possibly Viking), but in about 1000 a stone donjon was raised.

The castle was besieged in 1128 by the supporters of Thierry of Alsace. The remains of this early tower now form the cellars of the donjon that replaced it in the 12th century, built by Philip of Alsace upon his return from a crusade in the 1180s. He greatly enlarged the existing castle to control the burghers who were building towers in the city. Also from this period survive the windows of the castellan's apartments attached to the donjon, and the gatehouse, with a cross-shaped window in one of its rooms.

The castle was rebuilt and restored between the 13th and 14th centuries. The oval courtyard, which appears to rise out of the moat, is surrounded by a curtain wall with 24 projecting two-storey towers, or bartizans. Open-backed, each could have a wooden fighting deck inserted in time of need. Within the castle stands the count's palace, set on the curtain wall separated from the donjon, and other buildings with vaulted basements.

right: The bartizans on the curtain wall at Gravensteen.

In the early 14th century the burghers of Ghent twice besieged the castle; in 1301 fire was used to induce a surrender and in 1338 the attackers managed to breach the outer wall. Today the repairs made in the 14th century to the walls and gateway bear witness to these actions.

The counts used the living quarters for the Prince's Court of Justice from 1407 to 1708. It was sold in 1780, becoming a factory, but was restored between 1889 and 1908.

Beersel

Beersel Brussels is a moated castle built of brick as a forward defense to Brussels. Between 1300 and 1310 a circular enclosure was built, protected by a stone wall.

In 1489, during the "Revolt of the Towns," the castle was twice besieged and taken, suffering extensive damage in the process. However, it was mostly rebuilt in 1491 when three horseshoe-shaped towers were added to the walls—a shape designed to resist gunfire, and seen earlier at Fougères, suggesting French influence in the ground-plan. The towers are a precursor of the battery towers and double gates built in towns during the late Middle Ages.

There is a typically Flemish stepped style above courtyard level. Unoccupied since 1544, the interior is much as it was left.

Vianden

25 miles north of Luxemburg city stands the ruined castle of Vianden, on a rock overlooking the Our valley. The Romans and Carolingians had earlier used the site.

Built in the 10th or 11th century, the Counts of Vianden gradually extended the fortress in the 13th and 14th centuries to become one of the

left: The horseshoe-shaped towers at Beersel.

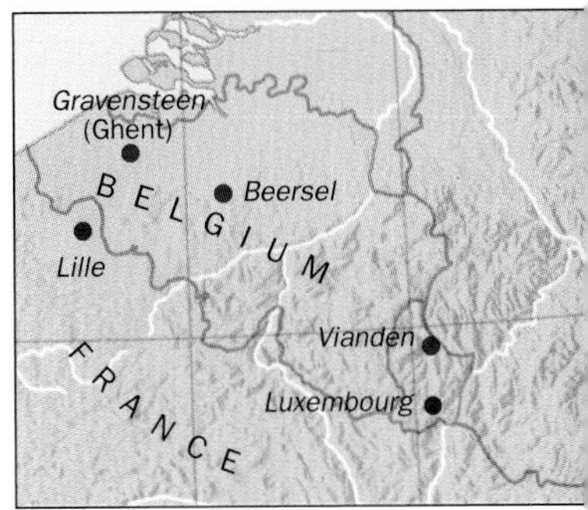

largest in Europe. There is an inner ward with a single round angle-tower and domestic ranges, and a lower outer ward, the castle being protected by three entrance gates.

The chapel, the small and the large palaces were built between the end of the 12th and mid-13th centuries. There is a delightfully decorated palace portal, while the chapel has a hexagonal opening through which the underground vault can be reached. The Knight's Hall is capable of holding 500 men. The "Quartier de Juliers" on the west side of the now destroyed large palace originated in the early 14th century.

From 1417 until the French Revolution the castle was owned by the House of Orange-Nassau, whose members constructed the early 17th-century House of Nassau. The castle was confiscated during the French Revolution but returned to King William I of Holland in 1820. Sold off, Vianden fell into ruin, but the grand Duke of Luxemburg transferred it to state ownership in 1977 and it was extensively rebuilt.

below: The palaces at the castle of Vianden.

The Netherlands

above: The brick castle of Muiderslot, with machicolated gatehouse and covered wall-walk.

Some 300 of the 2,000 or more castles which once existed in Holland survive. The country has very similar terrain to Belgium and again there are a large number of moated examples. Of regular and irregular plan, they utilize both natural and artificial water courses. A few examples of stone ring-walls survive at Utrecht, Horn, and Leyden, in a style of plan seen again at Ghent.

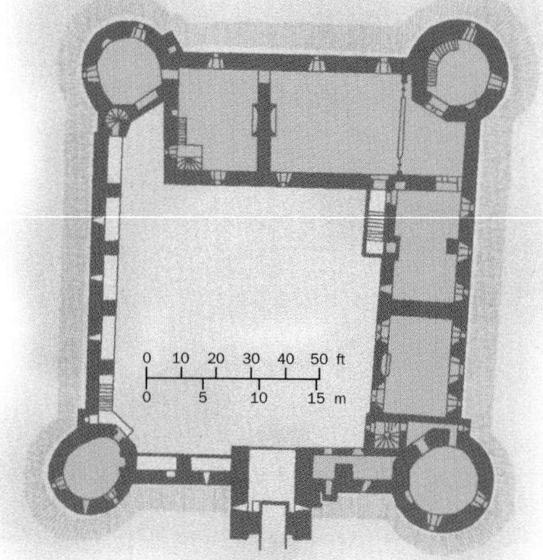

right: Muiderslot, plan of the castle

Floris V, Count of Holland, gave great impetus to castle-building in the 13th century with the building of Muiden, with French-influenced rectangular layout and round towers, and the Ridderzaal or great hall at Het Binnenhof, his palace in the Hague (now the seat of the Dutch government). The proximity of the prosperous Flemish cities was to influence the desire for comfort in later Dutch castles, and it is to this period that perhaps the best examples belong.

Muiderslot

Situated at Muiden in Noort-Holland, 8 miles east of Amsterdam, the Muiderslot has been fortified since about AD 1000. Count Floris V rebuilt it in 1280, but then moved his allegiance from Edward I of England to Philip IV of France. Discontented nobles seized him and, when the peasantry prevented them from taking their prisoner to England, assassinated him in the castle in 1296; the 13th-century castle on the site was subsequently destroyed. Some of Holland's most famous writers have described these events in their work.

The present castle was largely built between 1370 and 1386 by Albert of Bavaria and is one of the best-preserved brick castles in the Netherlands. It consists of a square enclosure sitting in a moat, and is similar to the sort of *randhausburg* seen in the Lower Rhine. The gatehouse is machicolated and a covered wall-walk runs the length of the curtain walls. On the north side was a hall, begun before the initial destruction, and on the east side is a residential wing, both running along inside the curtain walls. The Muiderslot was captured by the Duke of Gelderland in 1508 and again by the Earl of Leicester in 1586.

Valkenburg

Valkenburg, 7 miles east of Maastricht in Limburg, has the distinction of being the only hill castle in Holland.

The first castle was probably built in about 1115 by Gosewijn I, Lord of Valkenburg; a rectangular donjon within a surrounding wall with timber buildings. This castle was effectively destroyed in a siege by the count of Louvain in 1122. The 13th-century castle that was erected largely disappeared when it was besieged in 1329 by John III, Duke of Brabant.

Valkenburg was again rebuilt and in 1370 became the property of the Duke of Brabant. Rather triangular in plan, there are the remains of round towers at two corners, with a domestic range along one side and a lower court. There is a ruined 14th-century bent barbican, called a *dwingel*. Underground passages are hewn into the rock, possibly for use during medieval sieges.

Valkenburg was again besieged in 1465, 1568, and in 1632. Unfortunately Louis XIV or King-Stadholder William III blew the castle up in 1672 to stop the French making use of it. A chapel hewn inside the rock was used during the French occupation. The castle itself was not rebuilt and remained a ruin. In 1944 the Velvet Cave, reached from the passages, was used as a hideout during the fighting between Germans and the allies.

above: The ruins of Valkenburg.

Wedde

This fortress, standing on a hill, is a turreted castle in which a central tower is surrounded by a curtain to enclose the outbuildings. The rectangular tower was the first part of the castle to be built, probably during the mid-14th century.

A palisade protected the courtyard where the domestic buildings stood, but during the civil wars of the 1470s this was replaced by stone, itself updated in about 1530, when a hall was constructed to the north of the tower. A rectangular angle-tower projects diagonally from each corner of the curtain. It has since been rebuilt as a residence.

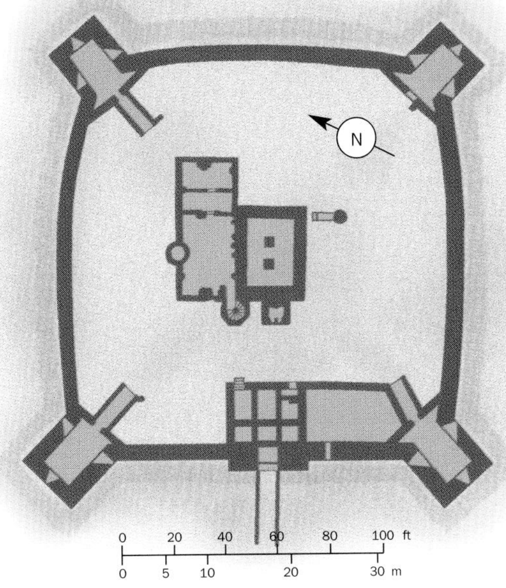

left: Wedde, plan of the castle.

Chapter Nine:
Gazetteer—Austria

Hilltop Castles and Water Defenses

Austria is rich in castles. As a nation, Austria formed a buffer against the threats from the East, and had no alternative but to defend itself.

At first Austria was threatened by Hungarian raiders, but as these were largely Magyar horsemen they posed little real threat to fortifications. Austria came under the German emperors and formed part of the Holy Roman Empire.

In 1493 its duke, Maximilian, became Emperor. In the 15th century the security of Austria was severely tested when Constantinople (now Istanbul, part of Turkey) fell in 1453 to the Ottoman Turks under Sultan Mehmet II. The way then lay open for a full-scale Ottoman Turkish invasion into Christian Europe. Under Suleiman I "The Magnificent" the Turks seized Belgrade in 1521, and Rhodes in 1522. Killing the king of Hungary in battle in 1526, they reached Vienna in 1529, but after an unsuccessful siege, the Ottomans withdrew.

below: The partially restored existing castle at Hardegg originally dates from about 1200.

1261	1278	1315	1386	1415	1485	1544	1683
King Ottokar of Bohemia captures Austria	Rudolf of Hapsburg beats Bohemians and takes Austria	Swiss defeat the Austrian army at the battle of Morgarten	The Hapsburgs accept Swiss independence within the Holy Roman Empire	Supported by the Holy Roman Empire, the Swiss take the Aargau region of Austria	The Hapsburgs are driven out of Austria by the Hungarians	Turkish forces campaign in Austria, eventually fighting to a draw	Turkish forces invade Austria, reaching Vienna, but are repulsed

After this crisis, the Hapsburg rulers of Austria could genuinely claim the title "Bulwark of Christendom" for their lands. In the 16th and 17th centuries several popes tried to arrange crusades through Austrian leaders. However, the Holy League of 1537–40 became the only true crusading union, and it was between the pope, emperor, and the republic of Venice.

Austria's mountainous terrain means that there is a great variety and combination of castle defenses. In the eastern part of the country particularly, the castle appears to have developed from much earlier Germanic prehistoric settlements, further fortified to meet the Turkish threat. This means it is often difficult to tell a bastion from a castle.

The stone tower was the main form of defense in Austria as it was elsewhere, certainly in the 12th century. At first it was the nobility and church leaders who built them, then knights in official positions and nobles whose titles came from offices increasingly took over. Often the tower was built before anything else, as at Steiermark. The towers at first were usually slim and square, useful more as defensive watchtowers than as a residences.

A quite serviceable, even spartan, hall would be built close by, the whole connected by a wall that hugs the contours more more closely in Austria than elsewhere. Thus in Styria, Carinthia, and especially the Tyrol, castles of irregular design blend into the mountainous landscape, some so narrow and inhospitable that it does not appear that they were often inhabited except when defense was necessary.

Evolving towers

Watchtowers at the heart of the castle can be seen at numerous places, such as Hardegg (*see page 89*). Such castles were built where the Hapsburgs had their influence, such as Switzerland, Bohemia, and Slovenia. The Burgenland, or "land of castles" richly deserved this epithet, though the terrain was not always favorable to building. Some watchtowers resemble Roman towers but are taller, and they were also being built late in the Middle Ages to command valley roads.

This period of castle-building largely ends by 1300. Already a shift toward additional domestic comfort is noticeable, with additional residential buildings in evidence. This was often done by extending the castle to accommodate such building work. By 1300 also, the watch tower was beginning to be used as a residence, achieved by erecting larger towers with wider window openings and better room layouts, or by adapting older towers. At Krempelstein, for example, comfort is given priority over defense. These towers can also be found in towns, perhaps under influence from northern Italy via the Southern Tyrol.

above: Anif is a *wasserburg* or water castle near Salzburg, built in the 16th century by the Archbishop of Salzburg and enlarged in 1803 by the Count of Arco-Stepperg.

The defenses of the castle were also changing. Parts of the donjon wall, barbican, etc. might be given entrenchments but walls rarely extended around the whole castle. Outworks also appear to take over from the storage rooms more usual in the earlier period, allowing barns, workshops etc. to be enclosed within the sphere of the main castle. Despite this new turn in the direction of comfort, the Austrian castles still often seem compact and severe when compared to those in Germany. Defense against external enemies, for the owner and the local civilians, would remain a constant menace for centuries.

The modern regions of Austria.

Great Towers

The slender watchtower, which may derive, like those in northern Italy, from Byzantine models, was superceded in the later 13th century by large towers more like the Norman donjon, though probably not directly influenced by them.

Friesach

Friesach in Carinthia is a fortified town with surrounding walls and a moat. There are three castles, all built by the archbishops of Salzburg, though the site had been known since 860 and several religious orders established monasteries and convents in the town.

To the north-west of the town is the largest of the castles, the Petersberg, built by Archbishop Gebhard before 1077 and given a large *bergfried* by Archbishop Konrad between 1124 and 1130, who also extended the castle. St Rupert's chapel within the castle houses attractive 13th-century frescoes.

Further building at the Petersberg was undertaken in the 16th century. The second castle, the Geiersberg, is located about half a mile north of the town itself, the *bergfried* preserved there being built in about 1130. In 1750 the castle was left to decay but restoration work was begun in 1912. On the south side of the town is the Virgilienberg, a small fortified priory.

below: Six courtyards encircle Rappottenstein.

Rappotenstein

The castle of Rappotenstein overlooks the River Kamp, 6 miles southwest of Zwettl. It was begun by Rapoto von Kneuringer (whose family built Aggstein and Durnstein) in the second half of the 12th century.

Rapoto erected a pentagonal tower on the south side of the castle nucleus, which itself is protected by high walls. There are some corbels

left: On Austria's border with Bohemia (modern-day Czech Republic), Heidenreichstein is a good example of an Austrian *wasserburg*.

on the tower walls that might have been designed to support wooden hoardings. Rappotenstein was a comfortable knightly castle such as those described by *minnesingers*, German poets encouraged by the Babenburg dukes of Austria.

The chapel of St. Pancras dates to 1348, while the domestic range on the north side of the inner courtyard—kitchen, vaulted hall, and the Archivzimmer—date to the second half of the 15th century. The curtain walls have Italianate merlons.

The large outer courtyard with its brew-house was built in about 1548, making a total of six such courtyards around the central nucleus. Also at this time the arcaded portico on the south side of the inner courtyard was added in renaissance style. The castle approaches are well thought-out and utilize the terrain, as does the main castle.

Heidenreichstein

Heidenreichstein is perhaps the most important of the Austrian *wasserburgen*. It stands 10 miles northeast of Gmünd in Lower Austria. It was begun in 1190 by the Burggraf von Gars. It was another castle of the minnesingers.

Heidenreichstein has a surviving 13th-century square *bergfried*, but most other buildings date from the 15th and 16th centuries. It has three round angle-towers with conical roofs; one is a great round tower whose hoarding is included in the conical tiled roof. It was reached by two drawbridges and a renaissance-era gateway. The great chimney stacks and privvies jutting from the walls demonstrate the later desire for comfort, sometimes at the expense of defense. The castle was besieged in the 15th century both by the Hussites (followers of Jan Huss, considered heretics and subject to largely German crusades), and by rebellious peasants.

Schloss Bruck

This castle lies half a mile west of Lienz in the Tyrol, perched on a crag overlooking the Isel valley. The castle was erected by the counts of Gîz between 1252 and 1277, and consists of a large rectangular Bergfried with an enclosure to the east. The Romanesque chapel was rebuilt in the 15th century but retains frescoes from both the 13th and 15th centuries. The Knights' Hall (Rittersaal) is well-preserved.

In 1442–3 the castle was acquired by the city of Lienz. The Hapsburg family took over the castle in 1500 and the defenses were modernized by adding an outer wall set with bastions on the south side. The castle now holds collections of art and cultural history.

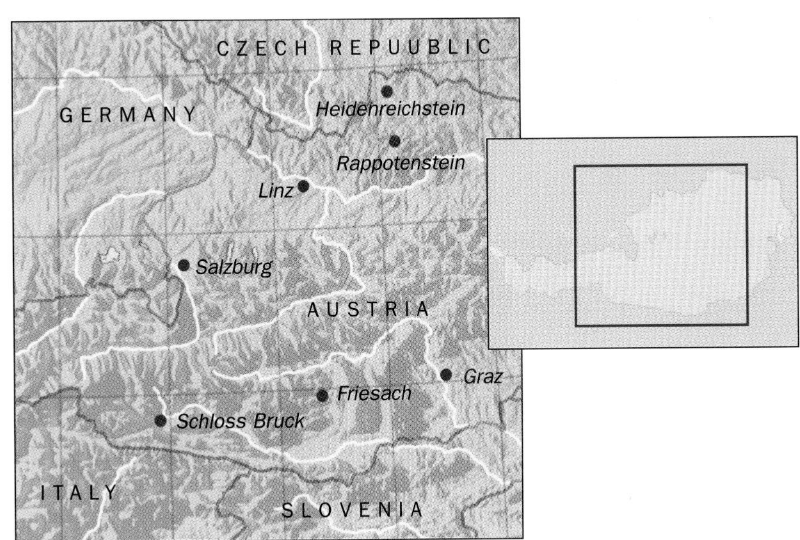

Hill and Mountain Castles

Austria has numerous castles set along crags and rocky ridges, many of which have irregular layouts as a result of fitting themselves to the contours of the hill or mountain.

Dürnstein

Four miles west of Krems in Lower Austria on a cliff that overlooks the River Danube, stands Dürnstein castle. It was probably built by the Kneuringer family in the early 12th century.

It has an irregular ground plan and is famous as the castle in which Richard the Lionheart was imprisoned by Duke Leopold of Austria after capturing him while on his way home from the Third Crusade. Richard had insulted the Duke during the crusade by having his banner torn down from the walls of Acre after its capture. He whiled away the time by writing poetry and wrestling with his warders, we are told. In legend Richard was found by the minstrel Blondel, who rode across the Empire singing a song under the windows of various castles until Richard heard and recognized it. A huge ransom finally secured his release.

Dürnstein was almost completely destroyed in the 13th century by Duke Frederick II of Austria. However, it was rebuilt and became the center of

below: Guarding a sharp bend in the Danube, the castle of Dürnstein overlooks the town of the same name.

above: A view across the long courtyard at Aggstein, high above the Danube.

the Kneuringer family's castles and their main residence. It still had an active military role when it was captured by the Swedes in 1645.

Aggstein

Aggstein is located some 8 miles northeast of Melk in Lower Austria. It was first built probably in the early 12th century by Nizzo, son of Azzo von Hezzmannsweisen, founder of the family Kneuringer.

The castle has been fitted along a narrow ridge high above the River Danube. There is a long, narrow but spacious courtyard with buildings along the south side between two outcrops of rock, on which are further buildings. The long extended shape is typical of castles in this part of Austria. Aggstein was seized by the Duke of Austria in 1231 and again in 1296, after which it remained in a ruinous state until the 15th century.

In 1429 Georg Scheck von Wald was granted the castle and rebuilt it much as it is seen today. The middle courtyard buildings, however, were added in the 17th century.

Runkelstein

Runkelstein in Italian Trentino-Alto Adige, under the Hapsburgs a part of Austria's South Tyrol, is perched on a steep mountain. Irregular in plan, it was built in the first half of the 13th century by the Vanga family, and has been modified over the centuries.

The noteworthy inner bailey lies on the north side of the castle. Within it the Vangas' palatial eastern residential buildings are set close to the side of the rock face, in the style of a west German *randhausburg*, and there are similar buildings on the west side. The interiors of the living rooms, including the hall of coats-of-arms, bath hall, and tournament hall, contain numerous excellent 14th-century frescoes and paintings. The summer palace also has frescoes, including the story of the lovers Tristan and Iseult. To the south the outer bailey fits around the ridge.

The castle changed hands several times, and in the 19th century Emperor Franz Joseph passed it into the care of the city of Bolzano.

Hardegg

Hardegg is on a rocky ridge above the River Thaya, about 8½ miles northwest of Retz in Lower Austria. A castle was probably first built on the site in the early 12th century, but the surviving fabric was begun c.1200. The town of Hardegg lay on the Austrian border and the fortress was strategically placed to provide a strong point against Hungarians, Poles, and Bohemians.

Hardegg is a large castle, provided with four huge towers, including a Romanesque watchtower, and two residential blocks. Restoration work began in the late 19th century. There is an extensive arms collection inside the castle.

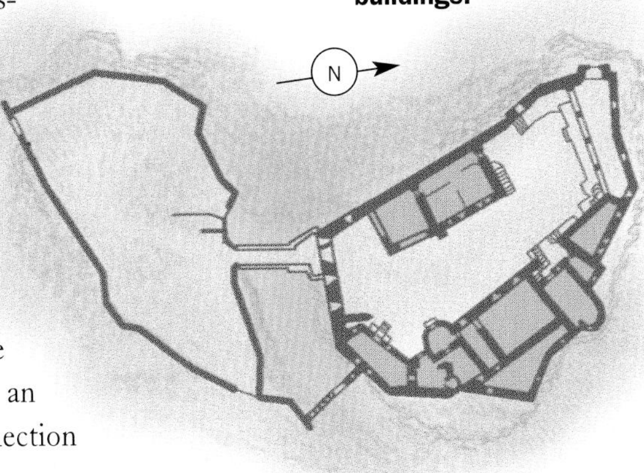

Plan of Runkelstein and (above) the palatial domestic buildings.

Bulwark Against the East

above: The impressive walls and towers of Hohensalzburg tower over Salzburg.

In the 14th and 15th centuries castle design in Austria changed somewhat, at first in response to a desire for more and better residential accommodation. From the 15th century, however, castles were strengthened against the threat of Turkish aggression via the Balkans. Major castles were the first to be strengthened, with bastions, casemates, and additional walls, a process that continued in the 16th century as the threat increased.

Hohensalzburg

This castle stands on the Mönschsberg ridge above Salzburg and is a mixture of work from several periods. It was first built to secure an Alpine route by Archbishop Gebhard in 1077, a papal supporter during the Investiture Contest between popes and emperors.

The earliest part to survive is the central Altes Schloss, although this was altered during the 15th century, especially under Archbishop Leonhard von Keutschach (1495–1515). He was responsible for the Golden Room decorated in 1501, including red marble spiral columns, carved wooden paneling with gilding and painting, notable wainscoting, and an amazing decorated ceramic oven. Decorated wainscoting is also seen in his other achievement, the Great Hall.

Hohensalzburg was also enlarged during the 15th century, with four round towers added to the curtain walls and a granery, while in the 16th and 17th centuries cruder outer bastions were added.

Archbishop Leonhard had to take up residence in the castle because of the hostility of the citizens and a peasant uprising. In 1525, despite all the defense works against foreign incursions, the castle underwent its only siege, during the Peasant's Revolt.

right: The long, winding approach set with numerous gates is a feature of Hochosterwitz.

Hochosterwitz

This very impressive fortress stands on the crest of a high hilltop in Carinthia, 5½ miles east of St. Veit an der Glan. A castle is recorded here as early as 960 and later belonged to the archbishop of Salzburg and the lords of Osterwitz, whose members provided the hereditary cupbearer from 1209. When one of the latter was caught by the Turks and died in prison, Emperor Frederick III pawned Osterwitz to the governor of Carinthia, Christof Khevenhüller.

The present castle at Hochosterwitz was largely built by governor Georg Khevenhüller, who purchased it in 1570. Work continued until 1586 on fortifying it against Turkish incursions. Unlike many Austrian frontier castles of this period, which had existing medieval bastions and other defenses adapted for cannon, the earlier fabric at Hochosterwitz has largely gone. The main nucleus is rectangular in plan and set with three round angle towers. The approach to the castle is extremely impressive; there are no less than 14 gate-towers and three ditches to be negotiated as the path winds up the hillside. The scale of such gate defenses is extremely rare; each was given a name. Little alteration has been made since the 16th century, and the family remained in charge of the castle.

Forchtenstein

Some 14 miles southeast of Wiener Neustadt stands Forchtenstein, perched on an outcrop of rock in the foothills below the Rosaliengebirge mountains. It was built in about 1300 by the Counts of Mattersdorf, who erected the huge prow-shaped donjon on the west side of the central courtyard. The nearly quadrangular enclosure has outworks with bastions. The castle passed to the Esterhzy family in 1622 and the residential areas were completely rebuilt. Moreover, artillery emplacements were then added. During the 16th and 17th centuries the castle was in the forefront of the wars against the Ottoman Turks. The well, which is 466 feet deep, was dug by Turkish prisoners between 1660 and 1680. It is fitted with a treadmill for winching the water.

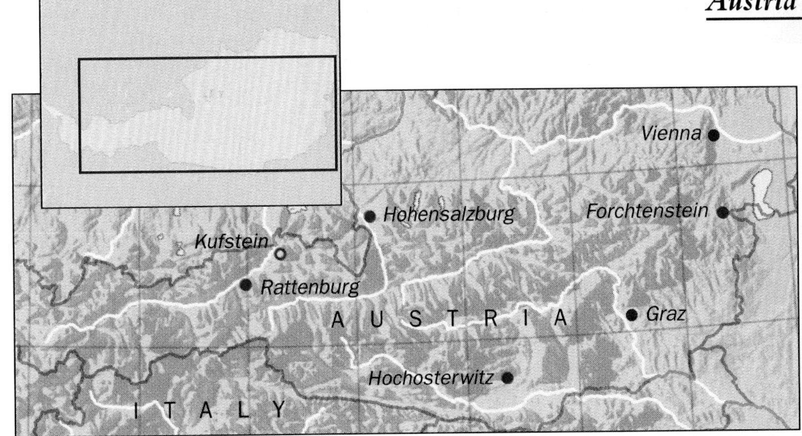

above: The great donjon rears above the walls of Forchtenstein.

Rattenburg

Rattenburg in the Tyrol, along with Kufstein and Sigmundskron in the same area, is one of the most powerful castles in the region. Rattenburg followed the ideal pattern in having a central strong bastion and a new large outer bulwark.

Plan of Rattenburg

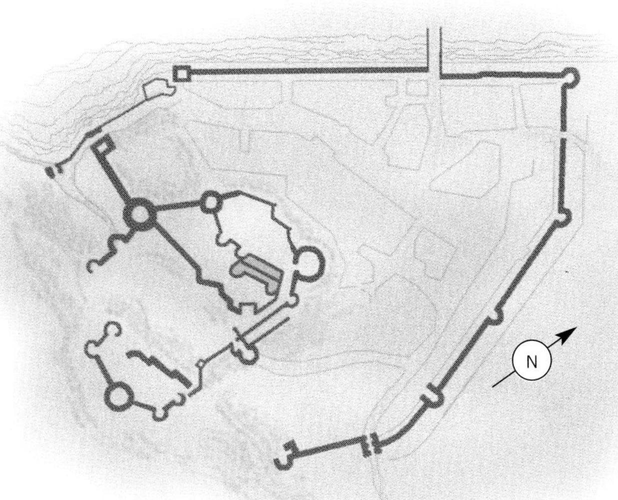

Chapter Ten: Gazetteer—Switzerland

Outside Influences on the Swiss

Despite its small size, Switzerland is full of castles, often sited on mountain crags or hills. They betray influences from the lands they border, namely France, Germany, and Italy, and share features with Welsh castles, since they used Edward I's Master Mason, James of St. George.

facing top: The stronghold pf Kropfenstein clings to a narrow mountain pass.

facing bottom: Part of Fribourg city walls.

below: The town of Murten in Canton Fribourg (Morat in French) still retains most of its enclosing walls, *chemin de ronde*, and towers. After his defeat at Grandson (*see page 99*), the Burgundian army of Charles the Bold was brought again to battle at the edge of Lake Murten/Morat in 1476 where the Swiss Confederation defeated them and ended Burgudian power in the region.

Although the Swiss had enjoyed freedom since the days of the Roman Empire, this was threatened in the 13th century by the oppression of the Hapsburg dukes of Austria. In 1291 three communities on the shores of Lake Lucerne, the Uri, Schwyz, and Unterwalden, formed an alliance that grew in strength as the Austrians were opposed.

As in Austria, the castles are often well-integrated into the terrain in which they were built, and as in Austria, the tower is an early and important feature of castle architecture. Gradually the towers were built away from the lowland farms and villages and were sited up hills, crags, or mountains, where they not only became more difficult to attack but also much more impressive to visitors, proclaiming the status of their owners. In many examples, however, this idea was abandoned, resulting in a number of village towers, such as Frauenberg. State-held castles, as well as some built by feudal lords, were usually provided with a tower.

It is difficult to draw a distinction between the watchtower and the residential tower in Switzerland, since residential and military functions overlap and blur the issue. As in Austria, comfort was mostly denied in order to maintain a well-functioning fortress. The ground floor of the main building was used for stores and a kitchen, and sometimes even a stable. The main residential building might occasionally take on the role of the tower. They could be set in a grotto, where the side of the mountain came down and only a frontage had to be built to block the passage through.

A good example of such a rock castle is at Kropfenstein. Tucked away securely wrapped in its rocky mantle, such strongholds are sometimes thought to have been the homes of robber knights, but there is no evidence to back this. Castles were built to command roads and mountain passes that would provide lucrative tolls from travelers.

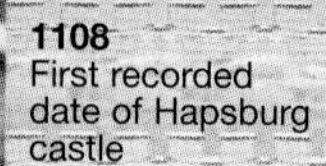

1108	1291	1291	1315	1319–53	1386	1444	1468
First recorded date of Hapsburg castle	Treaty of Rütli unites first three cantons of Swiss Confederation	Swiss cantons revolt against the Hapsburgs	Austria loses the Battle of Morgarten to Switzerland	Cantons Lucerne, Zurich, Glarus, Zug, and Berne join Swiss Confederation	Leopold II of Swabia is killed by the Swiss	Louis (later XI) of France calls off an invasion of Switzerland after heavy casualties	An invasion by Austria is repelled

A rich variety

As well as castles on mountains and set within water, there are also examples of other types. Rectangular fortresses are not common but several examples exist, in particular Marschlins in the Grisons canton, begun in the second half of the 13th century. It has similarities with the style of castle built by Emperor Frederick II in southern Italy, and since the bishops of Chur, who owned Grisons, were supporters of the Hohenstaufen emperors, the influence may come from there.

In the Vaud canton can be found castles with similar features, but here they are the result of contact with the House of Savoy. Later influence from northern Italy, with domestic features more prominent, comes in the late 14th or early 15th-century castle at Vufflens, built by a vassal of the Duke of Savoy.

The Late Middle Ages saw some castles extended with walls, as in Germany, but many were so well-sited on slopes that there was little that could satisfactorily be added. It was those with more gentle slopes that tended to be enlarged with outworks, those on flat ground receiving "keep" walls. A number of towns, such as Fribourg, were also given walls with flanking towers later in the Middle Ages, reflecting their rising power as money markets grew in importance. By this time townspeople and peasants were becoming dissatisfied with the nobility and their castles, seeing them as symbols of oppression.

Many Swiss castles eventually became bailiff's residences, such as Kyburg (Zurich) and Landvogteischloss (Bailiff's Castle), near Baden in the Aargau.

At this time also the Swiss spirit of independence grew increasingly militaristic. In the 14th century the soldiers of the Swiss cantons, armed with pikes and formidable halberds, were victorious over their Austrian overlords. In the 15th century they faced the powerful Burgundian dukes but the latter faired no better, and the death of Charles the Bold at the Battle of Nancy in 1477 ended attempts at domination.

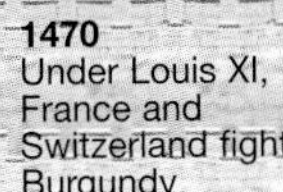

1470	1474	1476	1476	1477	1494	1499	1515
Under Louis XI, France and Switzerland fight Burgundy	Burgundy's Charles the Bold is defeated at Héricourt	Burgundy takes Grandson and slaughters the Swiss army	Burgundy meets Swiss army at Murten and is defeated	Charles the Bold is killed during the Battle of Nancy	Swiss mercenaries strengthen French campaign in Italy	Switzerland becomes politically independent of the Hapsburg empire	Switzerland defeated by France at Marignano, chooses to become neutral

Early Towers

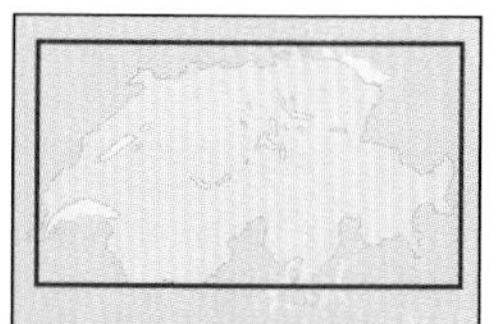

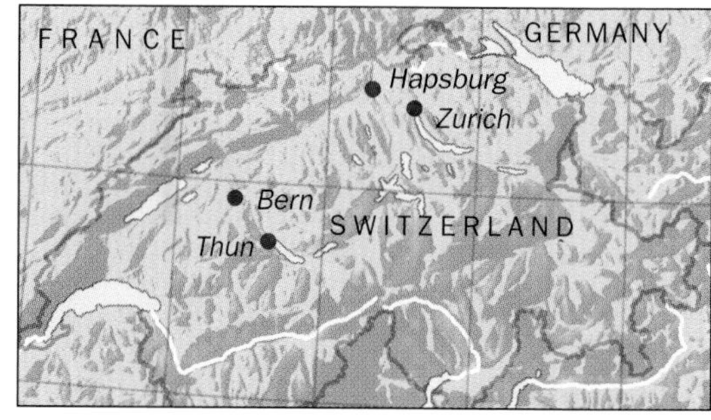

above: A reconstruction of the castle at Hapsburg, as it may have looked c.1250.

Watch towers and great towers were common features of early castle design in Switzerland, but the balance between living quarters and defense is often difficult to distinguish in these towers. They formed the nucleus of a castle and are often sited on hills or mountains.

Hapsburg

This castle is located near Brugg in Aargau, 27 miles northwest of Zurich. This is the castle from which the Hapsburg dynasty (dukes of Austria from 1282) took its name, though the family resided elsewhere from about the 13th century.

It was built on the top of the Wülpelsberg overlooking the valley of the Aar, and the first stronghold was begun in about 1020 by Radbot and his brother Werner, bishop of Strasburg. Many stone buildings were formerly erected in the 11th century. Although the *bergfried*, built from rusticated masonry, may date from the 11th century, the first documentary evidence for the castle comes from 1108 and it may actually have been built later in the 12th century.

In the 12th and 13th centuries a rectangular palace was built against the eastern angle of the bergfried and a wall was erected to form an enclosure. A ditch separated the old and newer parts of the castle, and during the 13th century the old eastern part of the castle was apparently gradually abandoned. A small square tower

left: The great donjon at Thun.

stands on the north side but was added in the 15th or 16th century.

In 1415 it was taken by the Bernese, and was handed over to Bern. In 1420 Hapsburg passed to the lords of Greifensee, who ceded it in 1457 to the town of Bern. Five years later Hans Arnold Segesser took over, and in 1469 the convent of Königsfelden received it. In 1529 the castle was returned to the city of Bern and much of the palace interior was remodeled and given wooden ceilings, paneling, and doors in Gothic style.

The eastern part of the castle was demolished in the 17th century. In 1804 it passed to the canton of Aagau and was restored in the 19th and 20th centuries.

Thun

Thun castle lies 17 miles southeast of Bern, dominated by a huge rectangular donjon. The castle overlooks one of the most important gateways to the Alps. The lords of Thun, who controlled the valley of the Aar in the 12th century, built their first castle a little nearer the top of the hill than the existing castle, erected by the dukes of Zähringen at the end of the 12th century. The plan of the pre-feudal large village with its widely-spaced buildings has survived. The donjon has a number of similarities to those in Normandy and is of impressive size, over 43 by 65 feet in area.

When the castle passed to the counts of Kyburg an additional stage was added to the donjon, visible from the range of plain arched windows. It was probably at this time that the huge hipped roof was added, bringing the castle to 138 feet high. Round corner towers were added, each topped with a tall octagonal roof. This work must have been complete by 1250, since it is depicted on the castle illustrated on the earliest surviving seal of the town.

Inside is one of the largest baronial halls in Switzerland, accessed by stairs added by the Kyburg family to replace ladders. The castle was enclosed by a wall, inside which domestic buildings were added south of the donjon.

Despite the great tower, Rudolf of Hapsburg appears to have stayed in a building in the courtyard in 1266. Additional building work was carried out at later periods. The Kyburg male line ended in 1263 and the Hapsburgs claimed Thun, calling themselves the Neu-Kyburgs. After changing hands twice Thun became the property of the Bernese in 1384. Some buildings were altered or added, such as the Executioner's Tower, but the castle remains largely intact.

below: The upper row of windows, hipped roof, and corner towers at Thun had been added by 1250.

Hill and Mountain Castles

The mountainous and rugged scenery of Switzerland meant that, like Austria and parts of Germany, many castles were spectacularly sited on peaks or on hills for defense and observation of the surrounding countryside. As in Wales, the mountains caused obstacles to an army, who could only use certain passes which might be controlled by castles.

Aigle

The castle of Aigle in the Vaud canton, 29 miles southeast of Lausanne, perches in the Alps like the eagle its name implies. A fortification was first built in the 11th century and the castle grew in the 13th century. In 1475 it was seized by the Bernese, who then built the present castle.

Its rectangular plan consists of a strong curtain with, at each of three corners, a slim round angle-tower rising up to a conical roof. In the fourth corner is a powerful donjon with a square turret on one side. An attractive covered wall-walk runs around the curtain walls, while a projecting guardroom on the wall above the entrance is rather like a box machicolation; the latter has its own fireplace and chimney.

Rectangular castles are rare in Switzerland and Aigle is a related type, the towers demonstrating influence from the House of Savoy. The donjon is surrounded by domestic structures but the courtyard buildings are not connected to the curtain wall. A similar type of castle is at Champvent in the Vaud canton.

Tarasp

Tarasp is an alpine castle in Grisons, 2½ miles southwest of Scuol. The first castle was built in the 11th century for the lords of Tarasp, who made it their base, from where they could watch the Austrian border. Several Swiss and Austrian families took control of Tarasp until it finally came into the hands of Duke Sigismund of Austria. It was taken over again in 1803 and restored in the early 20th century. It is now the private residence of the Grand-Duke of Hesse-Darmstadt, and is best seen from the top of the Kreuzberg.

Gruyères

The castle at Gruyères is in Fribourg, 3 miles southeast of Bulle, where it stands on a hill overlooking the fortified town below. The castle was mentioned for the first time in 1073, and was held by the Counts of Gruyères, who controlled the Sarine valley. Some 12th- or early 13th-century fabric survives; there is a square tower and an inner *enceinte* with later domestic buildings backing onto the walls. The eastern part of the town defenses may also date from this period.

In about 1250 Peter II of Savoy built the large

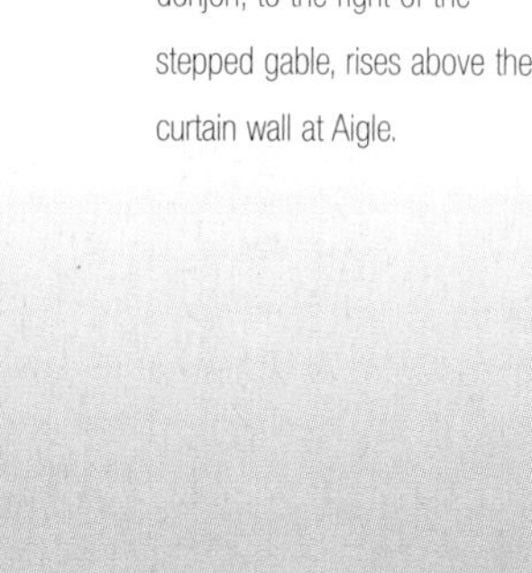

below: The tall roof of the donjon, to the right of the stepped gable, rises above the curtain wall at Aigle.

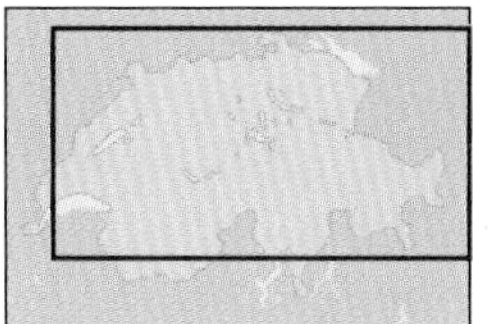

right: Tarasp perches on its crag near the border with Austria.

cylindrical donjon that sits in the south-east corner, 37 feet in diameter and vaulted internally. He probably reinforced and raised the outer *enceinte* wall at the same time, which allowed a large platform on the side of the inner courtyard. One of the towers shelters the chapel, mentioned for the first time in 1324.

Most of the rest of the castle is late medieval in date, following the destruction of much of the earlier fabric in 1480. Soon after 1500 comfortable domestic buildings were erected on the south side of the inner courtyard.

Nineteen counts inhabited the castle between the 12th century and 1554, when the enormous costs of building work crippled them. Fribourg purchased the castle in 1555 and held it until it was acquired by the Borg and Balland families in 1848, who set about restoring it. It was returned to the canton in 1938 and restoration continued.

Misox

Outside Mesocco in Grisons can be found the ruins of Misox castle, atop a rocky outcrop. The counts of Sax built the castle in the 11th and 12th century to guard the San Bernardino Gap and the Val Mesolcina. A curtain wall guards a powerful donjon. In the inner ward stands a chapel with a Romanesque campanile rising in five storeys of arches. The outer defenses at the foot of this huge castle enclose another church, the Chapel of St. Mary of the Castle, similarly with a Romanesque campanile and also a series of 15th-century frescoes, such as that depicting St George and the dragon. The castle was often besieged and was finally abandoned in the 18th century.

below: The cylindrical donjon built by Peter of Savoy at Gruyères stands beside the domestic buildings erected in about 1500.

Wasserburgen

above: The castle at Chillon makes good use of the natural defenses of Lake Geneva.

The Swiss lakes provided the opportunity for some impressive Wasserburgen, positioned for overseeing water-borne traffic and also as obstacles to mining and siege engines.

Chillon

The powerful castle of Chillon stands on an island in Lake Geneva, south of Montreux, which was occupied by the Romans and as far back as the Bronze Age. The castle was probably begun in the tenth century. It guarded the narrow pass between the lake and mountains on the route from Italy over the St. Bernard Pass, and acted as a toll station.

The castle was originally the property of the Bishops of Sion, from whom it was taken by the lords of Alinge, who built a square tower in the center of the present castle. From the beginning of the 11th century Chillon was held in fief by the Counts of Savoy, and the north tower (the Tower of the Dukes) was built (heightened in the 14th century, as was Alinge's Tower). However, Pierre Mainier reconstructed the castle in the 13th century for Peter II, Duke of Savoy, and it is this work that largely survives today, including domestic rooms mainly along the lakeside walls. The Duke's Chamber, modified in the 14th century, contains a ceiling and wall paintings of that date.

Three "D"-shaped mural towers in Anglo-French style were added to the landward defenses to increase their security. Conversely, the full-centered arches and low-rounded window arches used at Chillon—and typical of Savoyard work—are also seen at Harlech since they were both created by the Savoyard master mason, James of St. George.

Plan of Chillon showing the rooftops

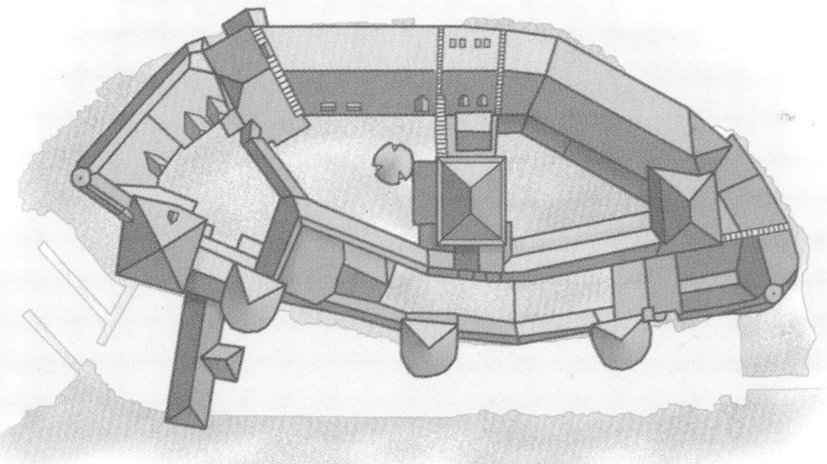

A new entrance tower was added in the 15th century. The entrance opens into the outer ward, which forms the first courtyard with military offices. The inner ward is divided into two courtyards by the donjon; the second courtyard has the prefect's quarters, magazines, and dungeons. The third courtyard to the north has the count's apartments and chapel; the fourth is the Curtain Courtyard by the "D"-shaped towers. When the castle became an artillery and ammunition store in 1836 the courtyard entrances were rebuilt to accommodate the passage of cannon.

In 1536 Chillon was captured by the Swiss (Bernese) who used it for their bailiffs and for stores and armor. Latterly Chillon was used as a prison. Lord Byron's poem *The Prisoner of Chillon* refers to François Bonnivard, a hero of the Swiss Reformation (freed by the Bernese in 1536), who was kept for four years in what had been a converted vaulted store-house. In 1798 the castle passed to the Canton of Vaud and was restored from the end of the 19th century onward.

Grandson

Grandson in Vaud is situated on the shores of Lake Neuchâtel. The first castle was built in the 11th century by the Lords of Grandson, but, as with Chillon, the present structure is largely the product of the 13th century. The *enceinte* is enclosed by a high curtain wall set with three round and two semi-circular mural towers. A *chemin de ronde* runs for 500 feet around the walls. There is a hall in Renaissance style, a chapel, and dungeons. On March 2, 1476 the Swiss Confederation defeated the army of Charles the Bold almost under the walls of the castle. It then became the property of the towns of Bern and Fribourg.

right: The landward curtain wall and a machicolated D-shaped tower, separated from the bank by water.

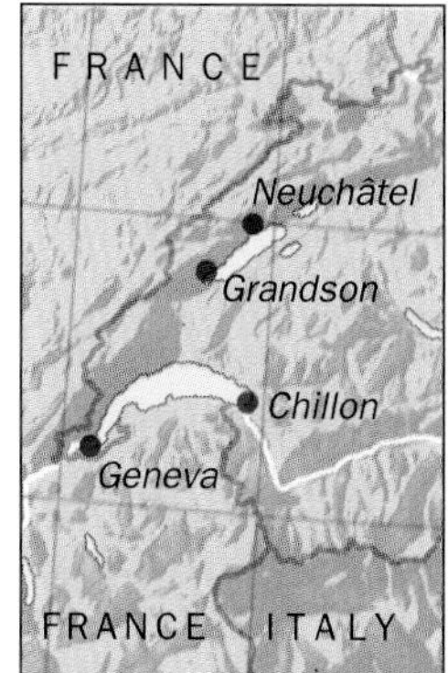

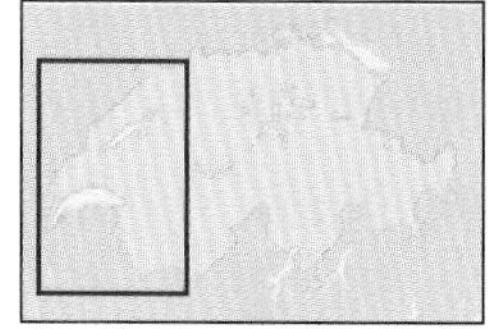

below: The loops piercing the upper walls at Grandson mark the *chemin de ronde*—the covered wall-walk.

Chapter Eleven: Gazetteer—The Iberian Peninsula

Spain Under the Moors

By the early 11th century, much of Spain had been overrun by the Moors. Series of workmanlike castles guarded routes and housed soldiers as disorganized kingdoms gradually recouped land.

The phrase "Castles in Spain" has become a cliché, but the country does possess numerous impressive monuments to its past, largely as a result of its turbulent history. By the middle of the eighth century, Muslim peoples referred to as Moors by the Christians had settled in much of the old Visigothic kingdom; their part of Spain and Portugal was called Andalus. In 1031 only about one third of the peninsula, roughly in the northwest, was under Christian rule, but now the Umayyad Caliphate collapsed and fragmented into petty states.

Meanwhile, the Christian kingdoms clashed with one another. There was no single king but several, such as those of Castile, Aragon, and Leon. One of the most famous names was the almost legendary 11th-century warrior, Rodrigo de Vivar, who seems to have been given the name El Cid (chieftain) by the Muslims, and who allied with Christians and Moslems alike in the maelstrom of power politics. The Reconquista, or reconquest of Spain for Christendom, did not begin in a crusading sense until the 12th century, and even then political and economic considerations were taken into account as much as, or more than, religious ideals.

below: The city of Toledo, with the totally reconstructed Alcázar in the distance, whose first tenant was El Cid.

The Spanish terrain of high mountain ranges, arid plains, and deep valleys also dominated the manner in which frontiers were set and wars conducted, while roads providing routes for armies. Castles were placed to guard roads, fords, or bridges, and were used as barracks for holding armed men. As such, the military aspect outweighed the domestic and castles in Spain often appear stern and workmanlike. But they were not the real goal for enemy forces, who much preferred to seize cities.

The Muslims had their own traditions of fortification, some of which they had adapted from the Byzantines. The garrison fortresses, or *alcazabas*, were geometric in layout, with square or wedge-shaped enclosures protected with walls and towers. They would remain the basic model for castles.

Controlling the Threat

At first the Christians used their own design, the tower keep. Round towers became very popular

986	1009	1037	1150	1236	1340	1385	1492
Emir of Córdoba completes conquest of Christian kingdoms in northern Spain	Christian kingdoms are re-established	Leon and Navarre unite against the Moors	Islamic Spain is controlled by the Almohad dynasty	King Ferdinand of Castile conquers most of southern Spain	Alfonso XI of Castile defeats Moors at Rio Salado	With victory at Aljubarotta, Portugal becomes independent of Spain	Spanish take Granada, ending Muslim rule, and turn eyes toward the New World

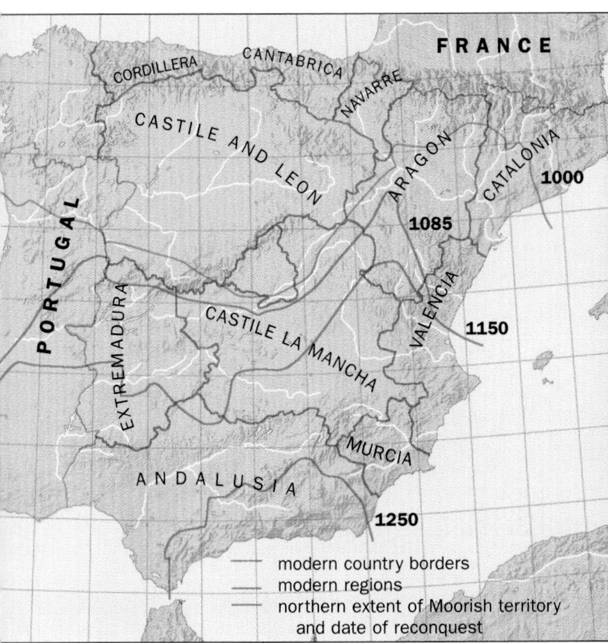

above: The 13th-century Molina de Aragon.

from the 12th century, assisted by the Spanish knightly orders, together with the Knights Templars and Knights Hospitaller, who brought the zeal of the warrior monks to the Spanish theater, and helped blend European and Syrian influences with those of the Muslims. The imposing walls of Avila, built between 1088 and 1091, were the work of Christian, Muslim, and Jewish builders.

The Reconquista was a slow process. Alliances and European aid led to significant successes, such as the capture of Toledo in 1085, after which the Muslims asked for aid across the sea in Africa from the fundamentalist Islamic Almoravids. Many hard struggles followed, but in 1150 another Islamic sect, the Berber Almohades, took over Andalus from the Almoravids. Gradually further Christian successes followed, such as the victory at Las Navas de Tolosa in 1212 and the taking of Seville in 1248.

Soon after, the Christians reached as far as the borders of Granada, which became a vassal of Castile. However, it was not until 1492 that a final push by the Catholic kings achieved the capture of the city of Granada itself.

The success in controlling the Muslim threat by the 14th century meant there was greater interest in European ideas, with Anglo-French influence in regular castle designs. The role of the garrison declined as a feudal-palace function finally appeared. The Catholic kings issued instructions in the middle of the 15th century to demolish castles, a policy that was only partially carried out. Some had been transformed into palatial residences, or became royal property and were given an alcaide (governor) and military personnel.

By 1588, the year the Spanish Armada blew itself to pieces around the north coast of Britain, many of the castles had fallen into disuse and were crumbling. Some were used during the Peninsula War (1808–13) between Napoleon and the British with their Spanish guerilla allies.

below: The extensive late 11th-century walls of Avila.

The Alcazaba

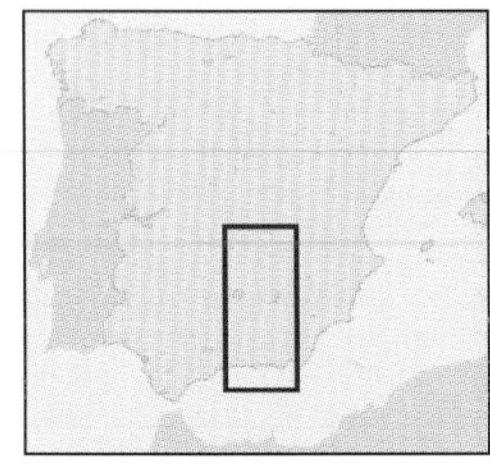

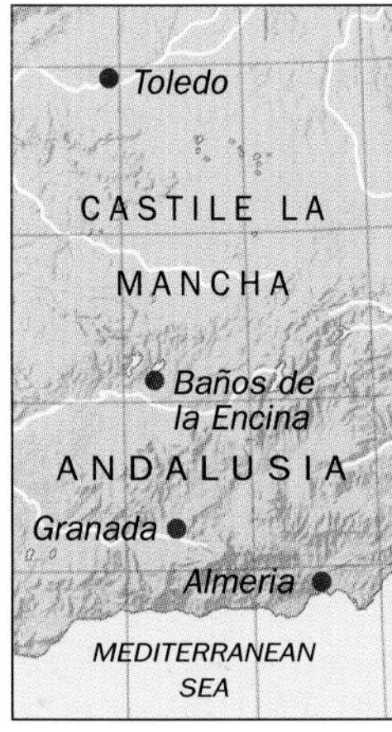

An *alcazaba* was a garrison fort used by the Muslims. A square or wedge-shaped *enceinte*, the walls set with square towers, it followed geometric patterns favored by the Muslims. The space inside—the *albacar*—was large enough to accommodate villagers and their cattle in times of trouble. The design influenced Christian castle-builders, while captured Muslim fortresses were often supplemented with Christian military features.

Baños de la Encina

This is a very good example of a Moorish *alcazaba*, fitted around a ridge above the village of Jaen, 7½ miles north of Bailén. Built in 967–8 by the Caliph Hakam II, it was sited to control a section of the River Guadalqivir. There are 15 square towers set along the curtain wall and a double horseshoe gateway of ashlar. This is typical Moorish castle design and demonstrates how advanced they were compared to the Christians.

Baños was taken by the Christians shortly before the Battle of Las Navas de Tolosa in 1212. It was they who added another enclosure, together with a *torre de homenaje*, this tower also acting as a victory symbol (*see page 104*).

below: Some of the mural towers set on the curtain wall of the alcazaba at Baños de la Encina, Jaen.

Alhambra of Granada

The Alhambra—Red Fortress—is at the end of the Sierra Nevada, above the River Darro to the east of Granada city. Begun in the ninth century, the *alcazaba* was largely rebuilt four centuries later by the Nazrites, the dynasty who ruled Granada after the decline of the Almohades, when the fall of Córdoba in 1236 threatened Granada.

A long enclosure is surrounded by adobe curtain walls and square mural towers, mainly built by Mohammed I (1236–73). At the western end he constructed the towered fortress of the Alcazaba, its eastern end separated from the rest of the complex by a ditch and strong wall set with the Homage and Quebrada Towers. In the 14th century another curtain was built, the walls forming a killing alley for enemies passing beyond the Gate of Arms. The western end of the walls was extended later.

To the east lay the king's palace. The Justice Gate is a powerful piece of Muslim architecture, with three right-angles in its vaulted passageway. The original entry to the palace, with its patio and mosque, have been destroyed.

Constructed between 1334 and 1408, the palace interior is an architectural delight. Perhaps the most famous area is the Patio de los Leones, surrounded by slim columns, its arches seemingly dripping with stalactite decoration. Other stunningly decorated rooms include the Sala de los Reyes, Sala de los Abencerrajes, Sala de las dos Hermanas, and the filigreed Mirador de Lindaraja.

The Alhambra and Alcazaba were surrendered

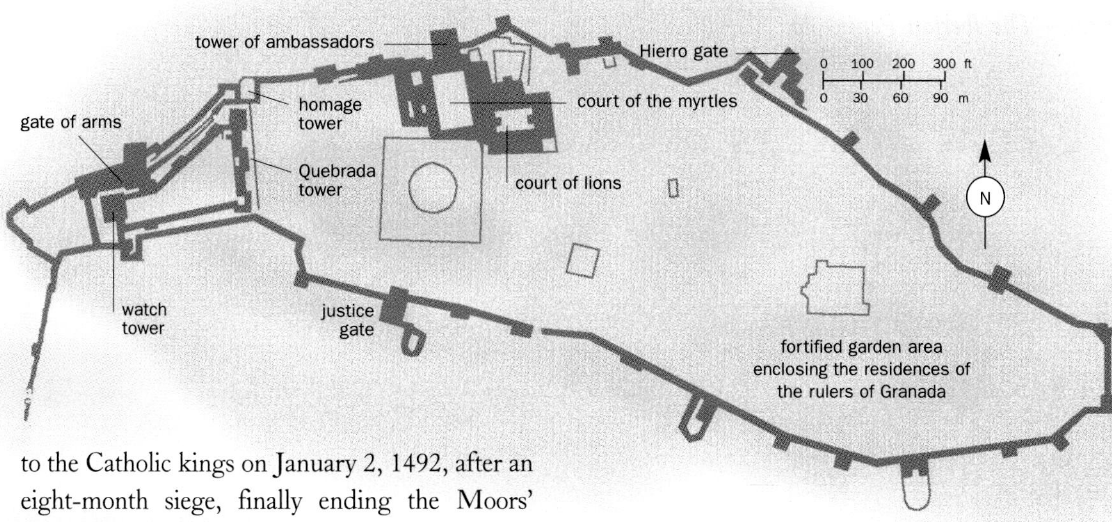

Plan of Alhambra of Granada, with the Alcazaba on the left, cut off by a wall.

to the Catholic kings on January 2, 1492, after an eight-month siege, finally ending the Moors' 781-year presence in the Iberian peninsula. In 1527 work began on the impressive quadrangular Renaissance palace of Carlos V, delayed in 1568 due to Moorish rebellion but resumed in 1579. The southern façade has a beautiful porch and the circular internal patio is surrounded by a colonnade.

The Alcazaba of Almeria

First begun in the late seventh or eighth century, this fortress guarded the town of Almeria, "mirror of the sea." In the 12th century it was conquered by Alphonso VII, who included Italian sailors in his enterprise. Ten years later it was recaptured by the Muslims, who strongly fortified it.

The *alcazaba* is built on the ruins of a Phoenician citadel and is irregular in shape, divided internally into three enclosures. The tower of La Vela sits on one side, while several wells or baths were provided around the enclosures. A gate leads into the second enclosure where the remains of the mosque now stands, plus six rooms underground. The third enclosure is set on rock foundations on the highest ground, cut off by a ditch and portcullis and further guarded by three towers and a donjon.

It remained in Muslim hands until the coming of the Catholic kings, and even then the last Moriscos sought refuge there after refusing to become Christians.

center: Alhambra of Granada, showing the tower of the ambassadors (left), homage tower (right), and the Renaissance palace behind.

below: The walls of Almeria

Great Towers

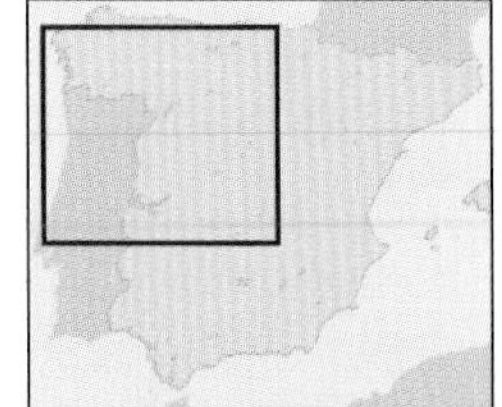

The earliest type of stone building erected by the Christians in Spain was the great tower—the *torre del homenaje* or "homage tower." This tower-keep of Galician Basque origin was also used as a symbol of victory. As with donjons, the door was placed high up.

A number of castles were built by the Order of Calatrava in the Campo de Calatrava, the plains between Christian Toledo and Muslim Córdoba seized by the Muslims from 1195 until lost after the Battle of Las Navas de Tolosa in 1212.

Albuquerque

This castle is 25 miles north of Badajoz on the crest of a massive rock outcrop, visible for miles around. It was built in 1354 on the orders of Alfonso Sanches, son of King Dinis of Portugal.

The walls have towers that betray Portuguese work in their square shape and pointed merlons, influenced by Muslim design. The walls and towers on the north side extend down the slope to enclose the town at the base. The approach to the castle itself is guarded by a series of flanking walls to produce a winding passageway. A large *torre*

del homenaje rises from the top of the pinnacle, and an extra-mural tower (*torre albarrana*) is connected to a barbican in the curtain by a monumental bridge, itself guarded by a drawbridge.

The year it was built, Albuquerque was unsuccessfully besieged by Pedro the Cruel; it was often attacked during the border fighting between Castile and Portugal. It was captured by Alvaro de Luna in the 15th century, but only through treachery.

Fuensaldaña

Fuensaldaña stands 4 miles north of Valladolid in Castile and was built c.1450 for Alonso Pérez de Vivero, treasurer to King Juan II. The castle has a rectangular *enceinte* with circular angle towers and small bartizans at the centers, where domestic rooms were established. The pleasing three-storied *torre del homenaje* is also rectangular and positioned across a short side of the curtain wall, reached via a high door and suspension bridge. It has corner turrets that rise to full height and bartizans to the centers of the longer sides. The towers and bartizans have machicolations and merlons of *mudéjar* work.

Viewed as a whole, Fuensaldaña looks like a Roman desert fortification, but the great tower decries the lordship of its owner. Unfortunately, three years later Alonso was thrown from a tower at Burgos by order of Alvaro de Luna, the king's favorite, and Fuensaldaña was probably never completed or inhabited.

left: The great *torre del homenaje* towers above the curtain walls of Fuensaldaña, which extend to one side of the rectangluar tower house, as the plan **below** shows.

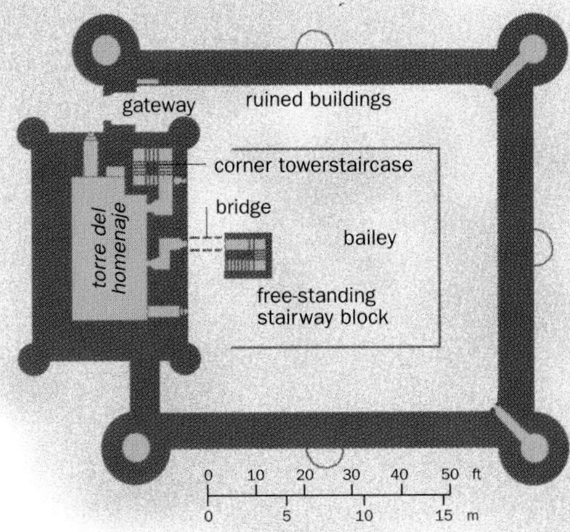

Guadamur

The small village of Guadamur, 9 miles from Toledo, has a fine castle, restored at the end of the 19th century. Dating from the 15th century, it is square with round towers at the angles of the curtain walls. The latter are angled inward halfway along, with machicolations and smaller round towers on the upper half. The enclosure is divided into three bays and domestic rooms and halls are connected by two rows of arches. A number of psalms and Latin prayers are preserved on friezes and moldings in the large rooms.

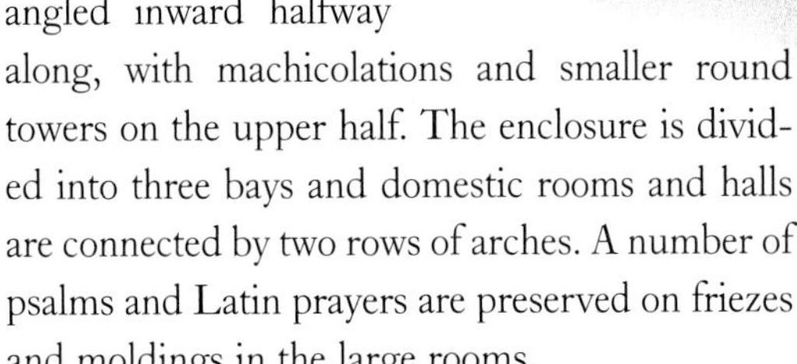

The impressive *torre del homenaje* is square in plan and sits astride the curtain. It has round corner bartizans and one each in the center of two sides. The corbels are adorned with strings of balls and the wall is carved with the lions, saltires, and diagonal bars of coats-of-arms, repeated on either side of the main entrance.

Calatrava la Nueva

This castle was built by the military Order of Calatrava from 1216 on a rocky prominence 5 miles southwest of Calzada de Calatrava, after leaving their earlier castle, also called Calatrava (now the old castle: *la Vieja*) between Toledo and Córdoba, from which they took their name. This had been taken from the Templars but lost during the Almohade counterattack; the Order did not get it back until their victory at Los Navas de Tolosa in 1212. The castle was not restored and the Order moved to la Nueva.

There is a large, round Romanesque church, towered and fortified, with a huge rose window, and a double *enceinte*, donjon, flanking walls, and monastic quarters. It has Moorish battlements and was probably built by *mudéjar* masons.

left: Guadamur, near Toledo, is a fine example of the *torre del homenaje*, and restoration in the 19th century has helped preserve some fine 15th-century wall decoration.

Gran Buque Castles

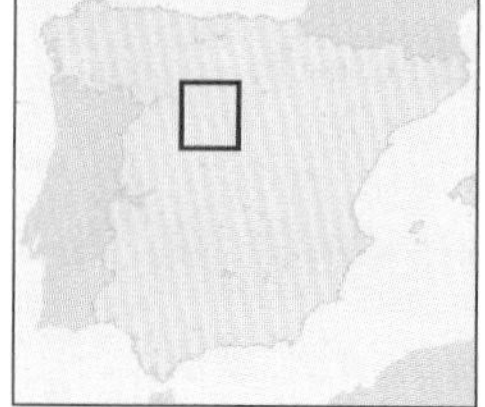

Many Spanish castles were built on crags, but the nature of such sites often precluded the construction of a large fortress. As armies grew and warfare required more mobility, some castles were built on hills or mountains where a more spacious stronghold could be placed, although the slopes could not be so steep. Some of these have the appearance of a great ship—the literal translation of *gran buque*. They are extremely impressive simply because of their shape and size. Combined with the fact that they are set on high ground, they give the impression of lordship, control, and impregnability.

Alcázar of Segovia

Alcázar of Segovia is one of the best-known Spanish fortifications. There was a fortress at its site—a narrow spur between the Eresma and Calmores rivers, within a deep gorge—in Roman times, and later the Muslims erected another.

The Alcázar—which means "palace" in Arabic—was built in the 11th century by King Alfonso VI, after Christians took control of Segovia. Alfonso constructed walls and towers and the castle became a favorite residence for the Castilian and other monarchy.

Over the centuries alterations were made to suit individual tastes. In the early 15th century, Juan II separated the old donjon, at one end of the line of walls, from his imposing *torre del homenaje* at the other. The latter, called Don Juan II, is the larger; it is rectangular in plan and decorated with machicolations, Segovian plaster work, and 12 bartizans. Internally it is decorated with *mudéjar* work, influenced by the Alhambra.

The square donjon at the other end is set with small round towers, whose conical slate roofs were added in the 16th century by King Felipe II. Here are six main halls and rooms in the first bailey, including the Great Hall of the Kings, which 15th-century chronicles recall as housing 34 gold statues representing the kings of Spain, a number increased to 56 by Felipe II. A narrow passage from the last hall leads to the second bailey, where the old donjon and a vaulted chapel stand. The interiors were badly damaged in a fire in 1862 but have been partially restored.

below: The great ship-shaped Alcázar of Segovia was enlarged after the Reconquista and the conical slate roofs—added in the 16th century—give the castle a more domestic air.

Peñafiel

Peñafiel runs along a narrow ridge above the town in Valladolid, overlooking the Duero Valley. The site was fortified in ancient times and the town was resettled under the command of Count Garcia Fernández of Castile in 1014. Legend recalls that when King Sancho took it from the Muslims in the 11th century, he drove his sword into the highest point and said: "From today, this will be the faithful rock *peñafiel* of Castile."

A castle was built here in the early 14th century by the Infante Don Juan Manuel, who wrote some of the most important works of Spanish medieval literature as a resident. King Alfonso X also lived here; a historian, he explained that kings should wear silks, gold, and precious stones, so the people could easily recognize them.

The present castle was built in 1466 by Don

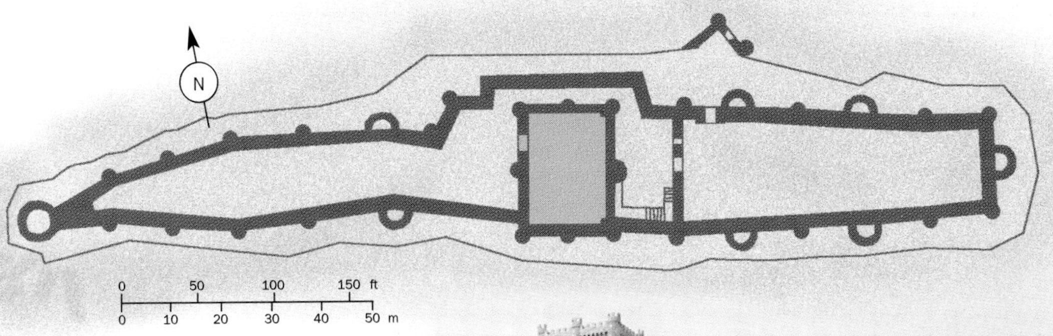

this page: Peñafiel defines the term *gran buque*, from the narrow confines of the inner bailey (**below left and on plan, left**) to its great superstructure donjon.

Pedro de Girón, Master of Calatrava. It is the best example of a ship castle in Spain, being only 74½ feet wide but 690 feet long. There is a double line of walls each side, which bow inward at each end to give an even greater impression of a ship. The inner curtain walls curve gently inward to a single cylindrical tower at each end. Along these each side of these walls are 12 cylindrical machicolated towers, with another two at the gateway. The wall-walk is nearly continuous.

A great tower, 111 feet high, with machicolations and bartizaned at corners and center, stands in the middle of the castle like a ship's wheelhouse and engine room. Peñafiel castle is protected by a dry ditch and reached via a bridge.

Castles in Castile

Castile was named after its many castles, and a tower forms the charge on its coat-of-arms. La Mota, Torrelobatón, and Coca are just three of the more interesting examples that still survive.

La Mota

Guarding a crossroads at Medina del Campo is La Mota, a large rectangular brick fortress of Moorish origin. Restorations from the 12th century eventually led to major work in the mid-15th century under the Christian architects Fernando Carreño and Alonso Nieta. The older *enceinte* was given a huge *torre del homenaje* in one corner, machicolated and bartizaned, together with an outer curtain wall pierced with gun-loops and set with round angle towers. The outer curtain also carries a *chemin de ronde*—a two-tiered vaulted passageway running inside the walls—and stairs in the angle towers. The *mudéjar* brickwork at La Mota is bettered only by Coca's.

The castle passed from the Fonsecas to the Catholic kings as a wedding present in 1475, their coats-of-arms preserved above the gates. Much of the interior has been lost. The most famous room is called "The Dressing Room of the Queen"—Doña Juana "La Loca" (The Mad One). Another room is connected with Cesare Borgia, imprisoned there until his legendary escape down a rope to a waiting horse.

Torrelobatón

This powerful castle, the best preserved in Castile, stands 9 miles north of Tordesillas, in Valladolid. It was built in the first half of the 15th century on the ruins of an earlier fortress by King Juan II. Bought by the Enriquez family, it became the seat of the Grand Admiral of Spain.

In style it is related to Fuensaldaña nearby; square in plan with round towers at three corners of the single surrounding wall. At the fourth corner stands a tall *torre del homenaje*, graced with eight bartizans; the entrance has a portcullis to block it off. The machicolations are false and decorative, yet the parapets have no crenellations, but are curved inward and made deliberately smooth to foil the use of grappling irons.

Torrelobatón was capable of withstanding cannon fire, so thick were its walls.

below: The *torre del homenaje* at La Mota (left) is surrounded by the outer curtain pierced with gun-loops.

In the early 16th century it was besieged for a week by *comuneros*, the ordinary citizens of Castile. Angry at King Carlos I's attempt to remove privileges initially granted because of their usefulness during the Reconquest, under Juan de Padilla they rose in rebellion against king and nobility. Torrelobatón surrendered but the *comuneros* were soon defeated in the field by royalist forces and Juan was executed.

Coca

At the confluence of the Eresma and Voltoya rivers, 30 miles northwest of Segovia, stands Coca castle. This impressive Hispano-Arab fortress was built for Alfonso Fonseca, Archbishop of Seville, in the mid-15th century, as a castle-palace.

In plan Coca is a rectangular concentric fortress; however, being built in the 15th century, the outer wall has a broad batter, with space for mounting cannons. Cross-shaped gun-loops and casemates for cannon are prevalent. The angles are covered by octagonal towers, while in one corner a square keep is accessible only from a right-angled approach via a bridge spanning the brick-lined moat. The Moorish artists left numerous marks of their work, such as the gateway in the wall surrounding the keep, with its horseshoe arch inside a pointed brick arch.

Alonso was very rich, enjoyed intrigue, and, like other Spanish nobles, used his wealth to build on a grand scale. His tastes are reflected in the decoration of Coca castle. The keep and angle towers sprout numerous bartizans, there is a riot of molded brick crenellation, and Coca is famous for the use of amazing *mudéjar* brickwork externally and stucco *mudéjar* interiors.

Despite its strength, Coca was never besieged, and was home to Alfonso until he died. In the early 16th century it passed to the dukes of Berwick and Alba.

left: The *torre del homenaje* and false machicolations below the smooth parapet at Torrelobatón.

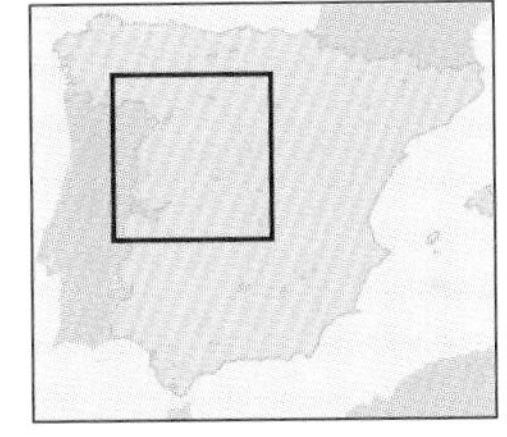

below: Gun-loops pierce one of the octagonal bartizaned corner towers of Coca's outer curtain, the inner ring rising behind.

Castle Palaces

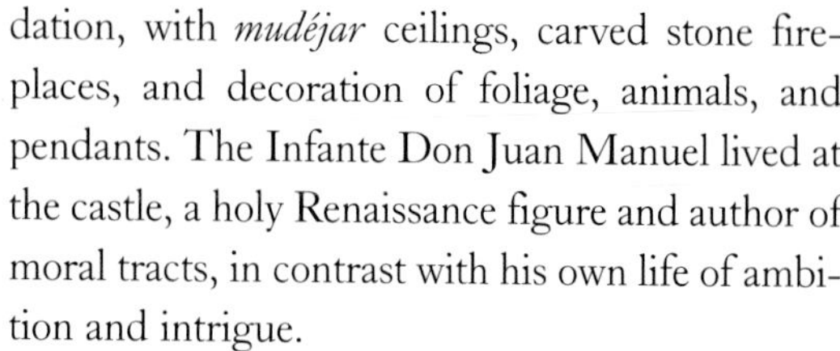

As in other parts of Europe, the removal of the immediate threat from the Muslims allowed an increase in luxury at the expense of the garrison. In Castile, especially, with its struggle between crown and nobility, the castle palaces of the nobility grew, partly influenced by French ideas but equally demonstrating a superb blend of Christian building and Arab decoration. Once Granada had fallen in 1492 and the Americas were opening up to Spanish adventurers, the kings became all-powerful in Spain. The era of great castle-building was at an end.

Belmonte

In the middle of the plain of La Mancha, 62 miles southwest of Cuenca, lies Belmonte castle, built c.1456 for Juan de Pacheco, Marquis of Villena. This ingenious geometric design comprises an *enceinte* in the shape of an equilateral triangle, within a wall shaped like a five-pointed star and triangular merlons. There are cylindrical towers at the angles with partially *mudéjar* crenellations, and an impressive *torre del homenaje* on the outer curtain near the gateway.

A low outer wall with triangular merlons follows the wall behind and has three gates. One is named after Princess Juana la Beltrajena, who used it in her night-time flight from the Marquis, who had betrayed Juana during her attempts to gain the throne.

In the middle of the castle, vaulted halls on the sides of the triangle provide the living accommodation, with *mudéjar* ceilings, carved stone fireplaces, and decoration of foliage, animals, and pendants. The Infante Don Juan Manuel lived at the castle, a holy Renaissance figure and author of moral tracts, in contrast with his own life of ambition and intrigue.

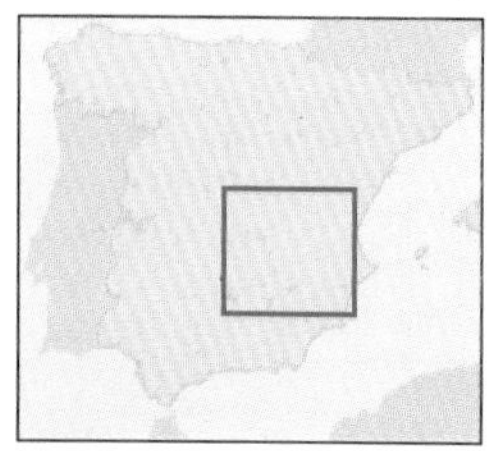

El Real de Manzanares

At the southern foot of the Guadarrama hills is El Real de Manzanares, 20 miles north of Madrid in a land once disputed between Segovia and Madrid. The earlier, 13th-century castle, built nearby in the hills, was rectangular with round corner towers and a *torre del homenaje* at the fourth corner. It was owned by famous 15th-century Spanish writer Don Iñego López de Mendoza, Marquis of Santillana, who was granted Manzanares by Juan II.

The older castle is visible from the newer one, erected in 1475 by de Mendoza's son, the first Duke of the Infantado. The last of the castle palaces, it is almost square, and has a curtain wall set with three corner cylindrical towers and a *torre del homenaje*. From each of the round towers on the western front rises another tower

left: Triangular merlons top the walls at Belmonte.

of lesser diameter, studded all around with stone bosses or balls. A chapel incorporating parts of a 13th- to 14th-century hermitage, complete with apse, was added to the east side. A low outer wall encircles the whole castle, with rounded corner bastions in front of the three corner towers.

In 1480 the second Duke of the Infantado added the *isabelino-mudéjar* gallery (that is, with highly ornate turrets) to the south side, probably the finest example of the flamboyant style in Spain. All this was the work of Juan Güas, designer of the church of San Juan de los Reyes in Toledo and the Duke's Guadalajara palace. He also built the octagonal turret rising from the roof of the keep, again with ball decoration, and the massive false machicolations.

El Real de Manzanares castle was meant to impress the eye by the force of its presence and decoration, as much as defend those within from attack. It may even be that the profuse decoration was meant to deceive the agents of the Catholic kings, who disliked new castles, as well as to captivate its owner.

below: Studded towers rise from towers on the walls at El Real de Manzanares, with the octagonal turret on the right.

Portugal

Towers and Citadels

Portugal is a land rich in castles. Its struggle for independence, which involved Crusaders from central Europe as well as the ubiquitous Moors, involved the construction and attack of many strongholds.

In 1137 Count Afonso swore fealty to his cousin, King Alfonso VII of Castile, for Portugal, and two years later took the title of king. Having achieved a victory over the Muslims at Ourique, he besieged Lisbon.

One of the most important events in the 12th century was the capture of Lisbon in 1147, partly assisted by the arrival of English, German, and Flemish crusaders on their way to the Second Crusade. The city walls were a tough proposition. The English built a siege tower that got stuck in the sand, while the Germans and Flemings failed to complete their mine.

However, a captured letter revealed that the Moors were short of food and had been refused help, and after a victory at Almada 80 Moorish heads were displayed to the defenders. A second mine collapsed the walls but the breach was filled with wood. Despite being cut off by the tide and vigorously opposed, a further siege tower finally reached the walls and the Moors surrendered. Now the port at the mouth of the Tagus was in Christian hands.

The rulers in Portugal tried to break away from Castile, reflected in castle-building from the 1170s to the early 13th century, when the Alentejo plains were seized. The threat from the Muslims to the south resulted in a number of strongholds being erected on the southern part of the Tejo Plain. Many castles were the result of rebuilding older structures or new construction, after the break away from Castile.

The weakness of Christian in-fighting in the peninsula gave the Muslims reasons to counterattack, but they in turn were pressed, as when in 1189 Silves in the Algarve fell. Sancho I (1185–1211) rebuilt castles and towns, founded new ones, and brought in settlers, notably the Military Orders—the Templars, Hospitallers, and Spanish Knights of Alcántara (Portuguese Avis) and Santiago.

Moorish Castle Design

By 1240 Sancho II had reached the coast of the Algarve, which was acknowledged as Portuguese in 1267. Portugal was now almost a complete kingdom. It did not stop internal unrest and wars with Castile, but under Alfonso III and Dinis

right: The castle of Almourol stands on a rocky island in the middle of the Tagus, close to the town of Constancia.

1097	1128	1321	1324	1382	1385	1411	1432
King Alfonso VI of Leon creates the county of Portugal	Afonso Henriques wrests control of Portugal from his mother, Teresa	Alter do Chão castle, Alentejo, built by King Pedro I	King Dinis adds a palace to Leiria castle	King John I founds the Avis dynasty	With its victory at Aljubarotta, Portugal becomes independent of Spain	Portugal and Aragon are at peace after 20 years of warring	Portuguese explore the west coast of Africa

left: Rectangular towers at Silves in the Algarve, spoiled by modern neon hoardings.

(1279–1323) Portugal gradually began to prosper.

Further trouble brewed when Ferdinand I claimed Castile and was beaten by its king, Henry II. The latter's son, John, then married Ferdinand's only daughter, and the furious Portuguese eventually crowned the Master of Avis as king and obtained English archers with which they won a crushing victory over Castile at Aljubarotta in 1385. This effectively secured Portugal's separation as a nation.

The tower and citadel are leading forms of castle in Portugal and can be seen in various forms. It appears as a single entity at Braganza, one of the largest fortresses in Portugal, the earliest parts dating back to 1187. The donjon also forms part of the citadel castle, as at Amieira, built in the second half of the 14th century by Alvaro Concalves Pereia, Prior of the Order of St. John. It was the military orders, notably Templars and Hospitallers, who helped to open up the country's borders. A less regular form appears in Alter do Chão, which was rebuilt under the orders of Pedro I in 1321.

The style influenced by Syria consists of a quadrangle with rectangular towers at each corner; the main tower sat at the entrance. This is a variety of a Muslim design. A number of castles have this form of workmanlike design, such as Trancosa and Silves. Square towers and turrets are common; the use of cylindrical towers is likely to indicate French influence. Nevertheless, the influence from Moorish design remained stronger in Portugal than it did in Spain.

1434	1444	1471	1494	1505	1515	1516–17	1521
The Azores islands are discovered by Portugal	Braganza becomes a duchy	Portugal establishes the trading post of El Mina (now part of Ghana)	The Treaty of Tordesillas divides the New World between Spain and Portugal	Portugal builds a fort at Sofala, east Africa	Hormuz, Yemen, is conquered and fortified	Portuguese trading posts are established in Ceylon and southern China	Portuguese colonies are established in Brazil

Castles of Several Cultures

right: View from the top of the donjon at Guimarães.

Influences on Portuguese castle design came from the Moors, which was long-lasting, Syria, via the Crusaders, and, later, France, largely seen in round towers.

Guimarães

This castle is situated on an outcrop of rock southeast of Braga (Minho). When Henry of Burgundy was made Count of Portucale by Alfonso VI of Castile in 1095, he built an *enceinte* castle which incorporated a tenth-century stone tower, making it a donjon. In characteristic Portuguese style, the donjon stands alone within the *enceinte* of walls. The crenellation is largely of Moorish type, the upper edges of each merlon rising to a central point.

In 1110 Afonso Henriques, the son of Henry of Burgundy and destined to be the first king of an independent Portugal, was born in the castle. In the 15th century Guimarães castle was partly rebuilt on a trapezoidal layout with square angle-towers, two of these acting as flanking towers to the gate.

Leiria

At Leiria in Beira Litoral, the castle looks down on the town from a position high on rocks. The site was of Roman origin; as a useful frontier castle on the southern borders, it was fortified by Afonso Henriques in 1135, four years before he was elected King of Portugal. However, after Lisbon and Santarém were taken from the Muslims in 1147 during the Reconquest, the castle's main purpose was lost.

In 1324, however, King Dinis built a small palace in the castle with a large rectangular citadel set at an angle above it. The curtain wall, following the contours of the rock face, had close-set mural towers. In the late 14th and early 15th centuries, the palace was altered by João I. An arcaded loggia now overlooks the surrounding countryside, decorated with carvings and chimney pieces.

Castelo de São Jorge

The name Castle of St. George was given to the fortress in Lisbon in the 14th century, the name coming from King John I. There was a rectangular Muslim *alcazaba* on the site when Afonso Henriques took it over for the Christians in 1147, and this partly determined the present shape. A donjon was added to the main wall of the castle.

above: The arcaded loggia at Leiria.

left: The machicolated corner galleries on the donjon at Beja.

There is some similarity with city fortresses in Italy, but the castle in Lisbon is stern and businesslike. However, the regular design, with its square corner towers, owes as much to Syrian influence, via the Military Orders in Portugal. There are inner and outer *enceinte*s, with deep battered plinths.

Lisbon's defenses boast 18 towers, 11 of which belong to the castle; one, the Portao Sul (South Gate), leads to the Rua de Santa Cruz do Castelo and the entrance of the old Praça de Armas square. There are twelve gates, seven of them leading to the parish of Santa Cruz do Castelo, and a barbican.

In the reign of King Sebastion the castle was restored and lived in, but the royal palace on the site later fell into neglect during the reign of the Spanish kings. It was used as a barracks and latterly as a prison. In 1755 Castelo de São Jorge was severely damaged by an earthquake, but restoration work began in 1910.

below: Castelo de São Jorge, overlooking Lisbon.

Beja

Beja in Alentejo stands on the site of a Roman fortification that in turn was built on by the Muslims. This was captured by Alfonso III (1248–79), who adapted the square tower *enceinte* on the hill to a castle on an irregular trapezoidal plan.

In 1310, during the reign of King Dinis, a donjon was added to the castle. The corners of the parapet are pierced by carved loopholes and there are machicolated corner-galleries below the 15th-century top-stage. On the first floor is star-ribbed vaulting with honeycomb corbeling and *ajimez* (arched and twin-lobed) windows, a sign of *mudéjar* work.

Castles Against Castile

After breaking away from Castile, Portugal still found itself threatened both by Spanish aggressors and the Moors. Castles continued to be modified or newly built, their importance and development affected by the presence of the Military Orders such as Hospitallers and Templars, as well as native Spanish Orders.

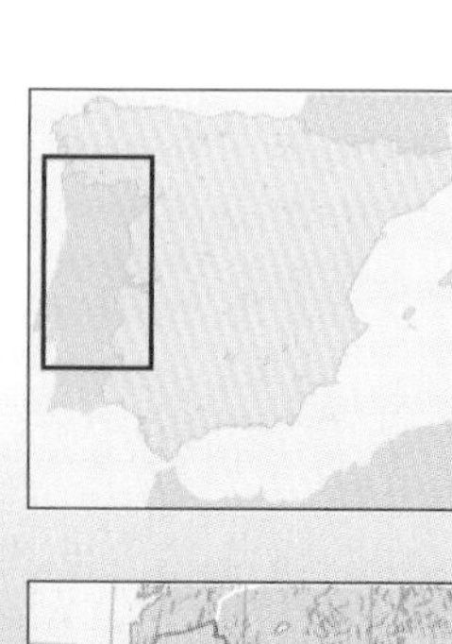

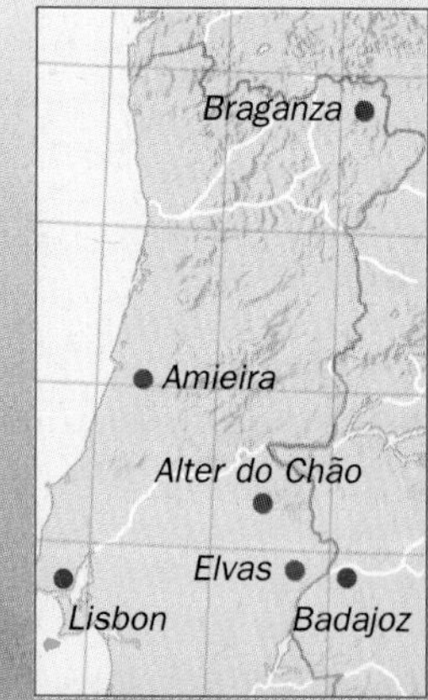

Elvas

Elvas sits proudly on a steep ridge, not far from Badajos in Spain. It is the largest castle in Portugal and an important frontier fortress set against Badajos across the border. King Sancho II took it from the Moors in 1226, when it was an important *alcazaba*.

There is a huge *enceinte*, some 3,286 feet by 2,133 feet, partly doubled, with square towers, a great donjon, and a *torre del homenaje* erected in 1448 by King João II. King Dinis also restored fabric in the 13th century, as did Manuel in the early 16th century.

Alter do Chão

This royal castle is situated to the south of Portalegre in Alentejo. An inscription says that it was built in 1359 by King Pedro I, which by our calendar would be 1321.

There is a regularity of plan so much more noticeable than in other Portuguese castles that it suggests French influence. It is almost square in layout, with a single *enceinte* and two round angle-towers with conical caps, the latter a feature common to many Portuguese castles. The third corner is occupied by a large donjon 144 feet high; the fourth corner has the square gatehouse tower angled to it, the crenellations of the wall tops running up to the gatehouse.

Braganza

Braganza lies in the Tras-os-Montes region and is one of the largest fortifications in Portugal. The castle, together with the walls of the town, date to 1187, when Sancho I took over and rebuilt an earlier fortification.

Within the *enceinte* stands a huge granite donjon, 108 feet tall, provided with bartizans at the corners. In the 14th or 15th century paired *mudéjar* windows were inserted on the south and east sides, perhaps as a result of the castle's proximity to the Léon-Castile frontier. The donjon is flanked by square watchtowers but is not

left: The massive donjon of Braganza.

detached, unlike most others.

In 1444 Braganza became a duchy—the dynasty originated here. From 1640 they took control of Portugal.

Amieira

Amieira castle is in Ribatejo Eoeste and was built in the second half of the 14th century by Don Alvaro Concalves Pereia, Prior of the Order of the Knights Hospitaller. This castle illustrates not only the presence of the Military Orders who helped to extend the Christian boundaries, but also their predilection for a regular form of layout, usually of rectangular plan.

The angle towers of the high inner walls are square, and one of them is constructed on a much grander scale, to form both a donjon and a gatehouse. A lower outer wall surrounds Amieira. This type of rectangular castle, with one corner tower at the entrance acting as the main tower, can be compared with similar styles in Syria, southern Italy, and the castles of the Teutonic Order.

below: The panorama of Elvas, perched on the hills above Spain.

Chapter Twelve: Gazetteer—Italy

Studied Italian Design

After the fall of the Roman Empire, Italy was invaded by Visigoths, and then Germans and Normans, held off by city alliances and wealthy ports. The fragmented country limited lords' resources, so the siting and design of Italy's small castles was all-important.

facing top: The tower at Termoli, originally built by Frederick II in about 1247, restored after an earthquake in 1456.

center: Plan of the 14th-century Sarzanello, north of Pisa.

below: The interior of Castel Ursino, Catania, which was built by Frederick II in 1239 more for comfort than defense.

Italy has a long classical tradition reaching back to the days of the Roman Empire, when Rome was the center of civilization. After the collapse of the western half of the empire, the balance shifted to the Eastern Empire of Constantine the Great, with his capital at Byzantium (Constantinople, now Istanbul) inaugurated in AD 330. From the fifth century, Italy, was settled by the Ostrogoths.

By the late eighth century the Franks in Germany and France were ruled by Charlemagne and, on a visit to Rome in 800, the Pope crowned him Emperor. Following his death in AD 814, Charlemagne's lands gradually evolved into France and Germany, but the German rulers, or Holy Roman emperors, continually looked to Italy, not least for their coronation in Rome. To compound matters, Norman adventurers carved out territories in Apulia and Calabria in the 11th century, then seized Sicily, leaving the Pope to juggle between Germans to the north and Normans to the south.

The German Hohenstaufen emperors invaded Italy a number of times in the 12th and 13th centuries but, when their line ended, the House of Anjou arrived to fill the gap. In the 15th century the *condottieri* mercenaries and other troops defeated incursions by numerous European and Turkish forces, but the French invasion of 1494 was the start of a military decline.

Except for parts of the south and a few areas in the north, feudalism never took root in Italy. Much of the nobility was itself based in towns. Numerous independent or semi-independent states emerged, while in the 12th century the north produced the Lombard League, a confederation of cities that opposed the encroachment of the German emperors. Meanwhile, Venice, Pisa, and Genoa became highly successful and aggres-

1194	1231	1260	1266	1277	1284	1388	1416
Holy Roman Emperor Henry VI conquers Sicily	Southern Italy consolidated under Frederick II	Siena city-state defeats Florence at the Battle of Montaperti	Charles becomes King of Sicily after France invades southern Italy	Milan is controlled by the pro-Holy Roman Empire Ghibellines	Genoa city-state defeats Pisa at the Battle of Meloria	Milan conquers Padua, Verona, and Vicenza	Ottoman Turks lose a sea battle against Venice

sive maritime cities, providing numerous ships for the Crusades, trade, and war.

Byzantine Influence

From about the 10th to the 13th century, the open settlements seen in Italy changed to fortified *castra*, which consisted of a curtain wall with a single freestanding tower. For security they were usually placed on a hill or other natural prominence. Later in this period the tower was often set in the wall itself for added strength, and flanking towers were added to the curtain. From the late 12th century the area used by the lord was given increased protection, and such fortifications became known as *rocca* or *cassero*, to distinguish them from the *castra*. *Castello* referred to a fortified village.

In the 13th century rectangular ground plans became increasingly common for castles, largely due to the efforts of Emperor Frederick II (1220–50), who was influenced by Byzantine fortifications he had seen during the Fifth Crusade. The donjon or *mastio* was also seen, as were castles consisting of a tower and a large palace, and castles with strongly fortified curtain walls and towers. A common construction detail was the use of forked merlons.

The unrest in Italy caused by the enmity between towns and nobility, opposing towns, and Italians and German invaders meant that numerous castles were built; however, they were often relatively small because of the limitations of the owners' financial resources. Often their lords were town-based, or the castle was dependent on

a town and was supplied by the surrounding *contado* or country area. Instead of spending on great military architecture, the designers utilized the contours of the terrain. They built outworks to keep an enemy at a distance (few of which have survived) and paid attention to the castle approaches.

In the 14th century machicolations were increasingly seen and walls were often scarped to thicken the base. In the 15th century the growing use of gunpowder saw the introduction of gun-loops, round towers, and the first artillery fortifications, which appeared toward the end of the century.

Sarzanello, plan of the castle

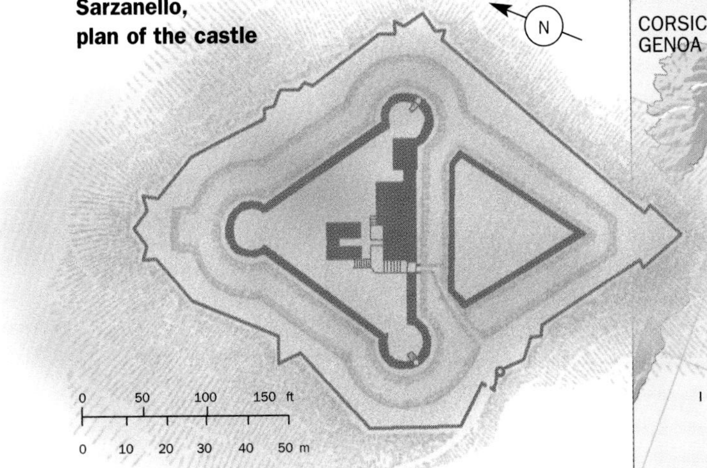

N

0 50 100 150 ft

0 10 20 30 40 50 m

The Italian City-States in the last half of the 15th century

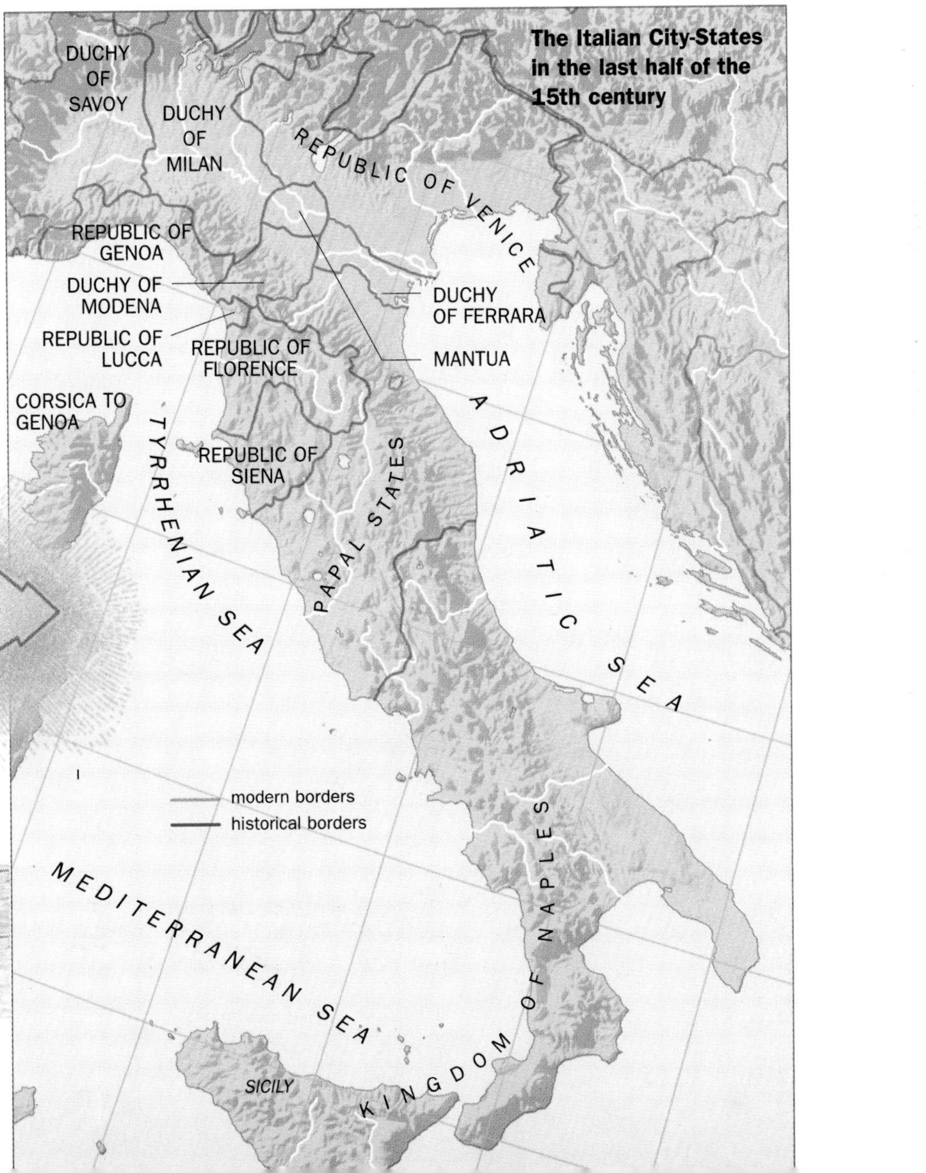

DUCHY OF SAVOY
DUCHY OF MILAN
REPUBLIC OF VENICE
REPUBLIC OF GENOA
DUCHY OF MODENA
DUCHY OF FERRARA
REPUBLIC OF LUCCA
REPUBLIC OF FLORENCE
MANTUA
CORSICA TO GENOA
REPUBLIC OF SIENA
PAPAL STATES
TYRRHENIAN SEA
ADRIATIC SEA
MEDITERRANEAN SEA
KINGDOM OF NAPLES
SICILY
modern borders
historical borders

1434
The de'Medici family gain control of Florence

1442–58
King Alfonso I of Aragon rebuilds Castel Nuovo, Naples

1511
Henry VIII is part of the "Holy League" against France's presence in Italy

Castles of Frederick II

The Hohenstaufen emperor, Frederick II, was known as *Stupor mundi*—The Wonder of the World. Cultured, cruel, and intelligent, he saw Italy as his by right. The popes distrusted him and, when the line ended in 1268, were delighted to be rid of the "nest of vipers." Frederick had consolidated southern Italy by 1231 and enjoyed the Muslim culture he found in Sicily. However, his castles were more reflective of the Byzantine strongholds he saw during the Fifth Crusade to the Holy Land. Many of his castles, such as Gioia del Colle in Apulia, had rich accommodation that is more worthy of note than his military designs. Indeed, Frederick may have personally influenced the decoration in a number of his castles.

Castello di Lombardia

This castle at Enna in the center of Sicily is set on a spur. Byzantine fortifications originally stood on this site, but the castle is usually attributed to Frederick II. There are three irregular courtyards surrounded by walls and defended by square towers, though unfortunately many of the towers have since collapsed.

Frederick is also credited with building the Torre di Federico, which can be found on a hill to the west of the Castello. This is octagonal and surrounded by the ruins of an octagonal wall.

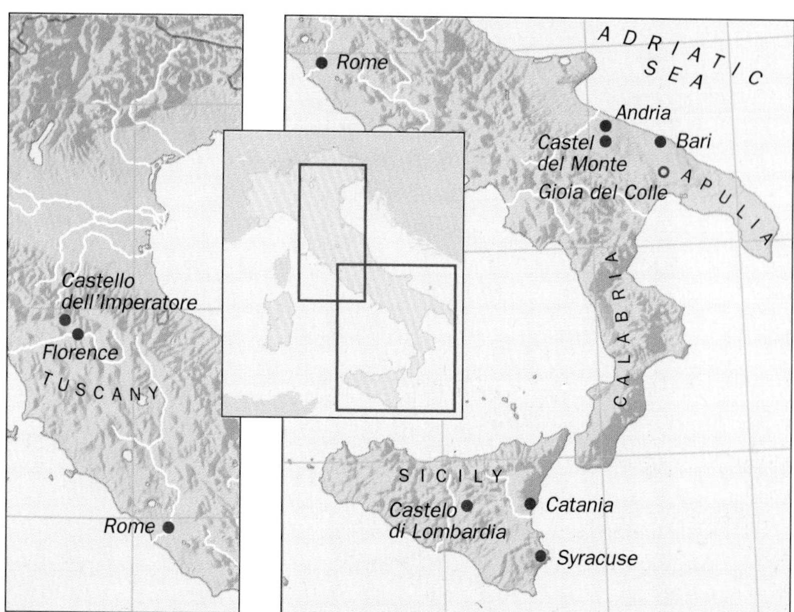

Castello dell'Imperatore

At Prato in Tuscany, 8 miles northwest of Florence, stands the Castello dell'Imperatore, which, as the name implies, was built by the Emperor (Frederick). It is the only one of Frederick's castle in central Italy that is in a good state of preservation, and was probably finished in or soon after 1241.

Castello dell'Imperatore is rectangular and set with square corner-towers. The walls are further protected by flanking towers of both square and pentagonal design, the square towers on the east and north walls being earlier work incorporated into Frederick's castle.

Castel del Monte

This famous castle, which German historian Ferdinand Gregorovius called "the crown of Apulia," is situated on an isolated hill about 10

right below: One of the courtyards at Castello di Lombardia.

miles south of Andria in Apulia, southern Italy. Frederick began work in about 1240, using the French master mason Philip Chinard.

Castel del Monte is octagonal in every way: the plan is a regular octagon, the courtyard is octagonal, and the eight angle-towers protecting the outer walls are octagonal. Moreover, there are eight rooms on each floor. The rooms are trapezoidal, the roofs supported by rib vaulting. The decoration uses marble and Roman-style features, including polychrome masonry inlay. The vaults are reminiscent of those in the cathedral of Le Mans.

Castel del Monte represents a fusion of classical and gothic themes, and is typical of Frederick's eclectic tastes and predilection for comfort. It is likely that the Emperor designed elements of the decoration, such as the portico. This castle is similar in plan to crusader work, and may be compared to that of Geoffrey de Villehardouin at Chlemoutsi in the Peloponnese in the 1220s, although the regularity of plan and lavish decoration place Castel del Monte as one of Frederick's best works. Equally, its shape has been likened to the chapel of Charlemagne at Aachen, where Frederick had been crowned Emperor, and with the Dome of the Rock in Jerusalem, which he had also seen.

There are bathrooms and water conduits, and possibly a mews for hawks on top of one tower (Frederick had written a definitive treatise on falconry). Though defensible, Castel del Monte seems to be a small palace and hunting lodge combined, prominently displayed on its hill.

below: Octagons abound at Castel del Monte, with its imposing entrance.

Castles of Several Cultures

facing top: One of the two round towers at Lucera.

These castles are examples of those constructed or rebuilt in Italy and Sicily by Germans, Normans, and Angevins.

La Zisa

The Zisa stands in Palermo, Sicily. The Normans who conquered the island in the second half of the 11th century built donjons like that of Roger I at Adernò. At first sight, La Zisa—the name is derived from the Arabic "El Aziz," meaning "The Beautiful"—looks like a rectangular donjon, but Arabic influence is strong.

below: La Zisa (view and plan).

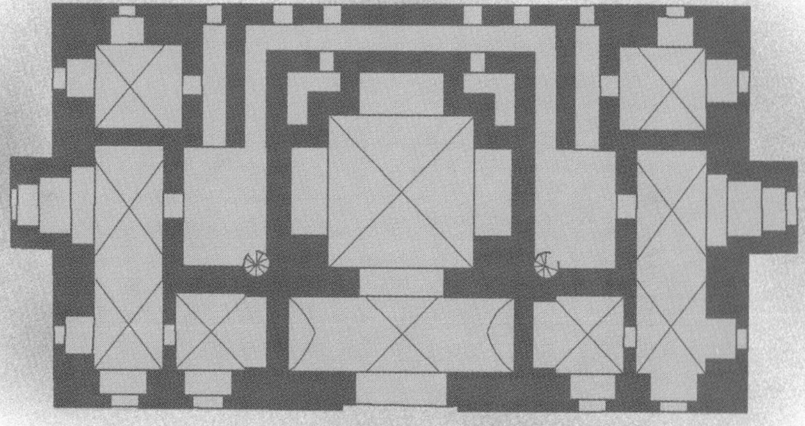

Built by William I in the 12th century, the walls are decorated with archivolts in relief and Norman-Gothic elements on the façade. The entrance in the middle of one side has high Arabic arches and opens into a long hall. Beyond is a two-story room in the middle of the tower, complete with an Arabic stalactite cupola and a fountain. The regularly laid out living rooms surround this central area on two floors; the third floor has one room originally with an opening in the middle of the ceiling, perhaps echoing the development of the Roman turreted fortress in Africa.

Also in Palermo is the Cuba, with a larger central room perhaps designed by William I in the 12th century, for banqueting.

Lucera

On a spur at Lucera, about 12 miles west of Foggia in Apulia, is Lucera castle. Frederick II built a castle here but this has been replaced—probably the only remaining vestige is the base of the great residential tower, 165 feet square. The sloping outer walls of this tower were pierced with loopholed galleries, and appears to have comprised two concentric rectangular walls, the upper levels possibly open to the sky to form a small courtyard. The upper stories were octagonal, the tower having been richly decorated and apparently filled with rich furnishings and antique statues. It survives only in a drawing of 1778, 12 years before it was blown up for use as building material.

Charles I of Anjou used Pierre d'Angicourt to plan the existing fortifications, built between 1269 and 1283. One side of the ditch in front of the spur is faced with a glacis of stone. Set in the glacis were steps up to a small gate in the wall above.

The castle within is a large enclosure, ideal for Charles to concentrate an army, ready for a campaign. A round tower is situated at each end of the ditch, called the Lion and Lioness, set on a large scarped platform to eliminate dead ground that was difficult to defend. Seven pentagonal towers are set between them; the rest of the curtain wall is strengthened by square towers.

right: Castello Caetani.

facing right: The foregate masks the Lion Gate and base of the tower at Castello dei Conti Guidi.

It was to Lucera that Frederick II imported a Muslim army, with wives and children, from Sicily, establishing a colony near the castle.

Castello Caetani

The town of Sermoneta, about 7½ miles from Latina in Lazio, is separated from its castle by a rock-cut ditch. An irregular quadrilateral in plan, the castle was held by the Anibaldi family in the 13th century; the rectangular donjon on the south side of the castle has been credited to them.

The curtain wall has rooms of several building dates set along the inner side. The hall to the east of the donjon was probably built by the Caetani family, who took over the castle in 1297 and modernized it in the 16th century. Though the Borgias also worked on the castle for a short time, the Caetani still own it today.

Castello dei Conti Guidi

This castle is situated at Poppi, about 25 miles north of Arezzo in Tuscany. Count Simone da Battifolle began the existing fortifications in 1274, which were enlarged and modified by Count Guido di Simone from about 1291. These comprise a fortified palace and tower. The small courtyard was partly rebuilt in the 15th century, from which date come a number of the room fittings and decorations.

Florence
Castello dei Conti Guidi
Arezzo
Rome
Castello Caetani (Sermoneta)
Lucera
La Zisa (Palermo)
SICILY

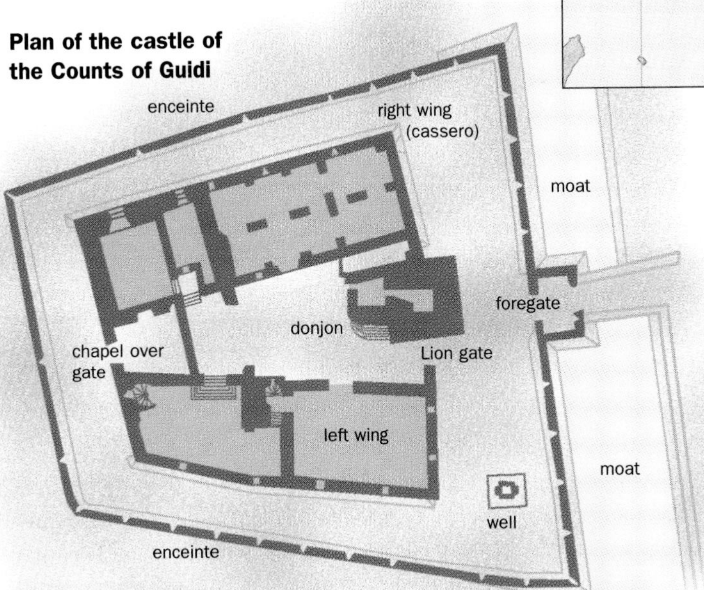

Plan of the castle of the Counts of Guidi

Urban Castles and Towers

above: Some of the surviving towers at San Gimignano.

The power of towns in Italy meant that many of the aristocracy were based in urban homes rather than in rural castles. Similarly, the burgesses within towns and cities were often wealthy and of some standing in Italian society. Quarrels between families perpetuated and many found it wise to construct towers to defend themselves, and also to proclaim their importance. These were usually tall, slim, and rectangular. Bologna once had 180 of these towers, of which only two remain. In Rome the Frangipani family built defenses inside the walls of the Colosseum, from which they opposed the papacy.

The cities built fortifications, fortifying walls, and public buildings, the most famous being the early 14th-century Palazzo Vecchio in Florence. Its trapezoidal ground plan was said to be forced, so it would not share a site once occupied by houses of the exiled Ghibellines. The large population is reflected in the 15 gates and 72 towers, part of a third set of city walls.

At Gubbio there is a complex of palaces, such as the Palazzo Municipale built by the consuls. The papacy also built new castles, even before it returned from exile at Avignon. One is the Rocca Pia, whose round towers glower at Tivoli, one of a number of similar castles. The papacy was often involved in wars with the tyrants, who had arisen in many northern cities. The Scaligeri, who rose in the 14th century, built the Castelvecchio in Verona.

In the 15th century warfare reverted from the use of foreign mercenaries who fought on foot in

right: Palazzo Vecchio, Florence.

below: Palazzo Municipale, Gubbio.

left: The machicolated walls and towers at Rocca Pia, built by Pope Pius II in 1460.

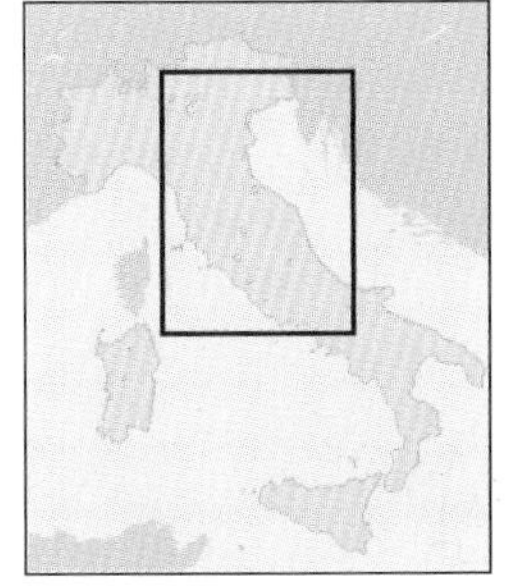

the field, to native mercenaries who fought cavalry battles and undertook long sieges of castles and cities. Sometimes the new artillery defenses were combined with residences, as at Sforza castle in Milan, rebuilt in 1450.

San Gimignano

The town of San Gimignano in Tuscany is a unique survivor of medieval Italy's wealthy urban past. During the Middle Ages there were 48 towers (some say 76) belonging to wealthy families, which stood up like church spires. Today, 13 of these towers remain.

Castel Sant'Angelo

East of the Vatican in Rome, overlooking a bridge over the River Tiber, stands the imposing bulk of Castel Sant'Angelo. The castle was built around the tomb of Roman Emperor Hadrian and was used as a fortress from at least the sixth century AD. Pope Leo IV improved the defenses when besieged by the Saracens in 846.

In 1080 Emperor Henry IV was deposed by Pope Gregory VII. This Investiture Contest between rival popes became a major catalyst for castle-building in Italy, Germany, Austria, and Switzerland. Henry invaded from Germany and by 1064 had seized Rome, while Gregory held out in the Castel Sant'Angelo. Normans from southern Italy assisted the Germans and Gregory was taken to Salerno. The fortress was often under attack and little of the original fabric survives. During the Renaissance various popes added lavish decorated apartments.

The castle was usually held by the most powerful family in Rome, but in the late 14th century by the papacy. Nicholas V (1447–55) added round towers to the corners of the tomb. Alexander VI (1492–1503) instructed the architect Antonio da Sangallo to modernize the corner towers of the fortress and add polygonal bastions to further strengthen them. These new bastions were designed to eliminate dead ground, and the sharply pointed form gradually found favor in Italy. Paul IV (1555–9), followed by Pius IV (1559–69), built the outer bastions.

Other fortifications in Rome

The Savelli fortifications are on Aventine hill, next to the Dominican center of Santa Sabina, and date from the 13th century. They consist of a castrum, home of the Savelli family, protected by a wall and square towers. The area is now laid as a garden.

Capodibove castle is about 2 miles outside the city on the Appian Way. The tomb of Cecilia Metella stands next to a fortified palace built by the Caetani family in about 1300. The large enclosure to the south may be earlier.

below: Across the Tiber from Rome stands the Castel Sant'Angelo.

Later Castles

In the 14th century there was an increase in the use of machicolated parapets, standing on stone corbels and as decorative as they were practical. In the 15th century the use of gunpowder led to the introduction of gun-loops and, by the end of the century, the first artillery fortifications. The great *condottieri* families saw the importance of castles in the disturbed conditions of northern Italy, although even these were as much statements of power and comfort as of military might.

below: The *mastio* towers above the walls of Rocca Maggiore, Assisi.

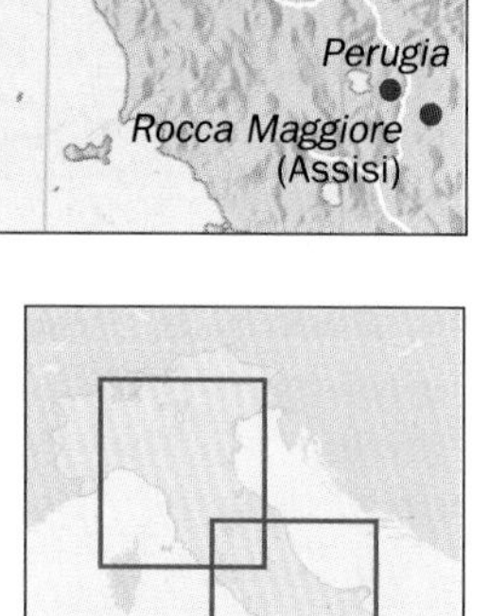

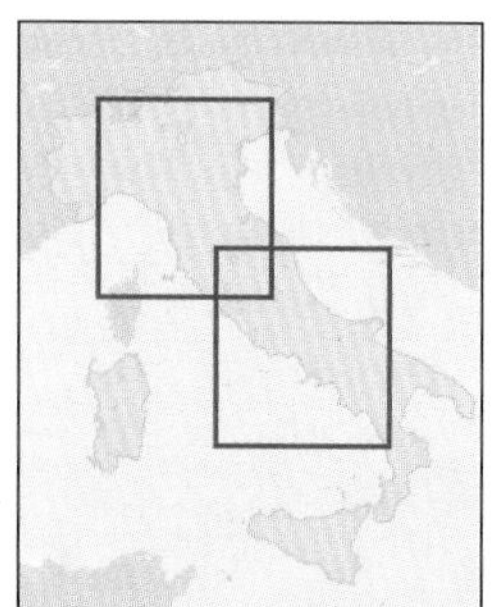

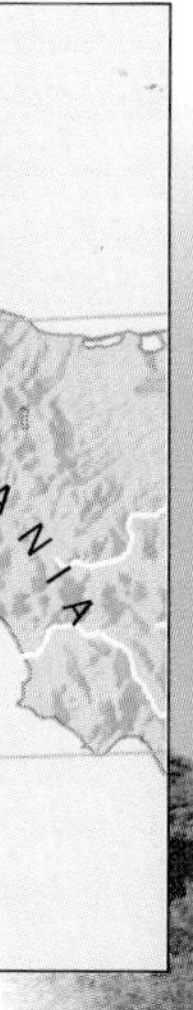

Castel Nuovo

Castel Nuovo stands by the harbor at Naples in Campania. Pierre de Chaule built a castle here for Charles of Anjou between 1279 and 1284, but hardly anything remains of this fortress. Between 1442 and 1458 the castle was rebuilt by Alfonso I of Aragon, using Spanish and Italian architects.

The plan is approximately trapezoidal, the curtain defended by large round towers similar to those used at other castles, such as the Rocca Pia at Tivoli (*see page 125*). There is a triumphal arch, built between 1453 and 1465, between two of the towers on the west wall.

Alfonso constructed a low outer wall in front of the main walls, almost in a concentric design. This outer wall is very thick and wide, however, and designed as a platform to hold artillery. Even so, when Gonsalvo of Córdoba besieged Naples in 1495, the engineer Peter of Navarre detonated a mine full of gunpowder under the castle walls, destroying the barbican. Castel Nuovo remained in use in the 16th century and beyond, because of its vice-regal connections.

Rocca Maggiore

Rocca Maggiore is at Assisi, 15 miles southeast of Perugia in Umbria, on a rocky peak overlooking the town. Emperor Frederick II stayed in the earlier castle on this site while a boy. The present castle was built by the papal legate, Cardinal Albornoz, as part of his preparations for the return of the papacy from exile at Avignon, and was first recorded in 1365.

It was perhaps constructed to a design by Ugolino de Montemarte, although it is likely to have remained unfinished by the time of the cardinal's death in 1367. The curtain wall around the large enclosure, set with angle-towers, and the *mastio* (donjon) were probably his work. There is a large palace with first-floor hall and a small courtyard.

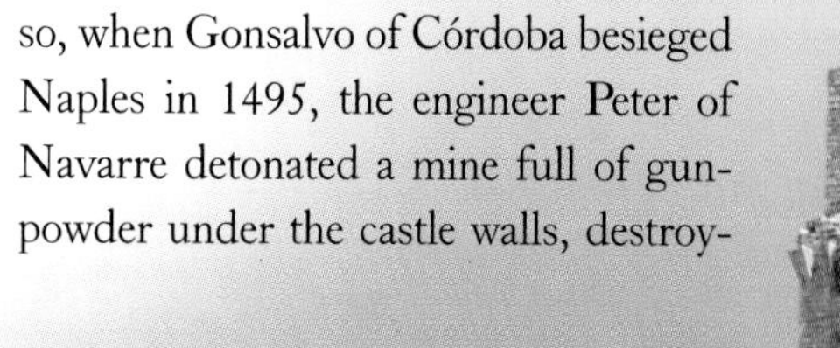

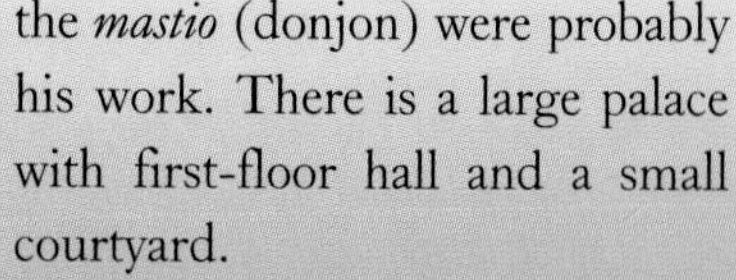

left: A low artillery platform forms the outer walls of Castel Nuovo.

Work continued on Rocca Maggiore castle, including the raising of the west and south walls of the curtain. In the mid-15th century Giacomo Piccinino built a 12-sided tower to the west of the castle but connected to it by a wall with an enclosed gallery along the top. In 1538 a round bastion was built near the entrance to the castle.

Castello Visconteo

This fortress is at Pavia in Lombardy, about 18 miles south of Milan. Galeazzo II Visconte, a member of one of the powerful families that had arisen in northern Italy, built the castle between 1360 and 1365. It was completed by Gian Galeazzo.

These families were aware of the importance of holding castles, and Castello Visconteo is one of the best examples of the 14th century trend to change the rich lord's castle into a palace. In his design Galeazzo wanted to incorporate a town palace with a cloister and castle, the palace intended for both public and private use.

The inner façade of two stories is arcaded with wide, two-light gothic arches. It is built to a square plan and is of impressive size, being some 470 feet. The building is of brick construction and its pointed gothic windows have terracotta surrounds facing the exterior, decorative but too large to be a practical defense. The moat is over 66 feet wide—the castle is reached by a bridge and drawbridges.

below: The elegant courtyard of Castello Visconteo.

Chapter Thirteen: Gazetteer—Scandinavia

Basic Scandinavian Castles

Isolated from central Europe, castles in Denmark, Sweden, and Norway evolved in different ways, Vikings using earth and wood fortifications later than other cultures, and bishops holding local power, rather than feudal lords. Advanced castles were built when influences and materials allowed.

The Vikings did not use castles, instead they created defensive communal burhs, as in Anglo-Saxon England, with ramparts and palisades. Four great circular forts have been found in Denmark, defended by a ditch and a rampart faced with wood. Aggersborg, the largest, is 787 feet in diameter. Inside, timber-paved roads divided the area into quarters, each with four wooden long-houses. These appear to have been built by Harald Bluetooth in about 980, during his struggle to unite Denmark.

Feudalism was hardly seen in Scandinavia, and the late appearance of Christianity meant that bishops held considerable sway. They supervised the first stone defenses in about the mid-12th century, rather than the nobles, who often preferred fortified houses, usually of wood.

below: Hamlet's castle of Kronborg.

Several of the 12th-century Danish *voldsteder* defenses were made as motte-and-bailey strongholds, often with a wooden tower, influenced from north Germany. Such defenses were also built in southern Sweden, such as Sölvesborg.

Stone towers were also seen in the mid-12th century. One of the earliest and best examples is at Bastrup in North Zeeland (Denmark), which has lost its upper part but was probably constructed in the time of Waldemar I (1157–82), who overcame the Slavs. His reign also saw the appearance of brick building in Denmark. The Danevirke—a large earthwork defense—was still the southern boundary and was partly strengthened by Waldemar with stone or brick walls.

In the later 12th century Knut Eriksson established towered strongholds along the east coast of Sweden to guard against pirates from Kurland and Ösel. Their foundation walls made them famous, those at Stockholm, Kalmar, and Borgholm being expanded later. On Gotland small rectangular or round towers called *kastels* were built from about AD 1200 onward, perhaps as refuges, lighthouses, or for storage.

At the end of the 12th century more complex

c.900	c.980	1013	1028	1066	1211	1319	1371
Harald Fairhair unites Norway's princedoms and becomes the country's first king	Vikings build Aggersborg fort, Denmark	King Sweyn of Denmark conquers England	Led by King Canute, Denmark conquers Norway	Harald Hardrada, the last Viking king, is killed at Stamford Bridge	Archbishop Absalom of Denmark builds a fortress which will later become Copenhagen	Norway and Sweden are ruled by Magnus VII	Magnus VII retires to Norway when nephew Albert of Mecklenburg becomes king of Sweden

layouts appeared, as at Nyborg in Denmark. In the 13th century the tower was gradually replaced as a central feature by the surrounding complex, as happened elsewhere, but in Scandinavia the materials were poor. The lay and ecclesiastical powers were the main bodies responsible for castles, while the nobles usually contented themselves with fortified houses. Scandinavian castles were workmanlike until the later Middle Ages.

Teutonic Influence

One of the earliest examples of the developed system of curtain with flanking towers is found in the town wall at Visby on the island of Gotland (Sweden). The developed form with round towers, which arrived first at Kalmar and then largely in Denmark, was borrowed from north Germany and the Baltic, via Rhineland and Westphalian influences.

In Sweden, Birger Jarl, the imperial administrator responsible for castles in Stockholm, Nykoeping, and Oerebro, made great changes. Towers and buildings became part of the structure, the curtain linking them together instead of standing within the surrounding walls. Larger though these castles were, they were not on the scale seen to the south in Europe.

The situation was similar in Denmark, as with Hammershus. It was not until the second half of the 14th century that the concept of round flanking towers was taken up properly, mainly under Waldemar IV (1340–75). Kalundborg displays similar features. Influenced by the fortresses of the Teutonic Knights, rectangular *enceinte*s with rectangular corner towers but no flanking characteristics could be seen at Tavastehus in Finland and Vaestervik in Sweden (now destroyed).

Gurre, plan of the Danish castle.

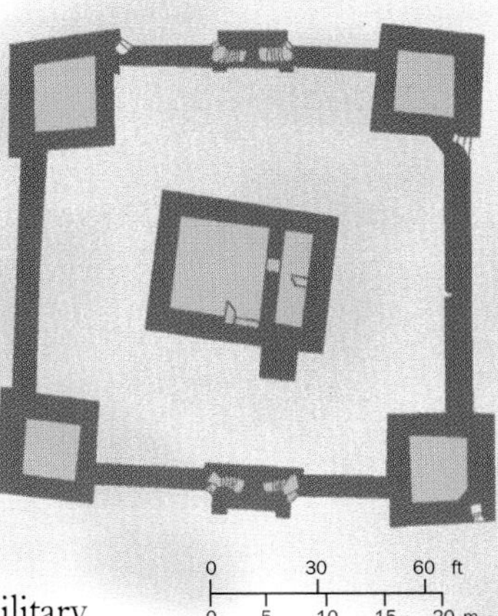

The tower did not disappear completely in Scandinavia in the later Middle Ages. It was developed as a residential area, though some retained their defensive purpose, especially those on the site of an older castle, such as Gurre in Denmark. Here the central tower probably has Romanesque foundations and stands within a roughly square 14th century *enceinte* with four square angle towers that project slightly. The wall here holds an important place in Danish military architecture, and was probably influenced by the Teutonic Order or Mediterranean styling. Gjorslev in Zeeland, seat of the Bishop of Roskilde, has a tower designed like a cross, similar to Trim in Ireland.

Toward the end of the Middle Ages the single-structure castle became common, especially in Denmark and Sweden. The aristocracy built these fortresses and older ideas were often retained. There is little evidence of any adaptation in respect of gunpowder, but still the thick defensive walls and isolated rooms of Glimmingehus, Sweden. Latterly, many Scandinavian castles were demolished or rebuilt to accommodate artillery, leaving scant remains.

below: Reconstruction of Krogen, showing the quadrangular plan favored by the Teutonic Order.

1397 Norway, Denmark, and Sweden are united by the Union of Kalmar

1423 King Erik of Sweden forms an alliance with the Teutonic Knights

1435 Eric of Scandinavia ends the Hanse dispute over Schleswig

1450 Danish King Christian I unites Norway and Denmark

1457 Christian becomes king of Sweden

1497 Norway, Denmark and Sweden are ruled by King John of Denmark after he conquers Sweden

1523 The Union of Kalmar dissolves after King Gustav makes Sweden independent

1532 Christian II loses the throne and is taken prisoner in Norway

Norway and Sweden

below: Changes in water level, as well as later additions, give the royal castle at Akershaus a more comfortable appearance than once would have been the case.

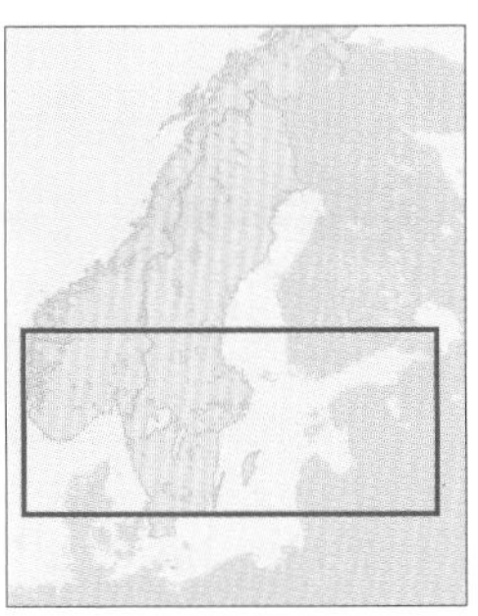

Norway was almost a stranger to feudal ideas from Europe, and royal and ecclesiastical castles were also few. Strongholds tended to be built near the coast or rivers, since its warriors preferred to fight on the water, and the geography of the country dictated that castles were usually moderate in size. Sverresborg near Trondheim is one of the oldest royal castles, with a gate-tower similar to Hammershus. Ragnhildsholm (now in Sweden) was a border fortress built in the 13th century and is a rectangular building with a projecting square tower. Tunsbergshus demonstrates Norway's most complete structure with flanking towers.

At the end of the 12th century Sweden faced the problem of pirates along her eastern coastline by constructing a number of castles. King Erik, keen to wrest northern Estonia for Scandinavia, concluded a treaty with the Teutonic Order in 1423 and, soon after, Krogen on the Oere Sound was begun, a castle even more obviously connected with the Order (today largely replaced by Hamlet's castle of Kronborg at Helsingør, the model for Elsinore in Shakespeare's play). A characteristic feature of Hälsingborg, Sweden, is the strong tower, probably built by Waldemar Atterdag in the 14th century.

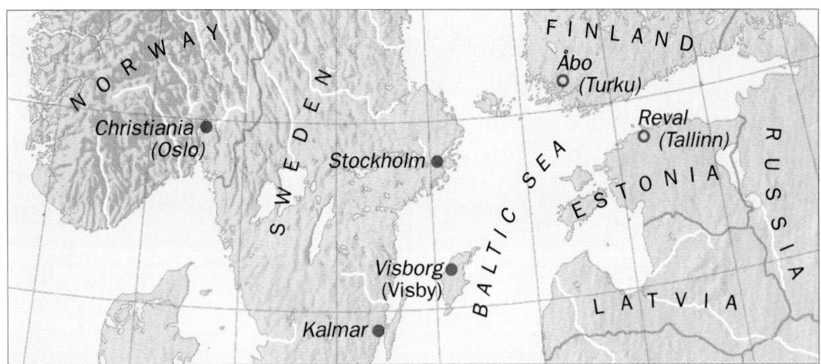

Akershaus

Akershaus is situated at Oslo (once called Christiania), Norway. The royal castle was begun by Haakon V Magnusson (1299–1319) in the new capital, but the castle was attacked but not captured in 1308, before it was completed. Work was finished at the end of the 14th century.

Akershaus castle stands on a rocky promontory, with sea and marshes for additional security—although the water level altered and new buildings were added, both of which have obscured this siting. There is a powerful central tower. The medieval fabric largely survives in the center of the huge complex, for the castle was enlarged and altered several times over its history and contains a number of styles of workmanship. A royal residence, the halls are still used for official functions.

Kalmar

This castle, known as "the Key to Sweden," was built on the southeast coast. The largest building after the walls of Visby, Gotland, it has been besieged over 20 times in its history.

The first castle was built in the late 12th century to counter attacks by heathen pirates, later rebuilt by Magnus Lådulus (1275–90). Kalmar castle first had an irregular circular wall, whose eastern front was slightly bowed, a donjon, a round tower on each corner, and two square gate towers, as at Gudenau and other Rhineland castles. The round towers were the first in Scandinavia, of French influence via the Rhineland and, for many years, the only examples.

However, Kalmar was much altered in the 16th century. Gustav Vasa radically modified it, building an outer rampart and thick round bastions for artillery. The castle has been used as an armory, prison, granary, and museum.

Visby and Visborg

Visby is on Gotland island, off the east coast of Sweden. Built in the second half of the 13th century, the 2½ miles of Visborg town walls have the earliest fully developed flanking towers in Scandinavia. There are 42 rectangular towers, ranging from 16 feet to 30 feet in height, probably influenced from the Rhineland, especially the walls of Cologne. Masons from Visby later built similar walls elsewhere, notably at Reval (Tallinn), which has semi-circular towers. Åbo (Turku) in Finland was also probably built by them.

In 1411, during the reign of King Erik, the Teutonic Knights built the castle of Visborg by cutting off the southwest corner of the 13th-century town wall. Visborg is severely plain, a square enclosure with square corner towers that only project slightly toward the field. It is also secular rather than ecclesiastical, the style based not on the conventual castles of the 14th century but the camp castles that later became popular. Erik was eventually chased out by his subjects but came to Visborg, where he remained for ten years. Parts of Visborg castle were demolished in 1679.

above: Reconstruction of the medieval castle at Kalmar, and (**left**) the castle today, with the outer rampart and bastions added by Gustav Vasa in the 16th century.

below: The walls of Visby.

Castles in Denmark

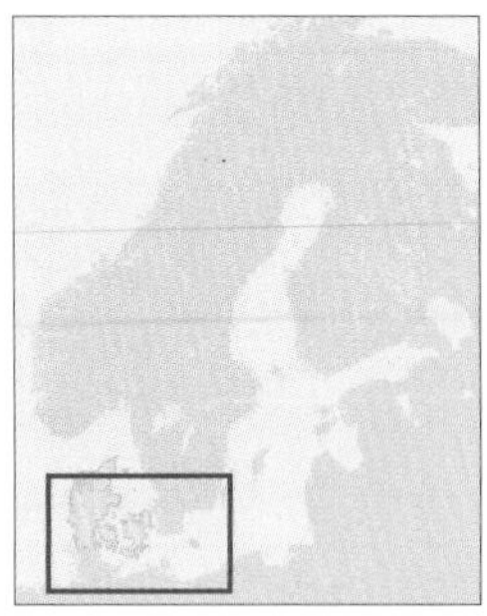

Søborg in Zeeland is one of the oldest Danish stone fortresses, founded by Archbishop Eskil in Lund in the mid-12th century. Originally there was a wooden octagonal tower on the site, standing on two four-cornered oak frames. Probably using the 11th century German palace complex of Goslar as a model, Eskil enlarged this into a roughly quadrilateral walled *enceinte*, with a rectangular palace next to the east side of the wall with a central staircase. To the north was a round building, probably a chapel, and to the south a smaller two-roomed building. In about 1200 Søborg was again enlarged.

Lilleborg at Bornholm, begun in the second half of the 12th century and almost destroyed in 1259, is the most similar to the Saxon fortresses. In 1211 Archbishop Absalom built the fortress that would form the nucleus for the city of Copenhagen, a work now almost totally destroyed. As the Danish monarchy grew stronger in the early 13th century, so the number of castles the king was able to directly control increased.

Nyborg

Nyborg is 18 miles southeast of Odense, on the island of Fyn. It is said to be the earliest royal castle in Scandinavia and, like Vordingborg, was built by Valdemar I, the Great (1157–82) to check raids by Slav pirates. Nyborg became the center of royal government for Denmark until 1416, when King Erik moved to Copenhagen, and was also the place where the Danish parliament met between the years 1282 and 1413.

Nyborg has turret-shaped half towers and a gatehouse on the east side, presumably of this early period. A palace was built against the west wall, echoed also at the fortress of Dragsholm. The foundations of this building remain.

After the government moved, Nyborg remained in favor as a residence for the king and was later used as an armory and a granary. However, in the war of 1658–60 the Swedes destroyed three-quarters of the castle and palace.

Vordingborg

Vordingborg lies at the southern tip of the island of Sjælland (Zeeland). It too was begun by Valdemar the Great against pirate raids. The original rectangular palace building was probably similar to that of Søborg and ultimately Goslar.

This early fortress was rebuilt by Valdemar IV (1340–75) and covers 10 acres, though now a ruin. An impressive curtain wall runs 2,295 feet and has semi-circular flanking towers built in brick, the whole enclosing two baileys and a small hill. The Gaasetarnet or Goose Tower is the best preserved example of a mural tower in Denmark.

Søborg, plan of the castle

Plan and reconstruction of Hammershus

Hammershus

On the island of Bornholm, 2 miles west of Sandvig, is Hammershus, a massive fortress perched on an inaccessible plateau formed by a granite outcrop. It is closer to Sweden and Germany than it is to Denmark, and was built in 1258 by the Archbishop of Lund during his contention with the king. Bornholm also has four fortified churches, specially strengthened against the Baltic pirates.

Hammershus castle has two baileys, the square inner courtyard entered through the *faestningsporten* gate tower and protected by a 30-foot high wall complete with flanking towers. There are houses along the wall, which connects to the central *manteltaarnet* that overlooks the castle. This is a huge square tower, the lower part probably of mid-13th century date, which was also the main entrance. A barbican protects the gate with, in front, a ravine to block the approach to the castle. The brick bridge over the outer moat survives.

The castle eventually came under the sway of the royal power. Despite its impressive setting, Hammershus was captured by the forces from Lübeck in 1525, although it remained in use until the 17th century, when partly demolished. Hammershus castle was restored in 1822.

facing below: Nyborg castle as it looks today. Elements of the original castle, which date from about 1200, have been incorporated in the various rebuilding programs from the 15th to the 18th centuries.

left: The great square tower dominates Hammershus castle.

Chapter Fourteen: Gazetteer—Eastern Europe and Russia

Invading Eastern Europe

There are many fine castles in the countries of Eastern Europe, an area much fought over, partly because it has suffered many incursions by foreign armies—Mongols, Ottoman Turks, and Teutonic Knights.

below: In a land much fought over, the castle in Hunedoara, Romania, used to be in Hungary, and was known as Vajdahunyad (*see pages 142–143*).

The Mongol horde from Asia entered Russia in 1237, capturing powerful cities like fortified Vladimir and the magnificent Kiev. After the latter fell in late 1240, the Mongols turned on Hungary and Poland, and routed a combined Christian army at Liegnitz and a Hungarian army at Mohi the next year. By spring 1242 they were heading for Vienna, and were only stopped by news of the death of their khan, which necessitated their return to choose a successor.

In the southwest the Ottoman Turks encroached into Bulgaria and, with the fall of Constantinople in 1453, pushed ever further inland. In September and October 1529 and again for three months in 1683 they besieged Vienna until relief arrived, when the Turks were driven off. Not until 1697 were the Turks decisively beaten at Senta.

Yugoslavia does not have many castles but does have many fortifications erected against the Turks, especially along the Danube Valley, with strongholds such as Golubac, probably built in the 14th century, its wall towers attached to rocks that stand in the river. Smederevo, begun in 1428, has a huge wall with closely spaced square mural towers, echoing Byzantine forms, down to the lines and patterns of bricks. A chain of defenses have rectangular designs with round or square towers.

From the west came the Teutonic Knights, or Knights of St. Mary the Virgin, the third of the great religious military orders. Formed in 1198, they lost their possessions in the Holy Land in 1291. From 1230 they had fought in Eastern Europe to pacify heathen tribes in Prussia, Livonia, and Lithuania and attempt to convert them to Christianity. They first entered the Kulmerland and neighboring areas. As they gradually conquered Prussia and Livonia in the 13th century, they built castles to hold down their gains and to protect the Knights from attack. These castles were, as with those of the Templars and Hospitallers, a combination of barracks and convent.

The Teutonic Castles

The first castles were needed quickly and Prussian castles were frequently adapted, often

1241 Mongols defeat Hungary at Mohi and Poland and Germany at Liegnitz

1261 King Otakar II of Bohemia takes Austria from Hungary

1344 King Louis of Hungary drives the Mongols from Transylvania

1386 Poland is allied with the duchy of Lithuania

1410 Christians defeat Teutonic Knights at the Battle of Tannenbeurg

1419 Followers of executed Czech religious reformer Hus rebel against German rule in Bohemia

1420 Hussites defeat King Sigismund of Hungary in Bohemia

1438 Albert of the Hapsburgs becomes King of Hungary

being set as sector castles. New castles tended to make use of the terrain and so did not usually display the square or rectangular plan that was usual later. The mid-13th century castle at Balga in East Prussia, for example, has an irregular layout to fit the contours of the shoreline. The rectangular plan may have been influenced by sights from the Crusades or derived from the Carolingians.

The early Teutonic fortresses were mostly of wood, until the native Prussian revolt of the 1260s was crushed, after which stone became more widely available. Between 1260 and 1290 the major castles of the Teutonic Order appeared, with a conventual house (*domus conventuales*) in the center. Usually four wings were set around a courtyard, these containing the chapel, chapter house, refectory, and dormitory. The chapel and chapter were joined first of all; large rooms were needed for the 12 friars who formed a community under a commander, the main ones on the upper floor.

The use of brick in these Baltic castles produced Gothic fortresses of imposing appearance. Marienburg had a brickworks in the outworks, and the use of stepped gables and large expanses of brick, relieved by blind sunken panels or colored bricks, shares similarities with churches and cathedrals in the Hansa towns and Poland.

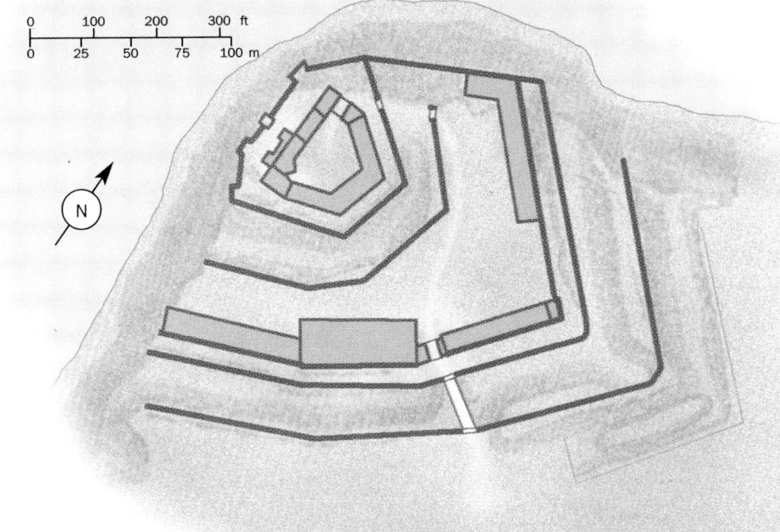

Balga, eastern Prussia, plan of the castle site.

Tall gables in some examples allowed north German brick ornament to be applied. Courtyards had arbored walks. Sometimes an earlier watch tower was amalgamated into the quadrangle of buildings, but substantial angle-towers were rare. Barbicans were popular, however.

It should be noted that, in reflecting the troubled history of this area of Europe, castles suffered severe damage during the Second World War. Happily, many have since been well restored.

below: The warlike towers at Golubac overlook the Danube.

1454–66
Teutonic Knights accept defeat and Poland's overlordship

Early Czech Castles

above: Hukvaldy.

below: Karlstejn—a grouping of five strongholds dominiated by the great donjon.

Of all the countries of Eastern Europe, Czechoslovakia has a wealth of castles that recall its importance on the map of Europe. The Germans were welcomed in Bohemia when they settled there and used their skills at forming thriving urban settlements, which helps to account for the siting of some fortresses close to towns, such as the Hradschin at Prague. Rulers saw the prospects of wealth from trade, and sure leaders such as the Premyslid dynasty encouraged German knights to settle as a balance to over-mighty Slav nobles.

Emperor Charles IV, son of the blind king of Bohemia, had been brought up at the French court and was a civilized, holy man. He saw Bohemia as the place to concentrate his power base, thus shifting the balance in central Europe eastward.

Hukvaldy

The 13th-century Hukvaldy castle is 25 miles south of Ostrava in northern Moravia, set on a hill above a game-preserve. Unlike many Czech castles, Hukvaldy is in much its original state. Hukvaldy town is famous as the birthplace of the composer Leos Janácek in 1854.

Karlstejn

Karlstejn castle commands an area $17\frac{1}{2}$ miles southwest of Prague from its hilltop. It was begun in 1348 by Charles IV, Emperor of the Holy Roman Empire and King of Bohemia, as a center of power in Bohemia, and completed in 1357. It also housed his crown jewels and huge collection of holy relics.

Under Charles IV, Bohemia experienced a "golden age." This is reflected in the concept of Karlstejn; it has the grandeur of castles of the period in France, yet in position, ground plan, and the lack of mural flanking towers except at the entrances, it suggests those of Germany. The wooden hoardings (modern restorations) betray a lack of stone machicolation that would have been at least partially evident in French castles.

Karlstejn has five separate towers, laid out in degrees of holiness, the strength of each related to the value of what lay within. The first, the well tower, is supplied by underground passages from the river. The second has the lodgings of the Burggraf (similar to a mayor), third the imperial palace and chapels, and fourth the Tower of the Virgin with its collegiate church.

The final stronghold is the huge donjon, 121 feet high. Inside is the Hall of the Empire and above it the Chapel of the Holy Rood, named after the piece of the True Cross Charles supposedly possessed, stored with the crown jewels. The chapel has golden vaulting, a rood screen, and a triptych by Tomaso di Modena. There are also some beautiful wall paintings by Theodoric, while a frieze below is set with 3,000 semi-precious stones. Other rooms in the castle also have painted medieval walls, such interior design perhaps a result of Charles' time as regent for his father in Italy.

During the wars against the heretical Bohemian Hussites in the 15th century, Karlstejn was held for Emperor Sigismund after all the other fortresses in the area had been stormed. In the 19th century the outer fabric was restored but the inside was preserved.

Zvikov

Zvikov, "the Queen of Bohemian castles," is 15 miles north of Pisek in southern Bohemia. Also known as Klingenberg, it is sited on a spur above the confluence of the rivers Otava and Vltava, now dammed to form a large lake.

In the 13th century Zvikov castle was the main seat of the Premyslid rulers of Bohemia; it was begun by Vaclav I and completed by Otakar II. Of their work survives the 30-foot high wedge-shaped and cylindrical watch tower and the shorter Marcomanni Tower (the name of a Germanic tribe that may have once occupied the area).

The remaining work is a Gothic construction of outstanding worth, following the style of a German castle. However, the chapel has wonderful 15th-century wall paintings, probably of French workmanship, while the residential building has an arcaded courtyard and a prismatic tower, unlike anything else in Europe.

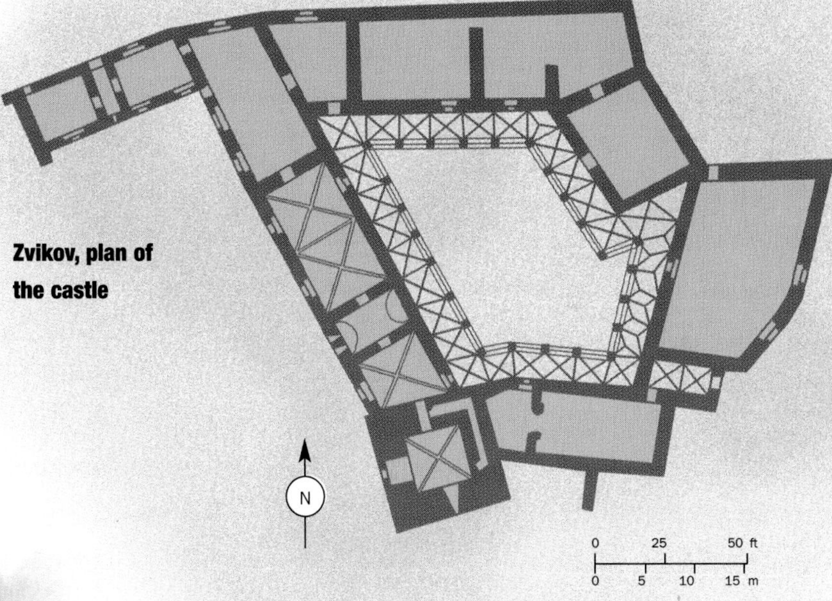

Zvikov, plan of the castle

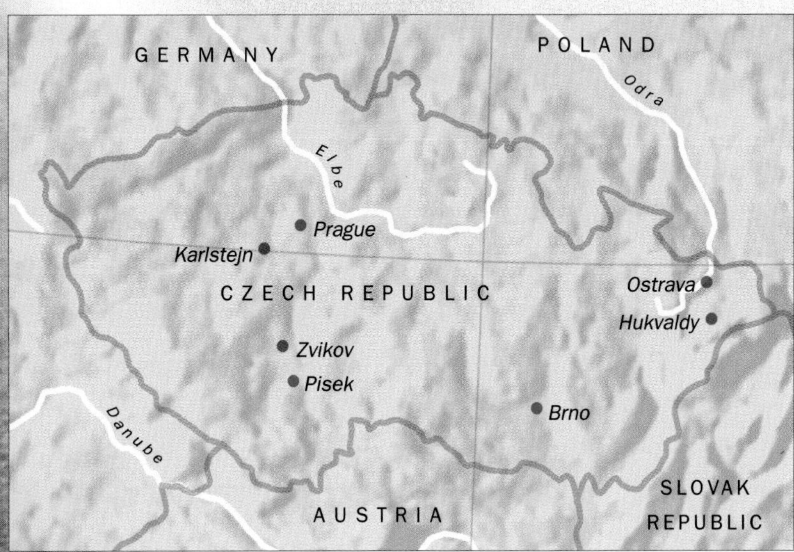

Later Czech Castles

facing top: Pernstejn, showing the residential tower.

During the first part of the 15th century much unrest in Bohemia was caused by the Hussites, the heretical followers of Jan Hus, burned at the stake in 1415. Largely from non-noble backgrounds, the Hussites made use of wagon trains to protect them; under the command of Jan Zizka, their guns and lethal flails, easily adapted from threshing flails, beat off crusading armies sent against them by the German emperor.

Krivoklat

Approximately 36 miles west of Prague is the town and fortress of Krivoklat. The latter was built on a hill within thick woodland, protected on three of its sides by the valley of Rakovnicky. The first castle of stone was erected at the end of the 13th century, during the reigns of Premysl Otakar II and Vaclav II. It was rebuilt between 1492 and 1522 and is triangular in plan.

The internal structures are noteworthy as containing some of the best examples of medieval Czech architecture. Krivoklat castle was partly restored and now contains a museum and the Furstenburg Library.

Kalich and Tabor

facing: Clever use of natural features made Krivoklat a formidable fortress.

In the Labe Valley east of Litomerice in central Bohemia stands the ruins of Kalich castle. It was built by the Hussites for their leader, Jan Zizka, an unusual occurrence, since the Hussites detested castles as symbols of the oppression by the Germans and the Holy Roman Empire, who saw the Hussites as a heretical threat. However, Kalich was built so that Zizka could change his name to Jan of Kalich (or Chalice), an emblem of the Hussite wish for communion in both kinds.

Zizka was a military leader of rare quality. In 1420 he went to the town of Tabor, the holy place named after a biblical mountain and founded by the Hussites 54 miles south of Prague. Set on a steep hilltop, it satisfied the Hussite's religious instruction to go to high places to await the coming of the Lord.

Already strongly positioned on a peninsula between the Rivers Luznice and Tismenice, Zizka fortified the town with double walls in a roughly hexagonal plan, each corner with a flanking tower.

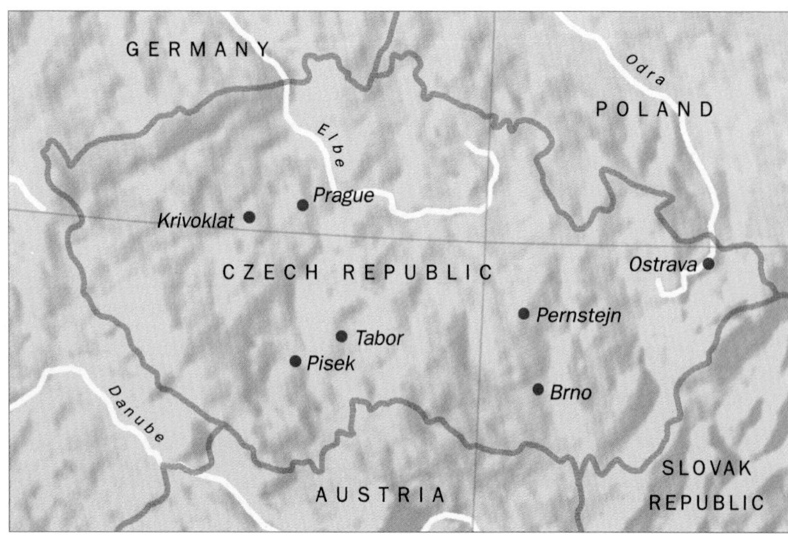

Pernstejn

Perched on its hilltop site 13½ miles northwest of Tisnov, Pernstejn castle overlooks the River Svratka. The castle was first built toward the end of the 13th century, but after the Hussite Wars of the 15th century the Holy Roman Empire had lost much of its influence and large tracts of church land were redistributed among the Czech nobility.

William and John of Pernstejn acquired this castle after it was damaged by fire in 1457; as was happening with other strongholds gained by nobles, they rebuilt it in a more modern and residential style, but also as a larger, more powerful fortress. Their work was continued for a further hundred years, mainly in the late Gothic style, and additions were made as late as the 17th century. It is now perhaps the finest castle in Moravia.

There are several levels, with five towers, four gateways, and two moats. White marble has been used to present a shining appearance to the onlooker, a clever idea all the more impressive due to the rarity of such stone in Moravia. The main residential tower is approached via a bridge from a powerful polygonal tower. The latter's top has turrets set around it that terminate at the bottom as machicolations, almost like box machicolations turned into bartizans. A parapet runs through the thick walls. The entrance hall is decorated with delicate cellular vaulting of high quality, carved c.1520.

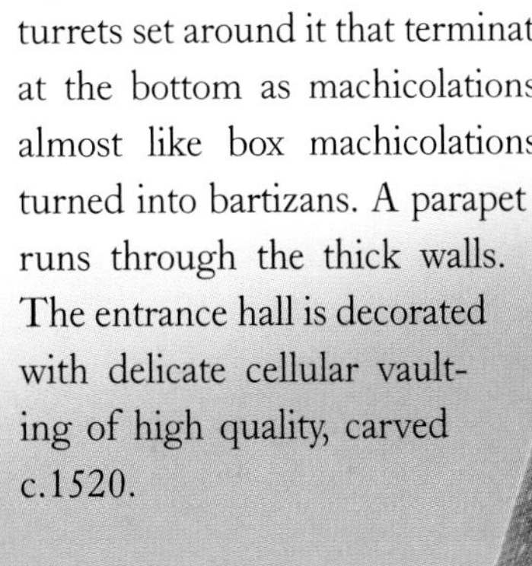

Castles in Poland

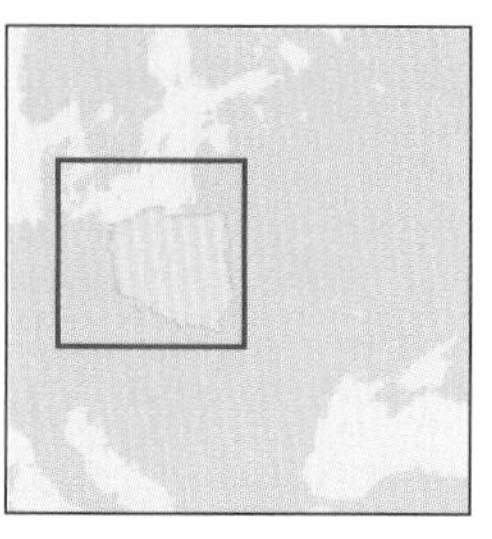

Poland has castles built by native rulers and some of the greatest works of the campaigning Teutonic Knights. In the 1450s King Wladyslaw renewed the war against the Order, ending with the Grand Master becoming a vassal of the Polish king.

Wawel

Wawel castle is set on a hilltop overlooking the River Vistula at Krakow in southern Poland. In the eighth century the Slavs built a stronghold here. In the 11th century, when Krakow had become the capital city of Poland, a castle was built on the site. It was enlarged in the 14th century, when the cathedral, which holds the tombs of early Polish monarchs, was rebuilt (1320–64).

It was the seat of the Polish kings during the Middle Ages and also a religious power base. In the 16th century the kings moved their capital to Warsaw but Krakow retained its religious and academic center. Similarly, much of the castle still has its medieval fabric. In the Second World War it was used as a residence by German Governor-General Hans Frank.

below: Wawel was once the power base of the Polish kings.

Marienburg

Marienburg, "the queen of all the castles" of the military Order of St. Mary the Virgin, lies at Malbork, 35 miles southeast of Gdansk. The Teutonic Knights were invited here in 1225 by a Polish duke, Conrad of Mazovia, who wanted to convert a pagan Lithuanian tribe, the Pruzzi. Grand Master Hermann von Salza met the challenge with ease.

Marienburg was probably a wooden castle first, speedily built in a potentially hostile environment. The new castle was a typical Teutonic design: rectangular in plan, built of brick, and serving both soldiers and monks. By 1280 Marienburg had two areas. The Hochschloss contained the chapter house, chapel, and *Wehrgang*—a decorated covered gallery with machicolations, perhaps indicating French influence via the Rhineland and Low Countries—while the Mittelschloss was the residential area. The courtyard was ringed with cloister-like galleries that connected the wings.

In 1309 Marienburg castle became the Order's headquarters. Between 1335–41 a tower and bridge over the River Nogat were added, while the Mittelschloss was rebuilt, notably housing the Master's Main Refectory, with its slim brick vaulting on granite piers. A third area, the Unterschloss of outworks, was added to the north, which included a brickworks and foundry.

Under Winrich von Kniprode (1352–83), the greatest of the Grand Masters, a new Master's residence was constructed as a wing of the Mittelschloss, under the direction of Rhenish architect Nikolaus Fellenstein. Amid its princely richness was the summer refectory, where a single pillar supported the vaulted ceiling, and underfloor heating in the winter refectory. The chapel was decorated with star vaults and enlarged to jut out beyond the east wall, unusual in a conventual buildings, and a huge figure of the Virgin and Child stood over Knights' graves.

In 1410 the Teutonic Order was soundly defeated at the Battle of Tannenbeurg by a Christian army, making their position as converters of the heathen very difficult. Marienburg was besieged that year by the Poles until dysentery forced them to withdraw. Despite this setback, Poles took the castle in 1457.

During the Second World War, Marienburg was used by Germany to hold prisoners-of-war. It has undergone restoration and reconstruction over several centuries, but remains a powerful monument to the Teutonic Knights.

Marienwerder

At Kwidzyn, 24 miles south of Marlbork (Marienburg), is another castle of the Teutonic Knights. Marienwerder is attached to the 14th-century cathedral overlooking the River Liva and was an impressive bishop's palace, with the conventual house predominant. There was probably a 13th-century wooden fortress on this steep bank before the castle replaced it, largely built in the first half of the 14th century.

An interesting and unusual structure at Marienwerder is the tall square *danske*, or sewage tower, with stepped gable roof. Reflecting the disciplines and views of the monastic orders, the tower is isolated from the main castle and reached by a covered gallery on five pointed arches. As a feat of engineering it ranks as the most impressive and expensive sewage system of the Middle Ages.

Marienwerder was very badly damaged during the Second World War but has been well restored.

below: The Hochschloss at Marienburg behind two lines of walls, with a pointed window of the chapter house at extreme right.

Hungary, Romania and Yugoslavia

After the Mongol invasion of 1241, King Bela IV of Hungary called in German and Italian builders to increase the number of castles, and asked his nobles to do likewise. Between 1304 and 1382 Hungary came under two Neapolitan Angevin monarchs, and French influences were felt.

Under Ludwig the Great (1342–82) Hungary grew in importance, also reflected in the number of new castles. Despite the efforts of John Hunyadi and his son, Mattias Corvinus, the Turkish threat increased. German settlers in Transylvania built strongholds, their churches surrounded by curtain walls with covered wall-walks, such as at Kelling, which has two *bergfrieden* and a moat. Castles often show modification in the 15th and 16th centuries as in Germany and Austria, first by the addition of round towers, as at Sebes or Trencsén, the latter having held off a Mongol attack.

The main front of Hunedoara (or Vajdahunyad), now in Romania, has the massive palace of John Hunyadi, with a gallery of oriel windows, Teutonic style. The main areas date to about 1430, round towers and bastions added later. Matthias Corvinus brought strong Italian influences, notably the 16th-century bastion.

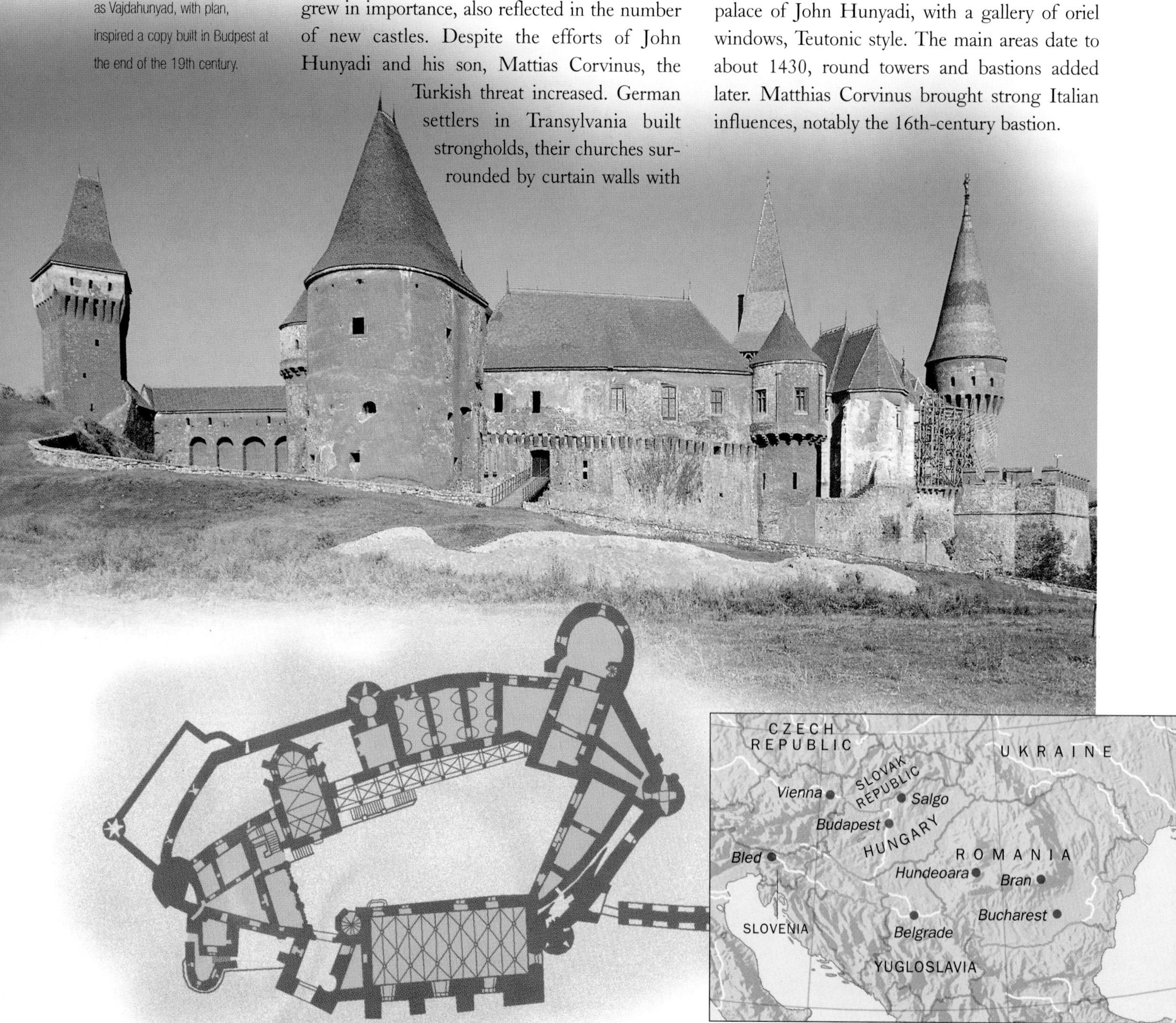

below: Hundeoara, also known as Vajdahunyad, with plan, inspired a copy built in Budpest at the end of the 19th century.

left: Bran has a more welcoming appearance than its association with Dracula would lead the visitor to believe, although the castle does have a blood-drenched history.

Salgo

Salgo is located outside Salgótarján in Nograd, 74 miles northeast of Budapest in Hungary. It seems likely that Salgo was built in the second half of the 13th century as a response to the Mongol threat. It is set high on basalt rock, with a pentagonal tower with very thick walls on the eastern side, and was so secure that it became the seat of baronial power.

In the 15th century Salgo castle was a fortress for the Hussites until it was taken by Matthias Corvinus The Just (1458–90). It later became the home of the Szapolyais family and István Werböczy, responsible for the codification of Hungarian law. The Turks damaged the castle and it suffered again when taken over by the Hapsburgs. Today it is a ruin, but the tower is well preserved.

Bran

Situated 15½ miles southwest of Brasov in the Transylvanian Alps, Bran is the most spectacular fortress in Romania. It sits on a steep rocky crag and controls the entrance to two valleys leading to Sibiu, an important city in the Middle Ages.

The first castle here was built from wood in the early 13th century; the existing structure was raised in 1377 by the men of Brasov to guard their city. Many medieval parts of the fabric have survived. However, it is with the legend of Dracula that Bran has achieved notoriety.

In the mid-15th century Bran castle was held by Vlad Tepes, the ruler of Wallachia. In his fight against the Turkish threat, Vlad used great cruelty to deter his enemies; one of his favorite forms of slow execution was by impalement on a stake. Vlad was also called Dracula, which means "son of the Dragon"—a reference to his father's title. In the 19th century, Bram Stoker used the castle and parts of its history when writing his infamous vampire novel.

Bled

Bled castle stands on a vertical bluff overlooking Lake Bled in Slovenia (part of the former Yugoslavia), 33 miles northwest of Ljubljana. The first fortress was built in 1004 to control both the lake and the town, itself founded in the time of Charlemagne and retaining its encircling walls.

In the 12th century Bled castle was given to the Bishops of Bixen by Emperor Henry II, who retained it until the 19th century. The bishops undertook work on the castle at various periods, much of which can still be seen. In the courtyard stands a well preserved and impressive Gothic chapel. Regent Paul used the castle as a favorite residence before the Second World War, and latterly it was often visited by President Tito.

below: Wall-walk and round tower at Bled.

Fortifying the Russian Frontiers

Early fortifications in Russia tended to be in the southeast, along the River Dnieper. In the tenth century many simpler earth-and-timber castles were erected along the forest edge and along rivers, from which troops could ride out to attack the nomads of the Steppes, which the Russians had failed to control. However, these castles were destroyed in retaliatory moves by the Qipchaq and Pecheneg peoples.

below: The Kremlin of Pskov bears witness to the effects of a modern war, as Russians crowd its bailey to pay their last respects to paratroopers who lost their lives in Chechnya.

Larger fortresses were built within Russia in the 11th and 12th centuries, often enclosing fields to provide food for a beleaguered garrison. Earthen ramparts were topped by a timber wall with wall-walk and an overhanging roof. Nearer the heartland were round forts of earth, rubble, and timber, a Slav type that had existed since the 10th century. Many of these fortifications were extremely large, but there was little use of stone or brick until the 13th century. Such timber strongholds were used, for example, in the Russian expansion west into Finnish territories.

In northern Russia defenses were similar, although less elaborate. Novgorod had a wall by the 11th century (some parts in stone, some in earth and timber), while Pskov may have had stone defenses in the tenth century. Stone walls were, like timber ones, given a pitched roof supported by posts at the rear of the wall-walk. Alexander Nevsky used small forts to defend the northwest frontier from the Lithuanians.

Facing the Teutonic Order

In the late 13th and 14th centuries stone towers rather like donjons were built, although added as a single entity on the weakest side of walled *enceintes* sited on a natural position, in a manner reminiscent of Hungarian and Polish practice. Many still relied on timber, however. Despite overtaking Novgorod as the chief city, Moscow's Kremlin, or "fortress," did not receive stone walls until 1367–8.

The effect of firearms on military architecture is seen more obviously in the Baltic than in Prussia, both among the native peoples and the Teutonic Order. Russian builders kept pace with their rivals; a Greek builder, Marcus de Grece, was a leading figure.

Ivanograd was a large border fortress facing the Teutonic Order's Hermannsburg across the River

1198
The order of the Teutonic Knights is formed

1237
Mongols invade Russia, Golden Horde khanate established

1240
Prince Alexander Nevsky prevents a Swedish invasion

left: Reconstruction of a timber-walled enclosure for a settlement.

Narva. It is a different form of castle to that of the Knights. In layout it is a long rectangle with round corner towers and square gate towers. A wall separates the far end, entered through another square tower, and there is a further enclosure projecting to one side, halfway along the *enceinte*. Ivanograd developed from the camp castles and border forts of the Balkans, which would also be taken up by the Turks. The Greek type of castle, such as that at Olofborg, reached from Russia to Finland.

As the Turks grew increasingly threatening, taking Constantinople, then almost seizing Rhodes from the Knights Hospitallers in 1480, the Czars followed other rulers and looked to the Italians for help in fortifying their strongholds. Already in 1475 the Italian architect Fioravanti was called in to improve the walls of the Kremlin.

bottom: Wall of the Kremlin of Novgorod.

below: Gate in the town walls of Reval (Tallinn).

1242 Prince Alexander defeats the Teutonic Knights at Lake Peipus

1325 Ivan becomes ruler of Moscow, but under command of the Golden Horde

1330 Construction begins on Riga, the first Teutonic castle in Russia

1339 Construction begins on the Kremlin

1380 Russians at Tula, Moscow, defeat a Mongol army

1395 Rival Mongol leader Tamerlane conquers parts of the Golden Horde's Russian territory

1453 War between Vasily II and cousin Dmitri Shemyaka ends with the latter's death in exile

1557 Russia invades Livonia, formerly held by Teutonic Knights

Castles of the Teutonic Knights and their Opponents

The Teutonic Order pushed up the Baltic from Prussia into Livonia and Lithuania, and finally into Russia itself. The Russians decided to end this aggression and, in 1242, Prince Alexander Nevsky defeated the Teutonic army at Lake Peipus at the "Battle on the Ice." The later conversion of the Lithuanians and their alliance with Poland undermined the Teutonic Order, culminating in its defeat at Tannenberg in 1410.

Riga

Situated in Latvia, Riga was the first castle built in Russia by the Teutonic Knights and became the seat of the rulers of Riga. Construction began in 1330 as the Knights expanded eastward. Later, Riga was controlled by the Livonian Order, or Knights of the Sword, a branch who settled in the

right: The castle in Riga, surrounded by the modern city and, **below**, the circular tower that today houses the city's museum.

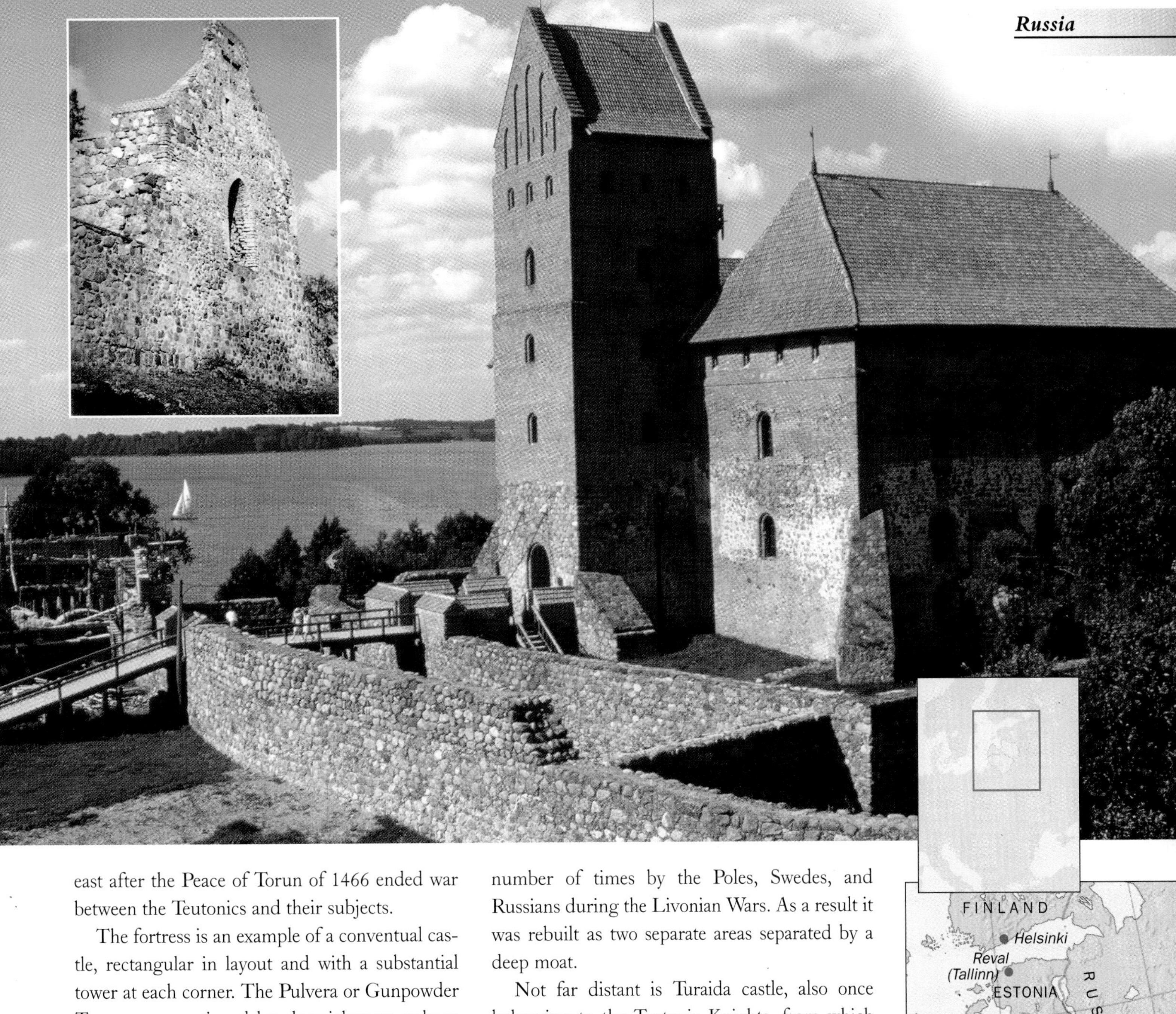

east after the Peace of Torun of 1466 ended war between the Teutonics and their subjects.

The fortress is an example of a conventual castle, rectangular in layout and with a substantial tower at each corner. The Pulvera or Gunpowder Tower was mentioned by chroniclers as early as 1330, but the present structure was built in 1650 and rests on oak foundations.

Under the Master, Wolter von Plettenberg (1494–1535), Riga was modernized, along with a number of other castles; diagonally placed cannon towers were added to the 14th-century building. The work was completed in 1515 and the castle became an influence on others in the east.

Riga sustained some heavy damage during the Second World War but has been extensively restored.

Sigulda

Sigulda castle is in Latvia, 33½ miles northeast of Riga. It was the second castle built by the Teutonic Knights in Russia, one of a number they erected in Latvia in the mid-14th century. In the course of the 16th century Sigulda was besieged a number of times by the Poles, Swedes, and Russians during the Livonian Wars. As a result it was rebuilt as two separate areas separated by a deep moat.

Not far distant is Turaida castle, also once belonging to the Teutonic Knights, from which excellent vistas of the countryside are visible. The story of Maja, the "Turaida Rose," who died when young but whose love lived on, is well known locally.

Trakai

Trakai is in Lithuania, 17 miles west of Vilnius. Because the town was set within a group of lakes, it was known as the "Town on the Water." The castle was built on one of the islands of Lake Galva, probably on a previously fortified site, by Witold, Duke of Lithuania (1398–1430), during the struggle of the Lithuanians and Poles with the encroaching Teutonic Knights.

The surviving castle dates from the 14th and 15th centuries. Its curtain walls have three large circular towers, and there is an impressive donjon.

above: The castle at Trakai is sited on an island in Lake Galvé.

inset: Sigulda.

Chapter Fifteen:
Gazetteer—The Middle East

Religious Battles in the Middle East

Crusader borders
Kingdom of Jerusalem after 1229
Modern borders
CYPRUS
COUNTY OF TRIPOLI
LEBANON
SYRIA
SYRIA
KINGDOM OF JERUSALEM
Jerusalem
JORDAN
ISRAEL

When Jerusalem fell to the Seljuk Turks, the Byzantines were aided by an army determined to free the Holy Land from the Moslem infidels. The region was later set with castles of the Templars, Hospitallers, Teutonics, and other knights with religious motives.

In 1071 the Byzantines suffered a great setback at the Battle of Manzikert, beaten by Seljuk Turks who had advanced into Anatolia. When Jerusalem fell to them, the Byzantine Emperor asked the West for aid. What he expected were bodies of troops to help his own forces. What he got was a huge army of knights, soldiers, and pilgrims (the bulk of whom were French), whipped up into a frenzy by Pope Urban II to save the Holy Places of Christendom.

The First Crusade set out in 1096, was hurried through Constantinople by the Emperor, and in 1099 besieged and took Jerusalem after a bitter struggle involving three siege towers. The butchery when the Franks, as the Muslims called westerners, surged through the streets is well recorded.

The Franks set up states in the Holy Land, run on similar feudal lines as their homelands. However, when Saladin rose to power to the 12th century, he united the Muslims and retook Jerusalem. The Third Crusade of 1189 saw the arrival of the gifted soldier-king Richard I, the Lionheart. Though a match for Saladin, he was aware of supply problems and how the settlers in

974 Byzantine Empire controls northern Palestine and Syria

1071 Seljuk Turks defeat the Byzantines at the Battle of Manzikert

1078 Palestine and Syria are occupied by Turks

1096 The First Crusade seeks to free the Holy Land from Muslims

1099 Crusaders defend Constantinople from the Muslims

1183 Saladin conquers Syria, becoming its sultan

1191 Acre and Cyprus are taken by crusaders

1229 Crusaders take Bethlehem, Jerusalem, and Nazareth by treaty

left: Between 1250 and 1254, St. Louis of France strongly fortified Caesarea, Israel, built on the site of the Herodian Caesarea Maritima.

Jerusalem would cope when the army went home; he did not try to besiege Jerusalem and finally withdrew. Only the Fifth Crusade under the Holy Roman Emperor, Frederick II, saw Jerusalem opened up through negotiation, but this too was short-lived.

A number of other Crusades followed in the 13th century, two under St. Louis of France attacking through North Africa. In the later 13th century, with the arrival of the Mamluks, an efficient army of freed slaves, the days of the crusader states were numbered. One by one crusader castles were taken and in 1291 Acre fell, the last Christian stronghold in the Holy Land.

The Knights of Religion

Major factors in all this were the knights of the Military Orders of monks. The Knights Templars, with their headquarters by the Temple Mount in Jerusalem, were set up in about 1119, while the knights of St. John, the Hospitallers, had originally provided care for the sick. In about 1198 these great orders were joined by the German Teutonic Knights, along with several smaller orders. The major orders accrued such wealth that they were far better placed than many to build and hold powerful castles, notably in frontier areas, and to recruit men via their European convents. The strictly trained warrior monks were a great strength in the Frankish armies.

When they first arrived the Franks found late Roman defenses, Byzantine fortifications, and Muslim strongholds. Their size was impressive: the city of Antioch, besieged in 1097–8, had 33-foot high walls set with 400 towers. Right from the start, however, the Franks built castles of their own. Though often using western styles and methods, they were influenced by the military buildings they saw in the east.

Castles were planted to guard road and river routes but there was no grand scheme to use groups of castles to block all paths into the crusader strongholds. Though they may appear to have been arranged in lines and often within sight of one another, as though to communicate, it is unlikely that a chain of defensive works was a conscious part of their planning. The castles were built at different times by different people, and remained as homes and administrative centers. Their use for holding garrisons was paramount in the assembly of field armies, often gathered from a number of strongholds, to meet the Muslims in the field. No major crusader castle in the late 13th century endured a siege for longer than about six weeks.

below: The ruined walls of Krak des Chevaliers, Syria.

1244	1268	1271	1272	1291	1307	1326	1387
Muslims capture Jerusalem	Mamluks sack Antioch and Jaffa	Mamluks take Chastel Blanc, Krak des Chevaliers, and Montfort castles	Crusaders and Mamluks agree a peace treaty	Fall of Acre to Muslims, the last crusader castle in the Holy Land	King Philip of France persecutes Knights Templars, seeking their wealth	Ottoman Turks begin to seize Byzantine territory	Mongol leader Tamerlane conquers Persia

Crusader Donjons

The donjon came with the crusaders from the west and, though of similar design, shows variations in style. Middle Eastern towers were often more squat than many in England and France. The lack of wood meant that floors were usually vaulted, while stairs were rarely of spiral form. The donjon was often surrounded by a *chemise* or wall, positioned much closer than was usual in the west. Others were set into curtain walls.

Edessa

Edessa was the first major Muslim fortress to be captured by western crusaders, in 1098. The castle and town are situated at Urfa in eastern Turkey. The site of an old acropolis had been taken over by the Byzantines and then the Armenians, resulting in a curtain wall with mural towers.

When the Franks captured it, they cut a ditch 40 feet deep into the rock, faced with large bastions of polygonal shape, to protect the castle from the town population, and added a square donjon to its defenses. A round tower was built in 1122.

below and facing: At Gibelet, curtain walls tightly enclose the donjon.

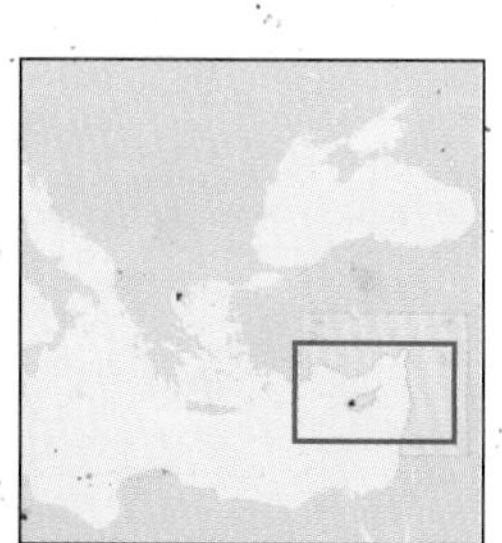

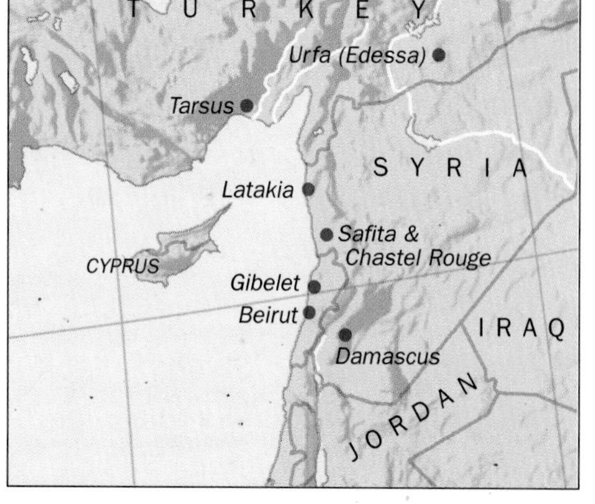

Gibelet

At Jubayl (Byblos) on the shores of Lebanon stands Gibelet, built in 1103 soon after the town had been captured by the Franks. At the southern corner of the town walls a large rectangular donjon was built, 58 by 70 feet in plan. Of the two internally vaulted stories, a cistern was set under the floor of the lower chamber. The first-floor entrance was reached by ladder, and straight stairs cut in the thickness of the wall lead up from there.

The wall-head defenses have now gone but were on two levels, as at Saône. The donjon was closely bounded by an almost square wall and square angle-towers (three being crusader work); on the north side, one angle-tower and a rebuilt square Fatimid tower acted as gate defenses from the town, liberally pierced with arrow loops.

Much of the stone used in Gibelet castle came from ancient Byblos, including temple columns, which were laid horizontally to strengthen the walls and inhibit mining. The large blocks of stone are *en bosse*, rather like at Saône, typical of crusader masonry, as are the drafted margins. In 1188 Saladin captured Gibelet and tried but failed to pull the great tower down.

Chastel Rouge

At Qal'at Yahmour, half a mile south of Beit Challouf in Syria, is Chastel Rouge (Red Castle). It was built by the Montolieu family in about 1112 as one of the donjons in the settlement of the County of Tripoli. The low, almost square ashlar tower ($52\frac{1}{2}$ x 46 feet) is set within a small square enclosure with a single curtain wall, inside which stone domestic buildings fill three sides. An outside stair leads to the first-floor entrance. The vaulted two-story interior was further divided on the upper story by a wooden floor. Straight internal and external stairs gave access.

Red Castle is similar to those built in the Kingdom of Jerusalem around Caesarea during the first part of crusader settlement. In 1177–8 it was given to the Knights Hospitaller by Raymond III. It fell to the Mamluks in 1289.

Safita

Safita (also known as Chastel Blanc—White Castle) is on a hill 12 miles south of Tartus in Syria. The early castle was sacked and then destroyed by earthquake.

The impressive donjon was built by the Knights Templars in the 1170s or after 1202 and at 60 feet is the tallest of the crusader donjons. A chapel occupies the ground floor and a hall above is reached by straight steps and divided by a row of pillars. This may have been the monks' dormitory. The donjon is surrounded by the remains of two *enceintes*, a (probably) rectangular inner one and oval outer one defended by at least two oblong Templar towers.

In 1188 Saladin refrained from attacking Safita. However, Baybars brought his Mamluks to Safita on their way to besiege Krak des Chevaliers in 1271, and this time the Master of the Order in Tortosa sent word that they should surrender.

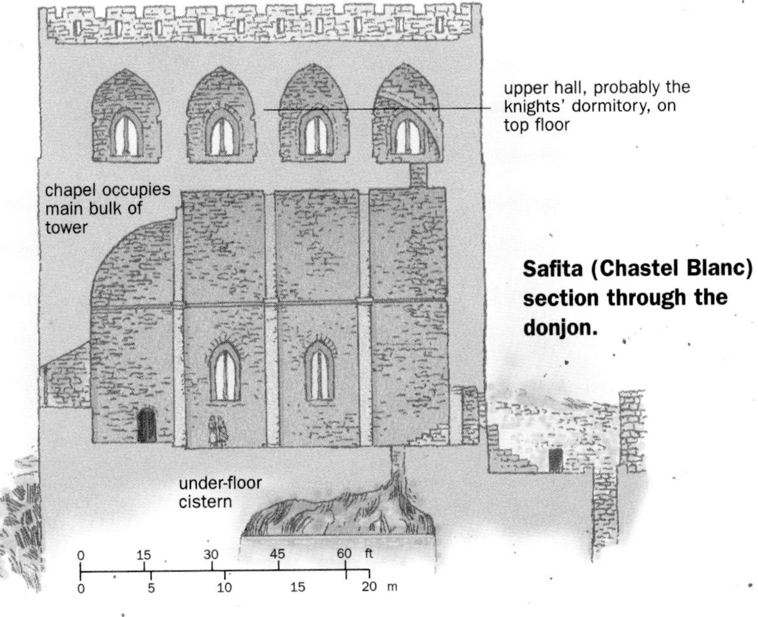

Safita (Chastel Blanc) section through the donjon.

Natural Sites

deep trench
donjon
crusader towers
cistern
chapel
Plan of Saône
lower enclosure gate-tower
N
0 200 400 600 ft
0 50 100 150 200 m

Where possible, the crusaders built their castles on naturally defensive sites. This was especially true in Syria. Neither isolated donjons nor enclosure castles were common in the northern states, except around the County of Tripoli, where the land was flat enough. Instead, advantage was taken of high ground, ideally if it was protected on three sides, such as at the confluence of two rivers, or on a coastal promontory. Then only the vulnerable fourth side needed extra attention.

Saône

Saône is one such naturally defended castle. Situated at Qal'at Salah al-Din, Syria, 18½ miles from Latakia, it stands on a long triangular site between two gorges. It began in the tenth century as a Byzantine fortress, complete with a large citadel. When crusaders obtained the site in the 1100s, they decided to strengthen it further.

The spur connected with the mountain at the east end; here they cut a huge ditch across the point of access, 90 feet deep through the rock. A pillar of rock was left standing in the ditch like a giant needle, to provide support for the bridge spanning the gap.

On the edge of the ditch they constructed a large square keep, its outer wall seeming to blend with the sheer side of the hewn rock. Internally the donjon was vaulted on two floors, which were supported by a central pillar. Round towers were also built above the ditch.

The crusaders extended the walls along the edges of the spur, building large square towers on the south side, but the north side was steep and required less fortification. On the west the lower enclosure of the Byzantines was fortified with square towers and a second ditch, but this was smaller than that on the east and was never completed. Two cisterns were included, one being of enormous capacity.

Despite its great strength, Saône fell to Saladin in 1188. He set up siege engines opposite the east end, while his son moved to the valley opposite the north side. Some of the stone catapult balls, weighing 100–650 lbs, can still be seen on the site. Following a daylong bombardment, Saladin's men stormed Saône and forced the castle's inhabitants to flee. The under-strength garrison took refuge in the keep but surrendered the next day.

The donjon (left) and a wall-tower at Saône, seen from the southwest, with smaller Byzantine masonry visible in the center curtain wall fragments.

left: Kerak seen from the south, with the great Muslim donjon that may have replaced an earlier crusader tower.

Kerak

Kerak, built in 1142 in "Oultre-Jourdain," is situated at El Kerak, 77 miles south of Amman in Jordan. The castle is set on a triangular plateau that extends northward from the mountain, separated from the town beyond by a rock-cut ditch. On all three sides the slopes drop into ravines.

Another rock-cut ditch, complete with reservoir, protects the mountain approach on the south—at approximately 65 feet it was wide enough to keep siege engines at a safe distance. Much fabric here has been destroyed, however. A long lower bailey runs along the west side.

The castle was well placed against caravans and pilgrims, which resulted in two unsuccessful sieges by Saladin. During the first siege of 1183 he ordered his men not to bombard one tower, since a wedding party was being held there. The garrison was finally starved out in a third siege in 1188.

Plan of Kerak

N
ditch separating castle from town
vaulted halls
original entrance
chapel
Muslim palace
glacis
Muslim donjon
0 100 200 300 ft
0 25 50 75 100 m

Castel Pèlerin

By contrast, Chastel Pèlerin (Pilgrim Castle) relied on the sea for defense—it stands on the coast at Atlit, 15½ miles south of Haifa in Israel. It was built in 1218 by the Knights Templar, assisted by a band of pilgrims, on a small promontory surrounded on three sides by the sea. The landward side was cut off by a rock-cut ditch, an outer wall crowned with a wall-walk and three towers (rectangular, unlike Hospitaller ones), and an inner wall with two very tall towers, all spaced alternately; one tall tower still stands. Behind were extensive crypts, halls, and an impressive chapel.

Chastel Pèlerin was besieged but never taken by the Muslims, and was held until the crusaders lost the Holy Land in 1291.

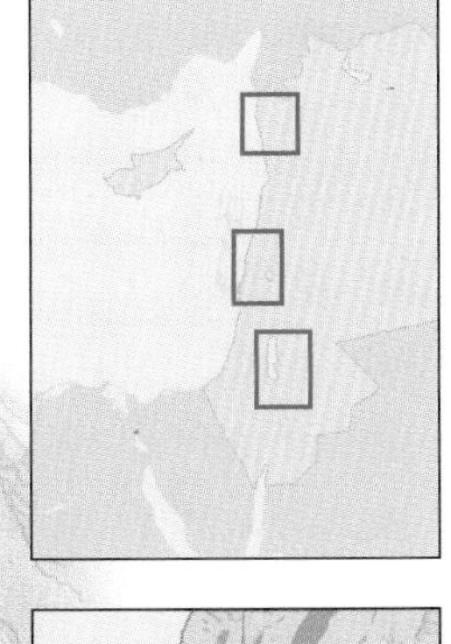

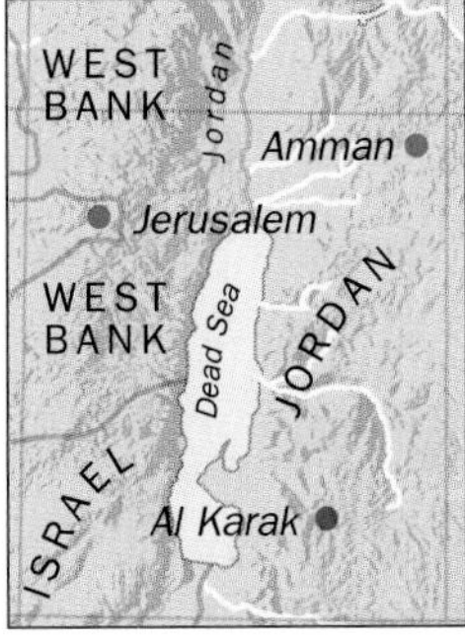

Castles of the Knights Hospitallers

facing: Margat, from the southeast, with the great round donjon. The tower below and left of the donjon is that undermined by the Muslims in 1285 and rebuilt.

The Hospitallers built some of the most impressive castles in the Middle East, before their expulsion in 1291 after the fall of the crusader kingdom. Being a religious order, their domestic arrangements also included the means of their devotion.

Belvoir

Belvoir castle is in Galilee, near Tiberius, on a hill overlooking the Jordan Valley. Shortly after 1168 the Knights Hospitallers began constructing the first datable concentric castle. The surviving structure has a roughly square plan and is one of the largest enclosure castles, being 427 feet by 328 feet.

The inner walls surround a courtyard with vaulted domestic ranges along the walls, and have square corner towers and a middle tower on the eastern side. The massive outer walls are lower and have an impressive talus and corner and middle towers, all designed to take the force of an enemy attack, further assisted by a deep dry moat. More vaulted ranges run along the inner side of these walls.

Perhaps 500 men lived here; there is an Arab-style bath in the outer court, while the inner court was the monastic cloister. Water was held in two rain-fed cisterns.

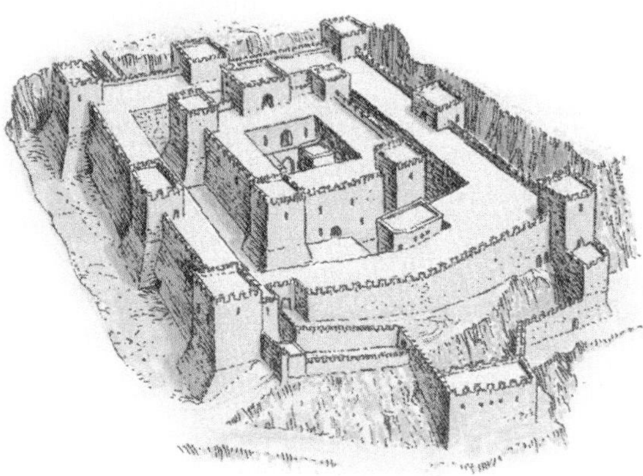

below: The concentric plan of Belvoir may owe more to symbolism than defense, the inner area forming the knights' private quarters.

right: Reconstruction of Belvoir.

After the destruction of the crusader army at Hattin in 1187, Saladin tried to starve Belvoir into surrender, but failed. The castle was too well provisioned, and the besieging force was surprised by a night attack. Saladin himself returned in March 1188, only to face torrential rain and resultant mud, the penalty of winter warfare. In the end, however, the walls were undermined and the garrison surrendered. Belvoir castle was destroyed but substantial ruins remain.

right: Krak des Chevaliers from the southwest, the side attacked by Baybars in 1271. The large corner tower and square tower on the outer walls were rebuilt afterwards by the Muslims.

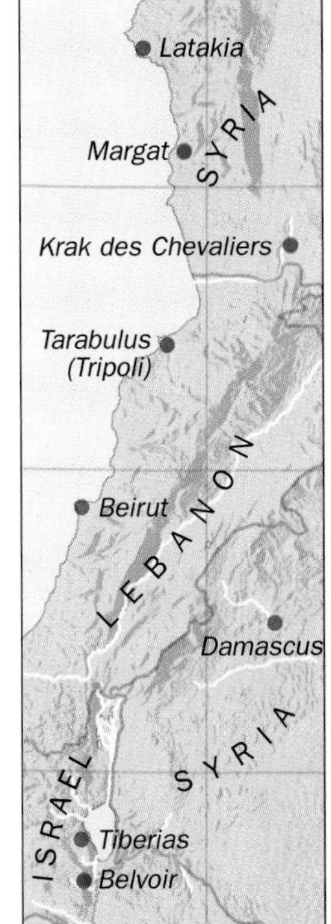

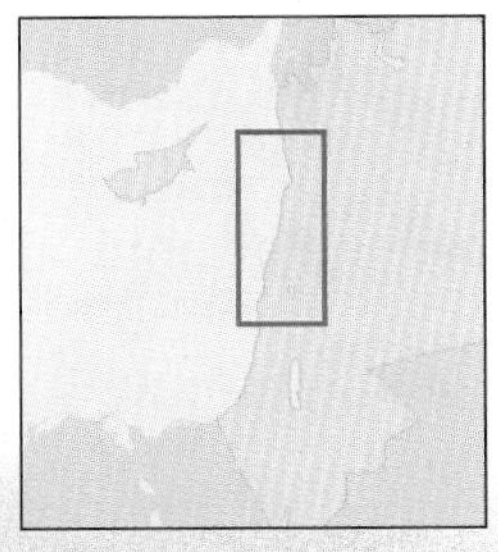

Krak des Chevaliers

Krak stands at Qal'at al-Hosn, near Haret Toukman in Syria. It is rightly regarded as one of the finest crusader castles. The first fortress on the site was a small rectangular 11th-century Arab structure called "The Castle of the Kurds," the wall set with square towers and built of masonry blocks *en bosse*. The Hospitallers acquired the fortress in 1142 and substantially altered it.

An enclosure castle and square flanking towers were built, repaired after the earthquake of 1170 and supplemented by a new chapel. Krak was further modified after another earthquake in 1202. New, larger inner walls were built in front of the old ones, creating a narrow passage, used as a shooting gallery. An outer *enceinte* had evenly spaced round towers and rare box machicolation. An elaborate covered way constructed with defended hairpin bends led to the inner halls and the chapel, decorated with rich carvings.

The Muslims referred to Krak des Chevaliers as a "bone in the throat of the Muslims." Saladin decided it was too tough to besiege, and the "principality" of Krak was the only significant inland area of the crusader states to remain in their hands continuously in the first half of the 13th century. Krak finally fell in 1271, when there was no chance of a relief force to save it.

Margat

Margat is at Qal'at Marghab, 2½ miles south of Baniyas on the Syrian coast. It began life as an Arab fortress in the 11th century but was acquired by the Franks in 1118. Severe earthquakes left the lord with serious problems, so he sold the castle to the Hospitallers in 1186 and the fortress was gradually rebuilt.

The outer walls follow the contours of the summit of the ridge, while the fortified triangular area was given an inner bailey behind a wide ditch. This irregular use of double walls does not constitute a true concentric castle. In this bailey were vaulted halls, a chapel, and a two-story cylindrical donjon 100 feet in diameter. The Mamluks besieged the place in 1285 and undermined the Tour de l'Eperon (Tower of the Spur); on learning of another mine under the donjon itself, the Hospitallers surrendered.

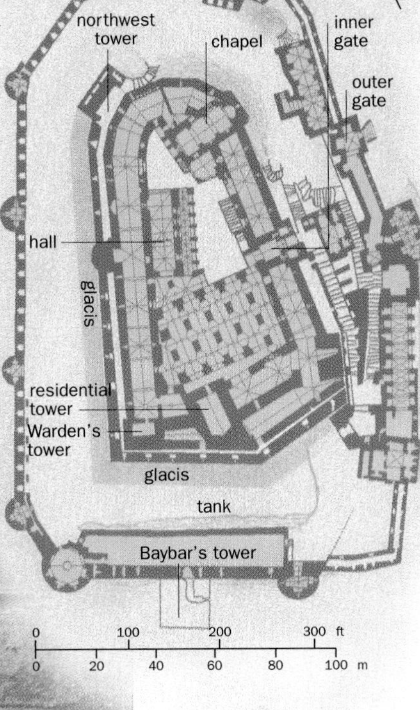

Krak des Chevaliers, plan of the castle.

13th-Century Castles of the Military Orders

The Templars, Teutonic Knights, and lesser military orders controlled castles, often in frontier areas, although even the Templars could not rival the wealth of the Hospitallers. Many of these castles are now in ruins. Saphet in northern Israel is a case in point; one of the most impressive castles held by the Templars, a good deal is known from written records but the site is very poor.

below: The sea castle at Sidon, seen from the southeast.

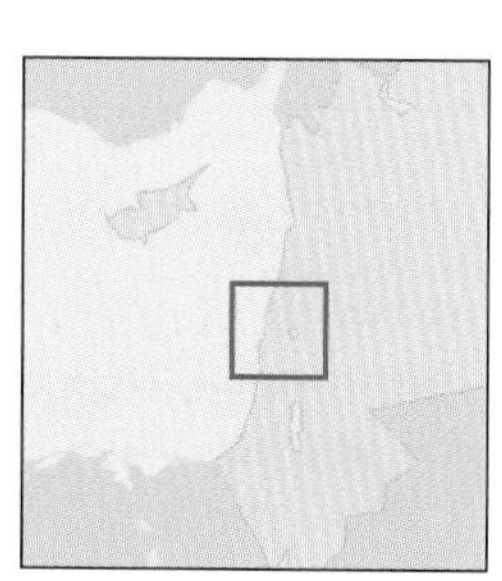

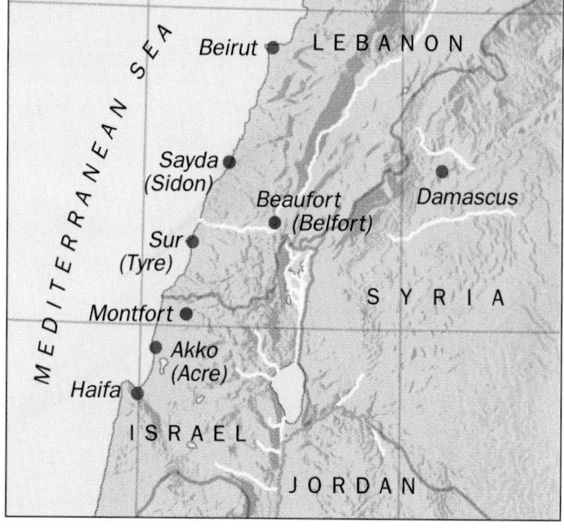

Sidon

Sidon, at Saida on the coast of Lebanon, was one of the most important lordships in the Kingdom of Jerusalem. It now consists of a ruined land castle and a somewhat smaller castle on the sea.

The landward castle was built at the apex of Sidon, an ancient acropolis. It was held by the Franks from 1110 but town and citadel were lost to Saladin's men in 1187, when the fortifications were dismantled. The populace seems to have disappeared but gradually built up again, only to be massacred in a surprise attack in 1253. St. Louis rebuilt the fortifications, now almost obliterated by the rebuilding work of Amir Fakhr al-Din in the 17th century.

In 1227–8, however, French, English, and Spanish pilgrims awaiting Emperor Frederick II's arrival during the Fifth Crusade began constructing a sea castle on a reef approximately 325 feet from the shore. The strongest side faces the shore, but the phases of building are not conclusive. Three square towers probably constitute the first phase, later strengthened by Simon de Montceliart, chief of St Louis' crossbowmen, who took refuge here in 1253.

Seven years later the garrison again sheltered here, when the Mongols attacked the town after an assault on their camp by Julien of Sidon. The Templars took control of the castle that year and it was probably they who enclosed the towers with vaulted shooting galleries and constructed the vaulted hall on the seaward side. Sidon was abandoned in 1291 when the Holy Land was lost.

Beaufort

High above the River Litani in southern Lebanon stands Beaufort castle (also known as Belfort). King Fulk captured the original stronghold in 1139 and constructed a castle here. The east side is guarded by a sheer drop to the river, while a rock-cut basin protects the north. A two-story 12th-century donjon in the middle of the vulnerable west wall protects that side of the inner bailey. There is a lower bailey to the south and a lower level court to the east.

The lords of Sidon held Beaufort until lost to the Muslims in 1190, but not before Reynald of Sidon fooled Saladin by promising to yield the castle, while Reynald secretly made repairs. It was recovered in 1240 and came to the Templars in 1260, who built a vaulted hall and a protective outwork on a plateau to the south. However, when Baybars and his Mamluks attacked Beaufort in 1268, he used the platform as a base for his own catapults.

Montfort

The ruins of Montfort, one of the last castles erected in the Holy Land, are on the crest of a ridge $2\frac{1}{2}$ miles northwest of Mi'ilya in Israel. The fortress was acquired from its owner by the Teutonic Knights in about 1229, who moved to this rocky site from the 12th-century castle of Chastiau dou Rei in its fertile valley. Montfort was reconstructed as their headquarters, suggesting defense was paramount at this time.

Where the ridge joins the hills Montfort is defended by a rock-cut ditch and a D-shaped donjon, resembling a German *bergfried*, on top of a cistern. To the west, a long undercroft probably supported a hall and chapel. Beyond this was another undercroft, probably with a chamber on top, and a wall curving around this end of the ridge 98 feet down the slope. A river ran along the northern edge of the ridge, and its mill was turned into a guest house in the 13th century.

Montfort was strong enough to withstand an assault by Baybars in 1266 but the lands around were severely ravaged and the Hospitallers lent the Knights some estates to cultivate. In 1271 Baybars led an attack that breached the outer walls and forced the Knights into the donjon, where they surrendered.

above: The hilltop stronghold of Montfort.

Beaufort, plan of the castle

below: The ruins of Beaufort.

Later Middle Eastern Defenses

facing top: The Tower of France and the Tower of Italy at Bodrum stand out above the castle.

facing center: The artillery outwork at Bodrum in front of the main castle

facing bottom: The massive round bastions at Kyrenia were added by the Venetians in 1544.

below: The land castle at Korykos.

The later crusader fortifications in the Holy Land were situated beyond the crusader states, lost in 1291. A number of these were the work of the Hospitallers, who moved their headquarters several times, to Cyprus, then Rhodes, and finally to Malta, where the Order survived until the 19th century. By contrast the Templars were suppressed in 1312 amid accusations of witchcraft and heresy, largely by Philip IV of France who coveted their wealth. The Teutonic Knights moved their headquarters to East Europe.

Korykos

At the western end of the Cilician plain, 16 miles east of Silifke on the coast of Turkey, stands Korykos castle. First fortified in 1111 by the Byzantine Admiral Eustathios, as a border castle against the territories held by the Franks and Armenians, it is an important example of Byzantine military architecture at the time of the Crusades.

It has a typical regular plan: two sets of concentric walls, the inner dominating the outer; many towers flank the inner walls, those on the eastern side set close together for extra defense. Korykos later fell to the Armenians.

In about 1216 King Leon II of Armenia built the fortified island castle several hundred yards offshore to guard the port. The land castle stands on a fairly level site, protected by the sea to the south and west and by a marsh to the north; a rock-cut ditch guarded the eastern approach. The inner wall of the land castle was constructed largely in the mid-13th century, while c.1360 King Peter I of Cyprus made further improvements. The builders utilized large blocks of antique stone, including a complete Roman gateway.

Bodrum

Bodrum is opposite the island of Kos on the west coast of Turkey. The castle of St. Peter's was begun in 1415 by the Hospitallers, on a peninsula they acquired in return for Smyrna (modern Izmir). Since they already held Kos, they then controlled one of the main channels used by coasting vessels.

Completed in about 1450, Bodrum has a single curtain wall and two large towers, called the Tower of France and the Tower of Italy, decorated with a number of carved escutcheon panels. Between 1501 and 1522 an impressive artillery outwork was built. Unfortunately for posterity, the Hospitallers used stone from the ruined Mausoleum of Halicarnassus, one of the Seven Wonders of the World. On finding the tomb and its decorated columns, they considered its superior quality before destroying it!

Kyrenia

Kyrenia, located on a promontory at Girne on the north coast of Turkish Cyprus, began as a Byzantine stronghold. On arriving in Cyprus on his way to the Holy Land in 1191, Richard the Lionheart soon captured the town. The Lusignan dynasty rebuilt the fortress.

In 1369 King Peter was murdered and Queen Eleanor of Aragon appealed to Genoa, whose army used the pretext to overrun Cyprus in 1373. Eleanor fled to Kyrenia, where the constable was holding out. The Genoese failed to capture it, despite pressing a siege by land and sea for some months in 1374, although the defenders had to come to terms eventually.

Another lengthy siege occurred in the 15th century, when the illegitimate James disputed succession to the Lusignan crown in Cyprus with his half-sister, Carlotta, who held Kyrenia. Venice

took control of Cyprus in 1473; the three huge round bastions and massively thick walls on the west and south side are Venetian work of 1544. The Turks found such defenses too difficult to capture when they attacked in 1570, and only achieved success through treachery.

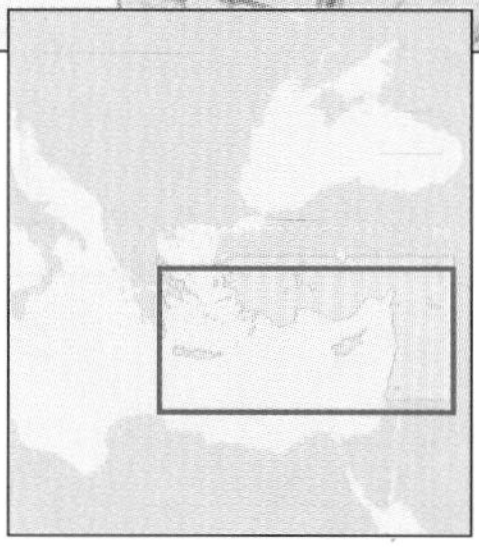

Chapter Sixteen:

Other Fortifications

Fortifications of the Muslims

Islamic fortifications have been documented in the Middle East and Spain sections of this book, but pre-Islamic peoples also used walled cities and towers. The Turks built fortifications, often concentric, with mural towers, and western Turks built isolated fortified towers in the mountains, similar to Chinese frontier defenses. Small fortified towns (*baliqs*) also used Chinese ideas, and by the 11th century were quite sophisticated, such as the Semiran capital of the Tarim Basin, with three sets of walls. The Volga Bulgars erected probably the largest earth and timber fortifications in the north of Turkish Central Asia. Wasit in Iraq had a double wall and moat and a low third wall some distance away.

below: The late 12th-century citadel at Cairo.

Much of the Muslim world had little in the way of rural fortification apart from frontiers, where *ribat*s probably served as watch-towers, and in poorly governed areas such as the Arabian peninsula. Even here sophisticated ideas could be incorporated, such as a double gate with portcullis. Byzantine strongholds were sometimes reused for larger frontier defenses, as in Cilicia. In Palestine the ribats tended to be fortified coastal towns, to guard against Byzantine naval attack.

After the Abbassid dynasty, more advanced fortifications were conceived. Aleppo had been too weak to withstand a Byzantine attack, but in the 11th century it was given a wall almost 50 feet high.

The Fatimids in Egypt and Syria built impressive works. In Cairo a fortified palace enclosure was similar to Baghdad, though smaller. The rectangular plan of the city had brick walls set with eight gates, either Armenian or Syrian in design.

In North Africa a large number of towns were fortified, especially on the coasts, as were those of Sicily and Moorish Spain. In Morocco and Andalusia a new form of architecture developed, broader structures capable of housing catapults. Andalusian town defenses often followed Roman work at first, but expanding cities in the plains adopted a regular plan, while those to the north were set around hills.

In the tenth century a series of huge fortresses was constructed in the mountainous border provinces, against Christian pressure, as well as small, isolated strongholds and round towers (probably used as beacons). Tabby cement, a mixture of gravel, earth, lime, straw, and bones, appeared at this time. The bent entrance, which requires the entrant to turn sharply after passing the gate, appeared in al-Andalus in the 12th century.

Consolidation in Islamic areas occurred in the 12th–14th centuries. Under the Ayyubids of the late 12th century, Cairo received a powerful citadel and the suburbs were drawn together. Larger walls and closer towers for trebuchets were the main feature of this period; the best example is at Damascus.

In the 13th century small castles and watch towers were built in southern Syria and Jordan as warning of crusader advances. In al-Andalus the external *albarrana* appeared, linked by a bridge to a curtain wall. Frontier hills had *atalaya* or watch towers.

The Mamluks built a series of fortified *caravanserais* along the main trade roads in the 15th century, consisting of walled enclosures with corner towers. Sultan Qait-bay's castle at Alexandria, built in 1479, is very impressive: a large central square tower with round corner turrets within a low walled *enceinte*, set with box machicolations and gun-loops.

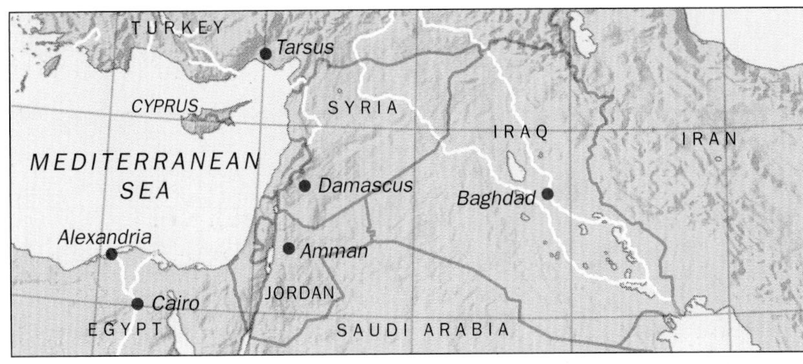

The Round City of Baghdad was built between AD 762 and 765 by the early Abbasid Caliphate. It drew on earlier work in Khurasan and Transoxania and was larger than anything seen before. The palace, surrounded by gardens, barracks, and administrative buildings, showed influence from Iran, with the ruler set apart, rather than of Islam. So the Caliph soon built a new residence outside, near the main parade ground. The outer and inner walls of the city served to produce an area for the senior men to live and work. The bent-gates of Baghdad (*bashura*) were also new in the Middle East, as a defense against horsemen.

Tarsus received a moat, 87 towers, six gates, and two walls in the late eighth century. By the tenth century the city only five gates, those in the outer wall being protected by iron—perhaps a portcullis. On the inner wall were 18,000 crenellations and a hundred towers, three provided with beam-sling mangonels on top and 20 others with smaller stone-throwers.

top: Sultan Quait-Bay's fortress, Alexandria, showing the box machicolations.

below: The fortified "desert palace" at Qasr al-Kharanah, Jordan, built in about 700, is one of the earliest Islamic buildings, probably a post for Umayyad armies.

Fortifications in India

above: The walls of Golconda.

Fortifications were well established in pre-Islamic India. The common form of defense was a wall set with towers that projected only a little way forward, both with a batter at the base, while the main walls had long galleries. In AD 630–45, Hiuen Tsang recalled that most towns and villages had inner gates, wide walls probably of bricks, fired or unfired, and towers or ramparts of wood or bamboo. Those with the means used dressed stone with a rubble core, while in Kashmir defenses were built in timber.

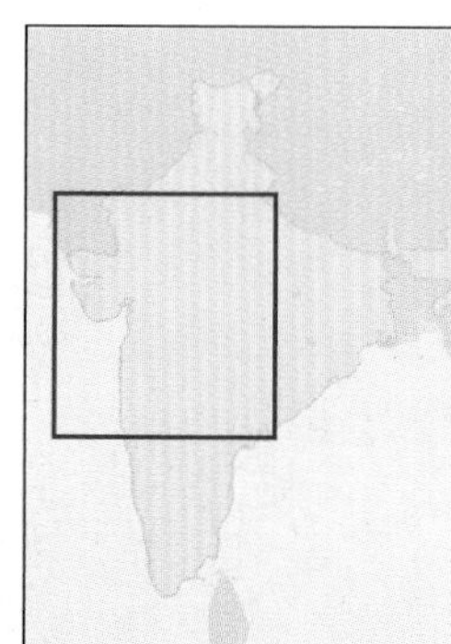

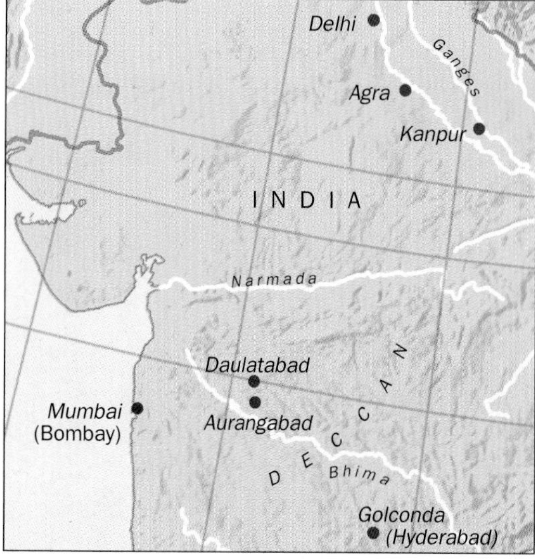

In the 11th century differences between Islamic and Hindu India fortresses materialized, but by the late 14th century both cultures used the ceremonial *chatris* or kiosk over the main gate, from which a ruler could observe those outside.

Under the Moguls in the 16th century, a large number of fortresses were erected. They were symbols of authority, many sited on hilltops to accentuate their power, but often more lavishly decorated than European examples.

Battlements tended to curve up to a central point, sometimes pierced by a loophole. The entrance doors might be fitted with rows of iron spikes, to stop an elephant battering them down. Fire or smoke were used to effect, including heated iron grilles to prevent them being opened, and spiked objects were rolled down onto attackers.

Delhi

Delhi has been rebuilt several times. Tughlakabad, the third city, was built between 1321 and 1323. The walls are made from a rubble core faced with rough-cut masonry, the whole strengthened by projecting bastions; both are provided with internal and external galleries.

The fortified tomb of Ghiyath al-Din Tughluq,

Sultan of Delhi, was built in 1325. Sitting in an artificial lake, it was part of the outworks of the city fortifications. The work is a mixture of Islamic and Hindu influence that would become typical of Islamic military work in India. Lal Qilah (Red Fort), one of the most important buildings in the city, was built in red sandstone by the Mughal Shah Jahan in the mid-17th century. The walls are some 75 feet high. Within is a complex of palaces, gardens, and barracks, including the Halls of Public and Private Audience.

above: Gateway to the Red Fort, Delhi.

Daulatabad

The ancient city of Daulatabad in the Deccan, central India, received a major castle founded in the late 12th century by King Bhillam of the Hindu Yadava dynasty. The present castle dates to the 14th century, when it came under the Mughal Sultans of Delhi. Built around a rocky outcrop, the walls have round towers with deep batters, supporting box machicolation typical of Indian military architecture. The main gate is decorated on either side with a carved elephant. Daulatabad castle was never taken by force, only by intrigue.

Golconda

The fortress and ruined city of Golconda lies 5 miles west of Hyderabad in Andhra Pradesh. In the Middle Ages the city was known for the nearby diamond mines, so its rulers could afford to lavish wealth on the fortress, one of the best in India. From 1512 it was the capital of the Qutb Shahi kingdom.

Constructed in stone, it consists of three walls. The outer wall protected the city, and has a ditch and bastions. There are eight gateways, tall enough to admit an elephant and defended by barbicans and box machicolations. The approaches were deliberately twisting and flanked by walls. Further up the hill, the fortress was protected by a double wall, 3 miles in circumference. Inside, a final set of walls were bonded with the rock to form an obstacle up to 33 feet thick. Palaces, mosques, and the royal tombs survive.

In 1687 Golconda was attacked by Mogul Emperor Aurangzeb, whose power base was in Delhi. After a four-month siege, soldiers scaled the walls during the night, but a dog began barking and roused the garrison, who pushed down the scaling ladders and threw hand grenades after them. The sultan presented the dog with a gold collar.

below: The Red Fort at Agra.

Fortifications in China

The most famous piece of architecture in China is the Great Wall, built during the Han and Chin periods. It was begun in 214 BC under the first emperor, Shih Huang-di, to prevent the nomads of the steppes from entering Chinese territory. Millions of slave-laborers were employed to build the longest wall on Earth—3,915 miles long, including its branches.

Parts of the Great Wall were older work joined on, and some was an earth and turf bank. However, long sections were of stone, an outer skin infilled with rubble, 29½ feet high and set with watchtowers every 200 feet, the paved wall-walk so wide horses could run along it six abreast. In desert regions an outer wall was built to restrain shifting sand.

Its sheer length made the wall difficult to guard and by the Middle Ages parts were in disrepair, while the border was mostly further north. In the 13th century Genghis Khan led his horsemen through an open gate. Much of the Great Wall was rebuilt in the 15th century.

In the north and west of China, a chain of large fortresses connected by watchtowers were built to guard the frontiers, the most remote built from layers of earth and brushwood, or reeds and clay. Fortified towns of regular layout were the main defenses and changed little until the introduction of guns in the late 14th century.

T'ang fortresses usually consisted of an outer earthwork 6½ feet high, within which soldiers could assemble for sorties. The inner citadel could also be used if the enclosure fell. In the Sung period animals were herded within the walls for pro-

below: The Great Wall of China is so long that it can be seen from the moon.

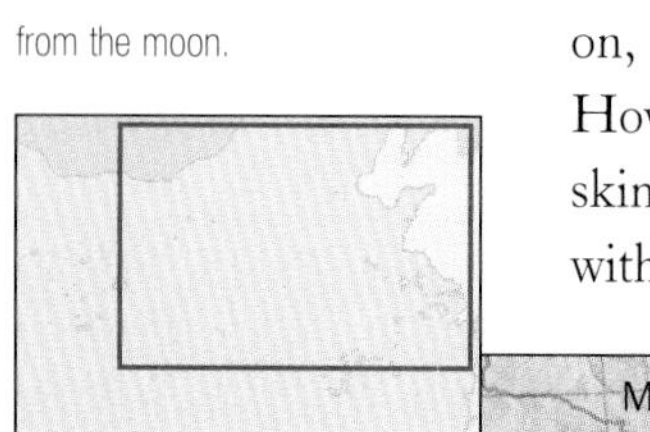

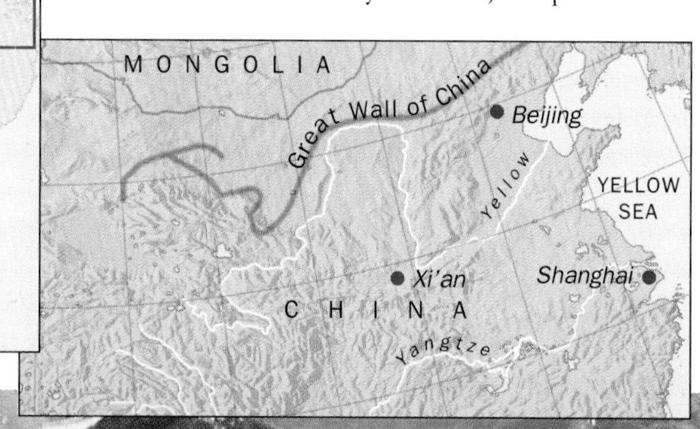

tection. The walls doubled in height during the 12th century, perhaps because of the improved performance of counterweight trebuchets. Korea tried to defend its northern frontier with Cholli castle, a wall stretching from the River Yalu to the east coast.

Chinese Sieges

Defenders expected to fight outside the walls, and so defenses were never developed to the extent they were elsewhere; there are no concentric defenses. In the T'ang and Sung periods counter-siege methods developed, which were later adopted in India and by the Muslims. Bowmen on the walls shot as the enemy approached, and then changed to pots of quicklime at the wall face, or even urine and feces. Only the men in towers were allowed to use bows and crossbows at this stage of the siege, and officers were a special target.

In the T'ang period torches were hung halfway down the wall to thwart night attacks, but burning bundles were used if an attack was begun. Mangonels were positioned inside the walls rather than on top. Smaller ones were used to strike people, including coolies bringing water; the larger catapults were aimed at their opposite numbers outside the walls, as might happen in Europe.

By the 12th century sandbags were used to protect mangonels, while water buckets were on hand to douse fire arrows landing on them. The larger, counterweight machines had a far greater range, while the Muslim mangonel (trebuchet) had an adjustable counterweight. Netting made from rice-stalks might be hung a little way in front of the walls to help protect them from catapult shot; they were raised or lowered by beam-slings that could also drop missiles on an enemy.

In the T'ang period the "Thunderstick"—a log covered in spikes—was rolled down walls toward assailants. By the Sung period they were made from clay and re-usable versions were roped to a windlass for retrieval. Chinese armies often used wooden palisades, bamboo, and thorns to defend their positions. As well as mangonels, extendible ladders, wheeled siege towers (some with extending platforms), vertically moving platforms, and multi-decked boats for sharpshooters were employed against Chinese fortifications.

above: Changan town walls (now Xi'An) in Shaanxi Province.

below: Quian Men, the Front Gate, once the main south gate in Beijing's city walls, it is now on the southern edge of Tianamen Square.

Fortifications in Japan

Fortresses were built in Japan from the Yamoto period (300–710), sometimes as temporary defenses. Samurai might live within a ringwork with ditch and palisade. By the early 14th century, wooden towers and strongholds started to appear in great numbers.

In 1500 Japanese society was still feudal. When Portuguese merchants brought gunpowder in 1543, there was a great impetus in castle building. In 1576 the warlord Oda Nobunaga erected a new castle at Azuchi, which also served as a palace, its crowning glory a seven-story tower called a *tenshu*, equivalent to a European donjon. Other rulers soon followed, such as Tokugawa Ieyasu at Edo. Cannons had not developed in Japan to any extent and castles provided a useful refuge against muskets and cavalry charges; the 16th and 17th centuries were thus the great period in castle building.

Castles were sited on hills, or set on platforms or rammed earth faced with large dressed stone blocks. Above this, the walls of the *tenshu* were built from a framework of wood filled with bamboo and clay, which was then plastered over, which also reduced the risk of fire. Windows were fitted with shutters, serving also as loopholes. Corridors connected the tenshu to smaller flanking towers, and other wooden buildings stood in the courtyards. These huge and numerous baileys, together

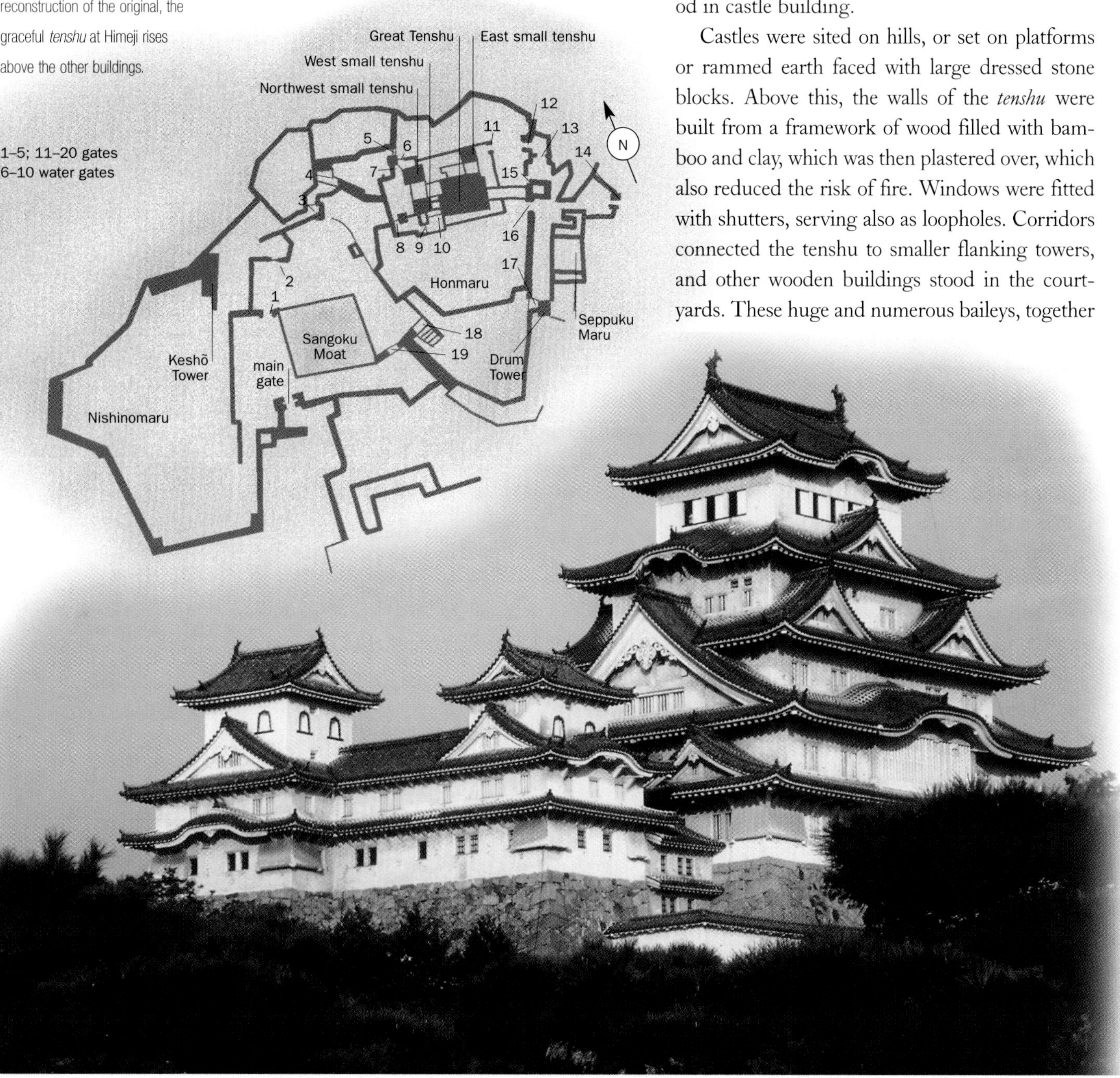

below: A recent concrete reconstruction of the original, the graceful *tenshu* at Himeji rises above the other buildings.

with gates and corridors, served to confuse and divide enemies, but especially kept them from firing at the *tenshu*. Gates, often iron-plated to lessen the fire risk, sometimes had a single-story tower.

The sea, rivers, and lakes were utilized as natural moats against mining, the latter technique established in Japan after Hideyoshi used it to take Kameyama in 1583. The main form of attack was an assault against the walls or a gate.

Himeji

The White Heron castle, on the Harima plain 62 miles west of Kobe, was fortified in 1346 by Akamatsu Sadanori. In 1577 Toyotomi Hideyoshi made it his headquarters and greatly enlarged it, including the addition of a three-story *tenshu*. Himeji passed to Ikeda Terumasa, who rebuilt and enlarged it from about 1600 until his death in 1614.

Set on two low hills and covering some 2,152,000 square feet, Himeji has 11 gates and seven connecting towers, with small *tenshus* to the east, northwest, and west of the *tenshu* complex. Nearby, the Great Tenshu sits on a thick granite stone base. It has seven floors (six internal plus the *ishigaki*), the upper ones resting on the stonework so they can move with any earth tremor, common in Japan. Above the stone base run rows of square gun-loops. The overhanging tiled roofs has eaves decorated with carved animals, while the overhang itself rests on beams to provide gaps between the roof and wall for dropping missiles.

Inside were comfortable quarters for the lord on the upper floors, with soldiers' sleeping quarters, kitchens, and corridors lower down. There were even beaters in case of fires.

Osaka

Built on raised ground running down the eastern side of the city, Osaka castle is guarded on the northern approaches by the River Hirano and on the west by the confluence of the Yodo and Tojima, though probably fortified in the 16th century by Oda Nobunaga, main building work began under Hideyoshi in 1583 and it was said 60,000 men almost completed it the following year.

The outer moat was 7½ miles long and gold leaf adorned the *tenshu* roof tiles. A castle town was built around the fortress. However, the stronghold fell to Ieyasu after sieges in 1614 and 1615, and was burned down.

The Tokugawa rebuilt on a massive scale, making Osaka, with Edo, the largest castle in Japan. The middle walls are 82 feet high and run for 1½ miles; the ditch in front is over 230 feet wide. Enormous stones of over one hundred tons were used at important areas such as gatehouse complexes. The five-story *tenshu* was destroyed by lightning in 1665, and most of the wooden buildings burned during the Toba-Fushimi Battle between imperial and Tokugawa troops in 1868. A slightly inaccurate concrete *tenshu* was erected in 1931.

above: The concrete reconstruction of the destroyed *tenshu* at Osaka.

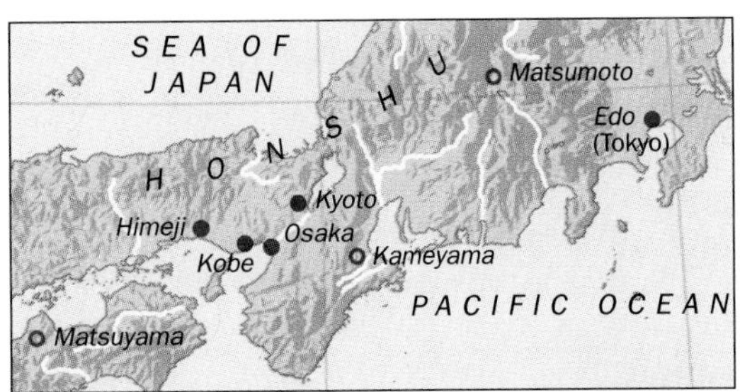

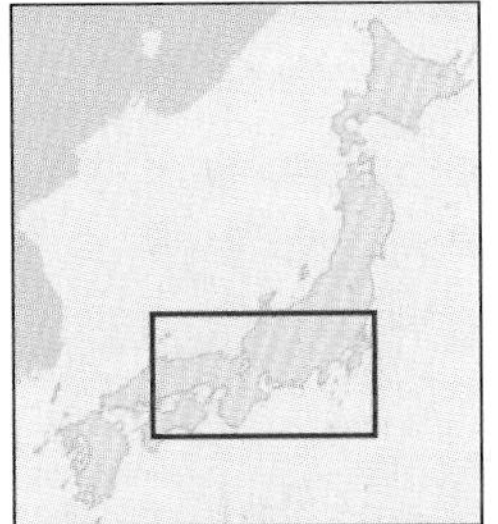

above: The tenshu at Matsumoto, in the central Japan Alps, a typical flatland castle begun in 1593.

left: Matsuyama, on the northwest coast of Shikoku, is a flatland-hill castle begun in 1602. The present Great Tenshu was rebuilt in 1854 and the smaller towers in 1969.

Fortifications in Central and South America

The Zapotec and Mixtec of Central America set up a number of states during the Classic Period (AD 200–1000), producing powerful cities such as Teotihuacán near Mexico City and Monte Alban in Oaxaca. From their eventual demise rose the Toltec, who fought against the incoming Aztec. Their city streets were arranged almost like a maze, deliberately designed to trap invading forces within them, as the 16th-century Spanish invaders later discovered.

above: Remains of palaces line the Avenue of the Dead at Teotihuacán, with behind it the Pyramid of the Sun.

The capital centers had walled precincts around the temples that doubled as firing platforms. Precinct walls might have battlemented tops, the merlons shaped like a trapezoid. Stepped pyramids, some over 100 feet high, could serve as refuges or citadels and were convenient launch points for throwing missiles.

Towns were used as last defenses when a battle was lost, but fortifications were not common, siege warfare techniques were simplistic, and lines of supply were weak. If earthworks and palisades were hurriedly erected, scaling ladders might be used, or pick-axes to undermine walls and battering rams against gates.

In 1458 Montezuma I ordered an invasion of Mixtec territory in the southwest. His huge army was driven back, only to be redirected to the great trading center of Coixtlahuaca. A great palisaded camp was set up but the blockade was broken by approaching relief forces. The Aztec moved on Tlaxiaco, drawing on the relief force and allowing Aztec contingents to scale the walls of Coixtlahuaca and seize it.

The Mixtec sometimes reused mountain ruins from the Classic Period, whose stepped agricultural stone terraces were ideal and could be used as refuges during battles. Otherwise they fortified naturally strong sites as palaces and temples. Tilantongo has three sides with steep drops, terraces, 10-foot high platforms, and residential structures, all obstacles to an attacker.

The Inca of Peru built a series of large stone fortresses outside cities throughout their empire, each with great storehouses and cultivated terraces. Others were built on major roads and along frontiers, these being smaller but with permanent garrisons. When the Inca conquered the Chimu they adapted their superior fortifications, notably the great series blocking the coastal plain from the Cordillera to the Pacific.

Paramonga north of Lima had three terraces, as did Caneta to the south. Paramonga's walls were 10 to 20 feet high with a parapet. Ramps passing through passages linked the terraces. The Inca used blockades or tried to lure enemy garrisons into ambush by pretending to withdraw.

Sacsayhuaman

The ruins of this fortress on its hill overlook the Inca capital of Cuzco. In about 1520 the ruler Pachacuti built Sacsayhuaman, the labor of

right: Monte Alban, Oaxaca, ruins of the Zapotec capital, built about 750.

above: A section of wall at Sacsayhuaman, with its perfectly cut and often massive stones.

20,000 people toiling for 60 years, at his royal city.

The terraced walls run along the hillside in lines, each section offset from its neighbor to form a zigzag effect. The stone blocks used were enormous, some weighing in excess of one hundred tons. They were assembled without mortar but the job was so precisely done that there was little chance of finding a weak spot. There were no battlements, just a smooth wall top. Within the walls were three stone towers, barracks for the garrison, storerooms, and a maze of tunnels connected the towers.

In 1533 Spanish conquistador Francisco Pizarro arrived at Cuzco and attacked it. Incredibly, there were only 130 Spanish soldiers, although they were assisted by native people who decided to turn against the Inca rulers. Their present ruler, Atahualpa, had been captured and killed by the Spanish; dismayed by the invaders' guns and horses—both unknown to this culture—the Inca retreated. Pizarro and his victorious soldiers entered the great fortress without firing a shot.

Three years later the Inca turned on the Spaniards and took back Sacsayhuaman, only to lose it again to the Spanish in Cuzco. Undaunted, the Inca besieged the city and three attempts to relieve the Spaniards were beaten back. Finally, in April 1537, Spain forced the Inca to withdraw. Unfortunately, much of this impressive fortress has been lost because Spanish settlers built houses from the stones.

below: The Inca inherited the strength of Chimu fortresses, such as Paramonga, near Lima.

Chapter Seventeen:

Siege Warfare

The Role of the Castle

The siting, design, construction, and history of many castles have been detailed in this book, but how did they operate in battle? Conflict was avoided where possible, but during the inevitable sieges the invaders had a series of tools and tactics to employ... and defenders had their counter-measures.

To any invader a castle represented an enemy position that, if not captured during the army's progress, could send out troops to harry his flanks or disrupt supply lines. This meant detaching troops to either capture or contain the soldiers within the castle.

right: This illustration from a 15th-century manuscript shows the Duke of Lancaster laying siege to Brest castle in 1373, during the 100 Years War. Cannon, ladders, and archers are deployed.

Equally, a king might find rebellious subjects repairing to their castles to defy his authority, a development that could herald a full-scale revolt. Belligerent neighbors might also besiege one another's strongholds if time and resources allowed.

Medieval warfare consisted far more of sieges than of risky battles. For example, despite Henry V's overwhelming victory at the Battle of Agincourt in 1415, he achieved little until he returned in 1417 and systematically eliminated French-held castles and fortified towns. It was at the siege of Meaux in 1421 that Henry seems to have contracted the dysentery that ultimately killed him.

facing: A castle under attack. The battering ram, slung under a mobile shed, is hitting the wall, where defenders have lowered a pad to muffle the blows. A mobile siege tower has been moved over a specially built causeway of earth and stones across the ditch. Soldiers attack via the lowered drawbridge, and a catapult on the top level shoots into the castle.

Strongholds were not always besieged. Sometimes the use of bribes brought a lord's castles into the hands of another. Conversely, the use of sheer terror, either by reputation or by physical demonstration before the walls of a fortress—with the assistance of captives or the heads of slain opponents—could be enough to persuade defenders to give up.

If surrender was not forthcoming when a besieger formally demanded a castle's submission, he was within his rights to sack the place and slaughter everyone within it. Messages could be sent to an absentee lord for advice, particularly if the opposing commander was of a gracious nature; moreover, many knights and squires knew one another from tournaments and recognized fellow members of the chivalric orders. Sometimes, however, castles were taken by surprise, trickery, or downright treachery.

Assaulting a castle was often costly in men and money. Surrounding it to provoke starvation was easier, and meant that having a well inside the castle walls was essential to its garrison. However, a blockade could lead to problems for the besiegers, who needed to hold together troops whose time of service had expired, pay mercenaries to remain, and evade disease in progressively insanitary siege lines. The latter was a real problem in the heat of the Holy Land.

Relieving Forces—and Boredom

Sometimes a commander could or would not wait; instead, he built a wooden siege castle, sometimes set within earthworks, and left some of his men to watch the enemy stronghold. This was also useful when attacking a town or city with long tracts of walls, especially in the Holy Land, where completely surrounding the target was difficult. Siege castles allowed an army to move on, but it might not prevent a relief force from bringing fresh supplies into the beleaguered garrison.

Even when completely surrounded, people sometimes slipped through enemy lines. This could be made more difficult by digging a trench in front of the lines, erecting palisades, or both. Sometimes they were also erected at the rear, to prevent attack from a relieving army. At the siege of Acre (1189–92) the besieging army led by Richard the Lionheart, among others, was itself "besieged" by Saladin's forces. The arrival of relief forces sometimes provoked a full-scale battle.

Sometimes attackers would burst out of the gates, or from specially built sally ports—small doors sometimes hidden away—to kill enemy troops or burn their siege engines. This is hardly surprising when it is remembered that knights were often among the garrison in a castle, and were happy to emerge and fight. Occasionally, bored knights from either side would formally fight each other. Fearless commanders threw open the gates and defied the enemy to enter.

Surrender was made by handing over the keys to the stronghold, after which the victorious besiegers marched in. The defenders were allowed to emerge with their arms and armor but, especially after a protracted siege, tempers might fray and a slaughter could take place, or formal executions as an example to others.

Taking A Castle

A fortress could be attacked in several ways. One of the most effective was by digging a mine underneath the walls. Occasionally the besiegers came up inside the castle under cover of darkness. Usually, however, the mine was dug under a wall, the foundations removed and wooden props used to shore it up. Smeared with fat and set alight, the wall was brought down as the props collapsed.

Bowls of water were watched for telltale signs of vibration, but mines were extremely difficult to stop. Countermines could be dug to break into the enemy workings, or a makeshift palisade built behind the threatened wall. The best defenses were a wet moat—the weight of water would collapse and flood a mine—or a bedrock site.

Sometimes a trench was dug to the walls, protected with timbers, so men with picks could prize stones from the wall. Battering rams might be used, or sometimes a bore whose pointed head dug into the fabric, but they were not so effective, and sack cloth could be lowered to deaden the blows, or a grapnel could catch the ram's head. Moveable sheds, known as cats, sows, or mice, were needed to protect rams' operators, and had to be covered with raw or wet hides against fire arrows and other combustibles. Ram operators also needed a causeway, constructed by tipping stones and earth into the ditch under cover of friendly fire.

Catapults were also used to breach walls. The mangon or petrary (such names also applied to other engines) used the torsion of a twisted skein of ropes to force the throwing arm upward. It had a flatter trajectory than the trebuchet, which appeared in the 12th century and worked like a seesaw, the shorter end pulled down to release the missile at the other end.

Traction trebuchets utilized teams of men hauling the arm down by ropes; counterweight versions used a box filled with tons of earth and stones for this task. Modern experiments have shown these machines to be highly accurate. They could consistently batter the same area of wall or shatter hoardings, wooden shuttering built out from battlements to command the wall base.

right: The torsion catapult's twisted skein of ropes flung up a throwing arm inserted into it to release a missile.

below: The ballista's bow arm shot a large bolt. The screw was used to wind the slider back when the bowstring was engaged on the trigger.

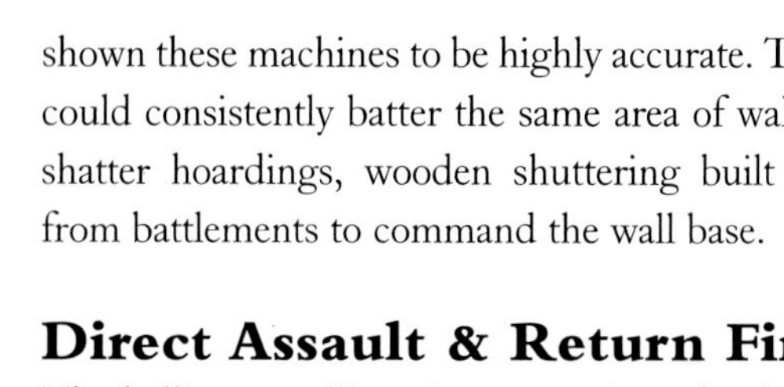

Direct Assault & Return Fire

The ballista was like a large crossbow fixed to a base and was used as an anti-personnel weapon, capable of skewering two or more men with its giant missiles. Early guns were little better than ballistae. By the 15th century, huge bombards could launch stone balls weighing 330 pounds .

Direct assault meant going over the walls,

unless a breach had been made by mine or artillery. The simplest means was to use ladders, often with hooks to grapple the wall-top and perhaps spikes to anchor them to the ground. This was extremely hazardous—the defenders tried to push ladders away with forked poles, and assailants could only arrive singly at the wall-top.

The siege tower, or belfry, however, was a far more substantial tool. Huge wooden structures higher than the battlements, towers acted like gantries, wheeled to castle walls to release men *en masse*. There might be a ram or shed at the tower's base or a catapult at the top.

Some were simply used as observation posts, or to allow archers to sweep the battlements. Cumbersome and vulnerable to fire, towers too were covered in hides. Sometimes they sunk into hidden pits the defenders had dug; one crusader tower had its drawbridge jammed shut by a beam from a defending machine; another was set alight from buckets of pitch winched out by defenders.

Defenders shot through arrow loops opening into embrasures in the wall thickness, though enemy archers hiding behind wooden mantlets could occasionally get an arrow through. Gatehouses were heavily fortified, at first by a single tower, then twin towers to hold soldiers. The passage had holes in the roof through which offensive material was dropped, or water to put out gate fires.

The turning bridge worked like a seesaw: weights on the inner end dropped it into a pit—another obstacle—as the front end swung up. The portcullis, a wooden lattice shod with iron, could be dropped swiftly, particularly when a sortie was being chased back to the gates. Multiple portcullises and gates were fitted to larger gatehouses.

Flanking towers allowed archers to shoot along them, while wooden hoardings might be replaced by bringing the whole battlement forward on corbels with gaps between. These machicolations were expensive and often confined to gatehouses and towers.

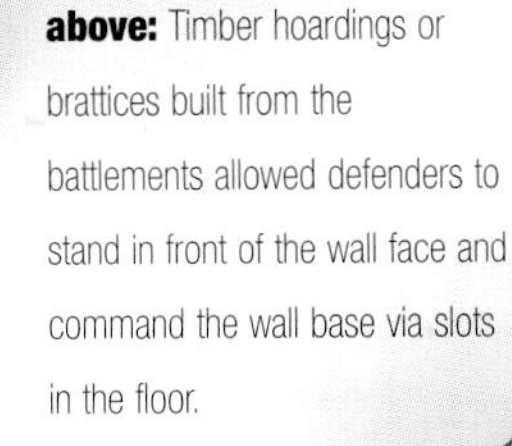

above: Timber hoardings or brattices built from the battlements allowed defenders to stand in front of the wall face and command the wall base via slots in the floor.

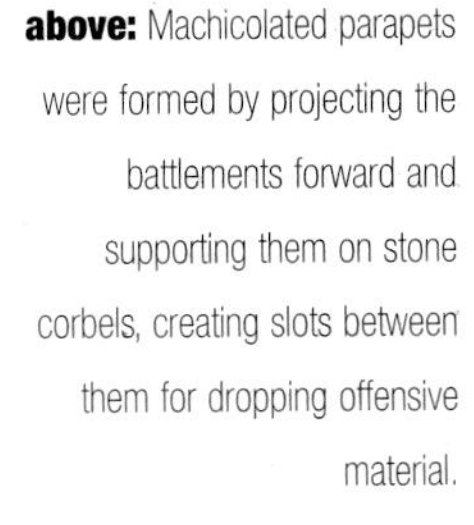

above: Machicolated parapets were formed by projecting the battlements forward and supporting them on stone corbels, creating slots between them for dropping offensive material.

below: A bombard about to fire and hurl a stone ball.

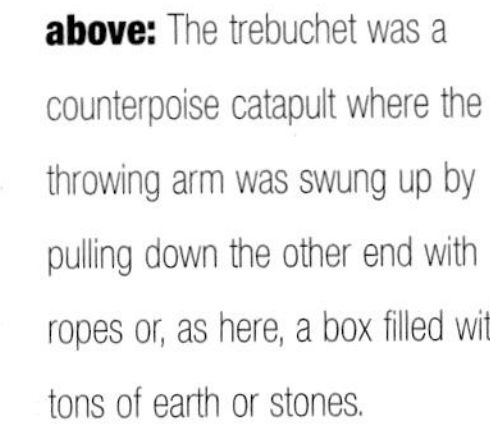

above: The trebuchet was a counterpoise catapult where the throwing arm was swung up by pulling down the other end with ropes or, as here, a box filled with tons of earth or stones.

Chapter Seventeen:

Fortresses

Refortifying the Castle

With the advent of gunpowder artillery, the castle had to evolve. The strength and angles of walls had to be modified to deflect greater firepower, and as castles became fortresses, they housed garrisons of soldiers, not rulers and nobles.

The development of guns c.1326 did not greatly affect castle design at first, but some countries adapted sooner than others. Italy and France, for example, made modifications at the end of the 15th century, changing the shape of castles more quickly than England did. In many places, the insertion of gun-loops low down in walls was the only real concession.

By the 16th century a desire for the comfort seen in great houses, together with more settled conditions in parts of Europe, meant that rulers and nobles visited castles less often. In France the château shows how the residential aspect of the castle grew at the expense of defenses, which are often poorly represented in such buildings.

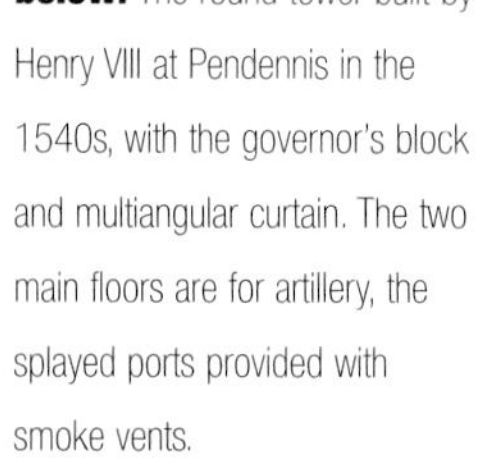

below: The round tower built by Henry VIII at Pendennis in the 1540s, with the governor's block and multiangular curtain. The two main floors are for artillery, the splayed ports provided with smoke vents.

Fortresses now emerged, defensive structures that also housed garrisons of soldiers. The residential aspect of a castle is excluded from a fort, which is more like a defended barracks. The shape of these strongholds is also different to that of most castles. Low walls fronting thick earthen banks were designed to absorb the force of cannonballs. Similarly, bastion tops needed to be broad enough and strong enough to carry cannons, including space and strength for the guns' recoil and its downward force. A whole new form of fortress thus emerged in the 16th and 17th centuries.

At first experiments were made with rounded or half-moon bastions, called lunettes. Henry VIII built a whole string of these along the south coast of England, such as at Pendennis in Cornwall, a typical small example. Soon, however, a new shape of bastion became popular.

It first appeared in the work of Micheli Sanmichele at Verona, Italy, c.1530–40, but may have originated from the eastern Mediterranean, perhaps Korykos in Cilesia (*see page 158*). In this shape the bastion points toward the field, the angle varying, while the flanks of the bastion are usually at right angles to the curtain. All the defenses were of earth with a battered revetment of stone, brick, or timber.

Angles of Defense

By the time Venetian engineer Giovanni Battista Zanchi published his book on fortifications in 1554, this star form was becoming common in fortresses and around towns. Eventually similar styles were taken overseas to colonial settlements in Asia and the Americas. In Europe many of these new fortifications were a result of the Thirty Years War (1618–48), while in England the civil wars also gave impetus.

In France the system for polygon walls of less than nine sides had a right angle between the face and flank of the bastion. It meant that there was an acute angle between the curtain and the flank itself, making it difficult to defend the face of a bastion from the flank of a neighbor. Instead, tenailles, ravelins, and other works were built in the ditch. Where the polygon had more than nine sides, the flank of a bastion might be perpendicular to the curtain. The Dutch engineers preferred to build bastions with flanks that were perpendicular to the curtain, the salient being either a right angle or frequently less.

The lines of defense—from the foot of the flank of a bastion to the salient angle of its neighbor—was no more than 720 feet for defense with muskets, or more if by artillery. This system was imported by the English, influenced by involvement in the Low Countries under Prince Maurice. The renowned Royalist engineer, Bernard de Gomme, was probably of Spanish and Dutch extract. Existing civil war bastion flanks sometimes had an obtuse angle, due to the terrain or, as at Carisbrooke Castle on the Isle of Wight, deliberately to guard the face of a bastion from the flank of a neighbor.

above: Guarding the Gironde, Blaye sits on the opposite bank of the estuary not far from Bordeaux, France. The picture shows the ravelin on the right, connected by a bridge to the main mass of the fort.

left: Castillo de San Marcos, built by the Spanish between 1672 and 1695 to protect St. Augustine, Florida, the first permanent settlement in the continental United States. Angled corner-bastions overlook the covered way, with the protective glacis beyond. The moat was usually flooded in emergencies only.

Round Forts and Star Forts

The round fort was gradually replaced in the 16th century by the star fort, named after its pointed bastions.

Deal

Deal Castle, actually a fort, is between the North and South Forelands of Kent, England. Begun in 1539, it was the last and largest coastal fort built by Henry VIII to protect the south from attack by the Catholic rulers of France and the Holy Roman Empire. It lay between two anchorages to protect fleets riding at anchor in bad weather.

There is a low central round tower from which six semi-circular bastions, or lunettes, protrude. These, however, only reach the first-floor level of the keep. There is a lantern (not the original) in the center of the tower and a clever double staircase. All the battlements of tower and bastions were added in 1732 to replace round parapets.

Tightly surrounding the inner defenses is a slightly lower outer curtain wall, the passage formed between them defended by gun-ports or musket loopholes low in the bastions. The outer curtain also has six bastions, the whole circuit pierced with gun-ports. Since guns could be mounted on the central tower and both sets of bas-

right: The broad artillery platforms provided by the bastions at Deal.

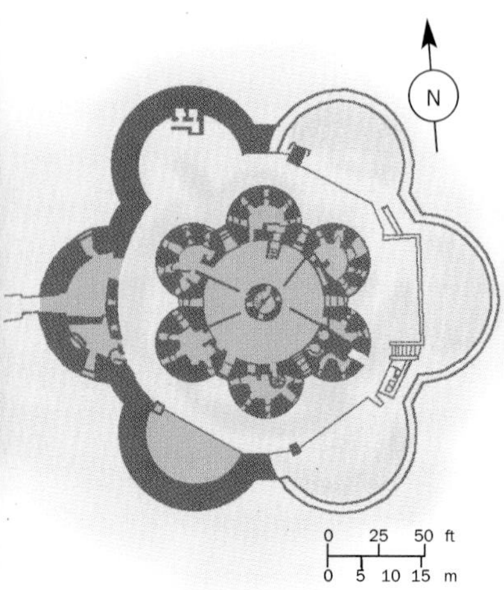

tions, five levels of guns were presented to an attacker, who first had to negotiate the broad ditch.

Originally the fort held a captain and 24 men, with kitchen, bakery, perhaps living quarters on the ground floor, more comfortable accommodation above, and stores in the tower basement.

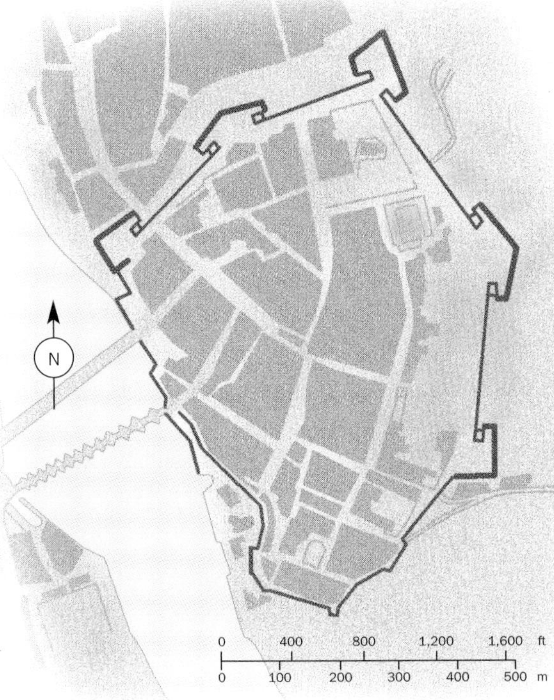

Berwick

The new defenses of Berwick-upon-Tweed, on the east coast of the English-Scottish border, superceded the medieval town walls and castle. In 1522–3 Henry VIII built artillery fortifications to the east (Windmill Bulwark) and along the river (Bulwark by the Sands), while in 1539–42 he added a circular masonry fortification (later named Lord's Mount) at the northeast salient. Smaller round gun-towers were added to the castle and wall.

A square fort was proposed for the east side of the city in Edward VI's reign. In 1558 Mary I ordered Sir Richard Lee, Surveyor of Fortifications, to replace the landward medieval walls and castle with a bastioned system, but most of the work was completed under Elizabeth I.

The main walls enclosed the southern part of the town, leaving the castle beyond to the northwest. Masonry walls 20 feet high were built, with five bastions with long orillons to protect small flanking emplacements of two stories. The counterscarp of the ditch protected the masonry and a sentry path around the bastions was guarded by low breastwork.

above: Fort St. Angelo on the promontory across Grand Harbour from the main town of Valletta.

left: Plan of the defenses of Berwick-upon-Tweed.

Valletta

This coastal city is the capital of Malta, the island taken over by the Knights Hospitaller in 1530. They refortified the old capital of Mdina, inland, and the precious harbors that would one day lap Valletta were defended. Fort St. Angelo was built on the promontory of Birgu town, and Fort St. Michael was set on a neighboring spit, connected by a chain boom and bridge of boats. A star fort, St. Elmo, was built to the northwest on another promontory to guard the entrance.

In 1565 Ottoman Turks led by Suleyman the Magnificent attacked the harbors and set up artillery where Valletta town now stands. They pounded Fort St. Elmo, which held out gallantly against all attacks, using "Greek fire," flamethrowers, and firework hoops. It finally fell, but Mustapha Pasha, who led the Muslim army, is said to have remarked, "If so small a son has cost us so dear, what price shall we have to pay for the father?" The Grand Master, La Valette, fired back the heads of recently executed Turkish prisoners.

A mine brought down part of Birgu's land walls, but the knights counterattacked. The Turks even tried a siege tower, but it was blasted by artillery. Relief forces finally arrived from Sicily and the Turks withdrew.

New star defenses were built around the new capital, Valletta. Fort St. Elmo was enclosed, the new bastions' walls 60–70 feet thick, and a great ditch cut off the landward side. Fort Ricasoli was added to the east and a square star fort on Manoel Island to the west.

Fortresses in the 17th and 18th Centuries

Fortifications in the 17th century took on a number of forms. Some towns were given a complete circuit of walls and bastions, or forts connected by a bank and ditch. Existing fortifications were sometimes further strengthened by the addition of bastions or ravelins. Many isolated bastioned forts were also built.

Similar fortifications were also seen in colonial areas; Fort James, built in 1697 by the British on James Island, Gambia, was one of a number stretching along the Atlantic coast from Senegal to Benin, set up by rival European nations in their quest for gold, ivory, spices, and, from the early 17th century, slaves. By the end of the 18th century some forts had towers with almost 30 guns and were very difficult to capture.

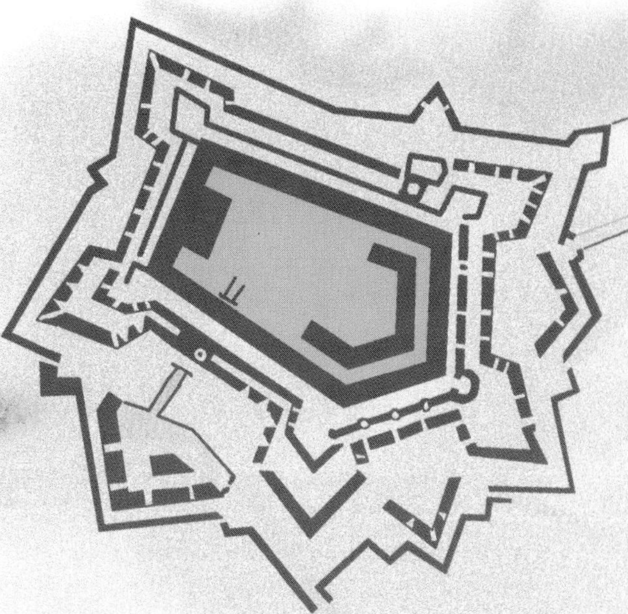

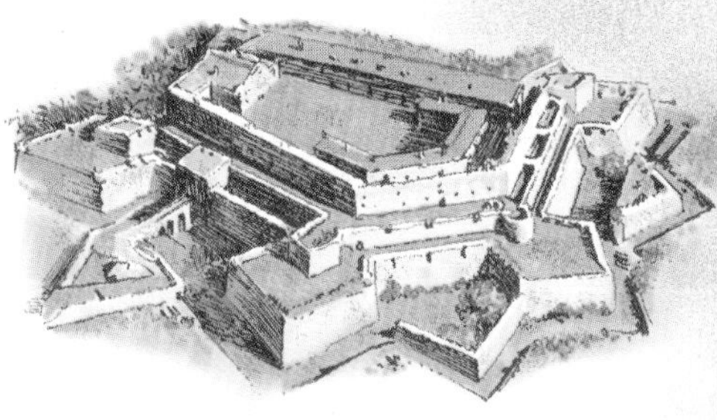

Plan and artist's impression of Fort Bellegarde.

Fort Bellegarde

On a precipice above the town of Le Perthus in Roussillon, France, the first stronghold was built by Peter III, King of Aragon in 1285, to guard the pass from Spain into France. Captured in 1674 and lost again, in 1678 Marshal Vauban's plans for a concentric pentagonal fortress were approved and the old castle demolished.

There is a strong counterscarp, while five bastions jut from the main enceinte. Within this curtain and above it was a second bastioned wall with a third line formed by the rear walls of the buildings in the center of the fort. There were barracks for 600 men, an impressive chapel, mill, bakery, kitchens, and hospital.

Gunpowder was stored deep in the bastions within ventilated chambers, as well as in buildings in the third line. One bastion on the second line is rounded, for reasons unknown. Beyond the fort were two small redoubts and an outlying fort 492 feet away. Spanish forces took Bellegarde in 1793, while the following year the French retook it after a 34-day siege.

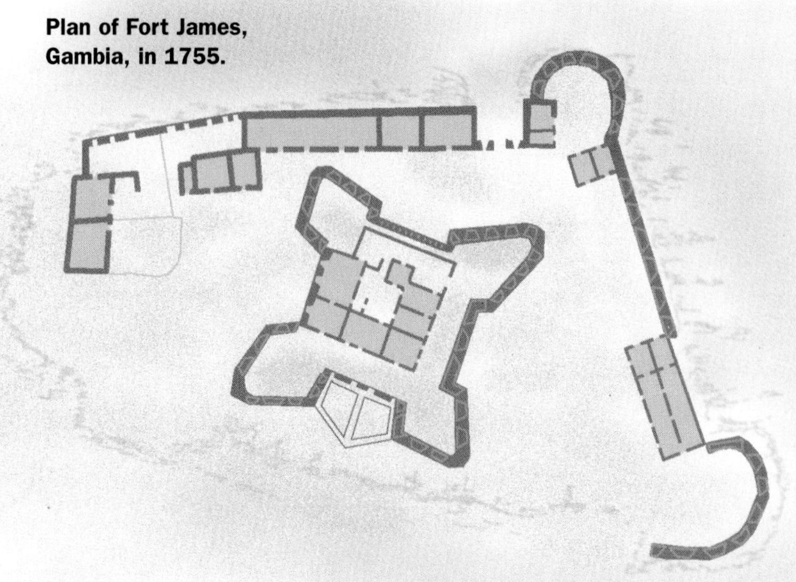

Plan of Fort James, Gambia, in 1755.

Fort George

This well-preserved fort stands on a sandy point projecting into the Moray Firth, 12½ miles

northeast of Inverness in Scotland. It was contracted by the Adams family in 1748 and designed by William Skinner, military engineer for northern Britain, when a new site for George II's army base had to be swiftly chosen, following the Jacobite rising at the Battle of Culloden in 1746. Work on Fort George was completed in 1769.

Polygonal in shape, the fort has six obtuse bastions for defense. Inside, all the army buildings survive intact: officers' blocks, barracks, ordnance and provision stores, and the chapel. William Skinner became the first governor, commanding 1,600 officers and men, plus an artillery unit. However, Fort George was so powerful that it never had to face an enemy.

left: The artillery fortification of Fort George.

Fort Ticonderoga

This fort in New York state stands by Lake George. It was built by the French in 1755 as a star-shaped earthwork and log defense called Fort Carillon to command the narrows through the lake, but was found to be partly ineffective. A small fort, the Grenadier Redoubt, was hastily erected.

In 1758, during the Seven Years War, 15,000 British soldiers were held off by the Marquis de Montcalm's 3,000 French troops in a massive breastwork west of the fort. In 1759 a multi-pronged attack drew French troops away and General Amhurst captured the fort with a loss of only 16 men. The British renamed it Fort Ticonderoga and, though the magazine had been blown up, Amhurst rebuilt it and erected a stronger fort to the north at Crown Point.

Allowed to deteriorate after the war, it was captured in a pre-dawn raid by Ethan Allen, Benedict Arnold, and a group of patriots in May 1775 during the Revolutionary War. George Washington and Benjamin Franklin visited the fort. The Americans built another fort on the hill across the narrow lake.

With Mount Independence, Ticonderoga became an obstacle to invasion from Canada, deterring a British force in 1776. In 1777 the British General Burgoyne recaptured it but the same year it was abandoned after the capitulation at Saratoga and was never garrisoned again.

below: Angled corner-bastions flank the entrance gate leading to the rectangular Place d'Armes at Fort Ticonderoga.

The Changing Face of Siege Warfare

By the 16th century, sieges had not changed greatly in operation, although the weapons employed were more advanced. Iron balls were taking over from stone ones, and guns were protected by gabions, drum-shaped wicker containers filled with earth. Catapults were disappearing from the field. Since the 15th century miners had sometimes used gunpowder instead of fire to bring down the props under a wall. Star shells illuminated the area and canister shot scattered its contents over a wide area. Bags of gunpowder were used to destroy gates, and high-trajectory howitzers and mortars became more common.

above: The Siege of Namur, 1692, painted by Martin Jean-Baptiste le Vieux.

Menno van Coehoorn (1641–1704) was a Dutch engineer. He reinforced the citadel complex at Namur, Belgium, in 1691, defended it the next year, and captured it in 1695. Coehoorn used energetic methods of assault, sending the best troops through breaches made by massed artillery, notably the miniature mortars he invented. In defense, he disliked the great French hornworks and their main rampart because they were costly and the revetment was easily seen. He favored hidden close-range flanking fire from redoubts in re-entrants, earthen fausse-brayes, and double-bastioned flanks, and room for troops to assemble for counterattack. He dug alternate wet and dry ditches; the latter, together with covered ways, were cut to within a few inches of the water table, forcing besiegers to bring earth to cross the ditch, since digging down would flood them out.

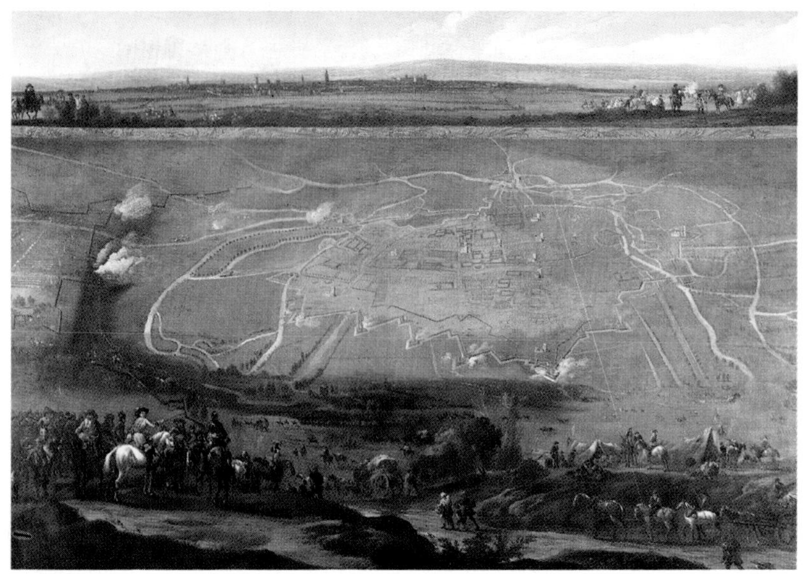

below: The Siege of Oxford, 1645, from a painting by Jan Wyck.

In France, the skill of Marshal Vauban (1633–1707) was recognized in sieges in the Low Countries. Vauban saw that the safest method to advance toward a fortress was not over the open ground but via zigzag trenches. These "saps" protected the men, stopped enemy artillery working down a trench, and confined blasts by the use of angles. At the end of a sap, troops entered a trench parallel to the enemy walls. Gabions protected the sappers as they extended the trenches to close in on an objective. As the saps moved forward, more artillery could be moved closer. Batteries of guns concentrated their fire at a few select spots in the defenses.

Setting the standard

Vauban used the wealth of France to build as he wanted, resulting in 160 forts and towns being built or refortified. In defense he relied on artillery, mainly 18- and 12-pounders, or less. To sweep the outworks of enemy soldiers he devised the idea of firing heaps of stones from mortars, an idea taken up all over Europe.

Vauban's bastions were less spiky than the Dutch and less obtuse and bulky than the Italians'. Flanks were sometimes straight, sometimes retired and concave and with orillons. Hornworks were sometimes used liberally. Existing fortifications might have to be considered, a citadel being built, then a rampart to the enceinte, before demolishing old defenses.

In his second design Vauban built hollow, loopholed masonry bastion towers which could be held even if the fortress was overlooked, such as Besançon. For his third system he added a casemated redoubt to the ravelin and recessed the center of the curtain to make flanks either side of the

bastion tower. This was the high point of bastion fortification.

The third great military engineer of the period was the Swede, Erik Dahlberg (1625–1703). He broke from Sweden's use of Netherlandish design, his most obvious symbol being the multistory casemate tower, used as island batteries, hilltop forts, or as keeps.

Vauban's work was digested and regurgitated in the 18th century by monarchs such as Frederick the Great of Prussia, with some modifications. However, costs raised questions of the necessity of permanent defense. In 1776 Marc-René, Marquis de Montalbert, brought out a work that supported far-reaching principles: Many guns were needed for defense; the heavily indented bastion trace should be replaced by the long curtain with artillery casemates (doubling as barracks), with a huge three-story caponier projecting from it—this "polygonal" system could fit ground contours more easily; detached forts should cover the main fortress. Much of northern Europe, Germany especially, took up this idea, but France refused.

above: The Siege of La Rochelle, 10 August to 12 October 1628, from a 17th-century painting by an unknown artist after an engraving by Jacques Caillot.

Romantic Ruins and 19th-Century Forts

above: Stone facing blocks hide the brick walls of romantic Neuschwanstein.

In the 19th century many castles decayed or were plundered for materials. Castles were seen as symbols of oppression and imprisonment, which appealed to 19th-century poets—indeed, some were turned into gaols. They also encouraged feelings of nostalgia for a lost past, for peace and order. By contrast, some new castles were built as follies by wealthy men captivated by the past, but the real business of war continued in less romantic forts.

By mid-century the "polygonal" plan fort was used in Europe. Less expensive and more compact than earlier bastioned versions, it could concentrate firepower on the enemy but still command a wide field of fire, while the garrison could shoot from firing steps around the scarp wall. Detached forts, set within range of neighboring forts for flanking cover, could provide the same cover as long lines of walls around a town, with separate long- and close-range armament.

France's old-style defenses, which concentrated on flanking fire not on siege batteries, were shaken by the Franco-Prussian war of 1870, but they quickly put up redoubts modeled on German practices. Some ring-fortresses in western Europe were enormous complexes; by 1898 those at Antwerp extended for 66 miles (106km).

Neuschwanstein

This impressive fortress towers above the Pöllat River gorge in the Bavarian Alps of Germany. It was begun in 1869 by King Louis II of Bavaria, sometimes called "Mad" King Ludwig, who grew up in nearby Hohenschwangau castle, but was unfinished on his death in 1886.

It employed modern technology: running water and flush toilets on all floors, hot water for the bath and kitchen, and a warm-air heating system. A spring 656 feet (200m) above provided drinking water.

An outer skin of limestone blocks hides the brick walls behind. Louis created some beautiful interiors: The two-story throne room was created as the Grail-Hall of Parsifal, with a Byzantine-inspired dome suggestive of Hagia Sophia in Constantinople. The third floor rooms recall the legends that inspired Wagner, of whom Louis was a patron. In turn, Neuschwanstein castle inspired the Sleeping Beauty Castle in Disneyland.

Fort Nelson

Fort Nelson lies at Portsdown at Fareham in Hampshire, England. It was begun in 1860 amid

right: Fort Nelson, looking inland, with the pointed redan in center foreground. Of the three long white roofs, the outer flanking pair are survivors of the original ten Second World War anti-aircraft ammunition sheds.

fears of a French threat. It was inspired by the German system, being polygonal in plan and one of several fortresses around Portsmouth harbor and the Royal Dockyard.

The north side has an obtuse arrow-head wall; the barracks are to the south and covered with earth. Tunnels allowed swift, safe access around the fort, while the powder magazine was hidden under the parade ground. The main armament was 68-pounders on the gun platform, 13-inch mortars in three concealed vaulted batteries, and lighter guns in caponier and barracks, for flank defense. In the later 19th century the Armstrong RBL (Rifled Breech-Loading) gun was employed. When Fort Nelson was completed in 1871 it was already obsolete, the French threat having passed, but it was kept up for maneuvers until disarmed in the early 20th century. It was used as a transit camp in the First World War and an anti-aircraft magazine and adjoining battery in the Second World War. It latterly fell into decay, but was leased to the Royal Armouries in 1988 to become a national artillery museum.

Hearst Castle

Hearst Castle is on a rocky crag above San Simeon Bay, midway between San Francisco and Los Angeles in California, some five miles inland. Its 127-acre estate was created by American millionaire William Randoph Hearst and named La Cuesta Encantada—"The Enchanted Hill." Work began in 1922, and a huge team of designers and craftsmen took three years to construct the main building, the Casa Grande, a Mediterranean Revival mansion. Work continued on additions until 1947.

Julia Morgan, trained at the École des Beaux Arts in Paris, worked with Hearst on the design of the castle, which combined features from several decorative styles and historical periods, mainly from Southern Europe, but constructed from modern materials such as iron, steel, and cement. The material was stored at the port of San Simeon until it could be hauled up the mountainside, along with Hearst's art treasures until the mansion was ready to receive them.

The guest cottages were finished first, including the Casa del Mar, Casa del Monte, and Casa del Sol, in a style echoing the Italian Renaissance. Although called cottages, the Casa del Sol, for example, boasts 18 rooms, including four bedrooms and four bathrooms. When the Casa Grande was completed it comprised 130 rooms. An assembly room on the ground floor was designed for Hearst's visitors to gather.

Hearst was a pioneer in the production of newsreels and movies (producing, among others, *The Perils of Pauline*) and the mansion therefore has a theater, also on the ground floor. Here too are the dining room, morning room, and billiard room. Hearst's private suite and study—the Gothic Suite and Gothic Study—stretched across the whole of the third floor.

The upper floors include a pantry and kitchen. The Doge's Suite was built in the Italian style with a balcony inspired by the Doge's Palace in Venice. Four cloister rooms are flanked by an open walkway. The library houses 5,000 books and an important collection of Greek vases. The castle also contains some of his collections of silver, furniture, antiquities, fine and decorative arts, paintings, tapestries, religious textiles, and oriental rugs.

Underground storage vaults were built into the final design. There were even bedrooms set into the tall bell towers. The mansion is complemented by an esplanade and beautiful gardens, which included marble sculptures and pools. Hearst, who had five sons, died in 1951.

below: The Casa Grande dominates the complex at Hearst Castle, California.

Forts in the USA

North America in the 19th century was the stage for two very different forms of conflict. Stone or brick forts used in the Civil War were replaced in the face of increasingly powerful artillery, thick earthen banks added to absorb the impact of round shot and shell bursts.

The clash with native Americans was caused by the persistent flow of settlers and soldiers pushing further and further west. Forts used by the US soldiers in the west were largely of timber, though adobe was sometimes used. They ranged from crude clusters of shacks, such as Fort Ruby (built to protect mail routes from Native Americans), to large collections of buildings that at least catered to the comforts of the men.

right: Artist's impression from a contemporary photograph of the short-lived Fort Ruby built in 1862 in Nevada.

Fort Sumter

Fort Sumter stands on Sullivan's Island at the entrance to Charleston Harbor. Named after a Revolutionary War patriot, it was begun in 1829; four sides of its 5-foot thick brick walls were designed for three tiers of guns within casemates, the fifth (with officers' quarters) for only the third tier, 135 guns in all. Barracks for 650 men ran along the two flanks.

It was still under construction early in 1861 when the Confederacy decreed the evacuation of the few Federal troops under Major Robert Anderson. President Lincoln ordered a supply expedition but the Confederates opened fire on April 12. Most of Sumter's 60 guns pointed out to sea and, unable to withstand the pounding, Anderson surrendered two days later. The Civil War had begun.

From April 1863 until January 1865 Federal forces pounded Sumter into rubble, firing some seven million pounds of metal, but it was only evacuated when Federal forces were advancing. In 1948 Fort Sumter was declared a national monument.

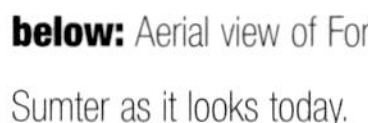

below: Aerial view of Fort Sumter as it looks today.

9-foot palisade covered a third of a mile, with 25 guns among 15 32-foot high mounds, with internal bombproof rooms and powder magazines, and an underground passageway guarded the landward side.

An attack by Federal forces in December 1864 failed but a second attempt on January 12, 1865, by ships under Commander David Dixon Porter and over 8,000 infantry, resulted in the capture of the fort three days later. Only a partially reconstructed palisade and a few mounds remain, due to sea erosion.

Fort Fisher

The Confederate forces built Fort Fisher in 1861 on a neck of land at the mouth of Cape Fear river in North Carolina to protect Wilmington and keep off Federal ships. Until July 1862 it comprised several sand batteries mounting less than 24 guns. Colonel William Lamb, greatly influenced by the Malakoff Tower at Sevastopol in the Crimea, expanded the defenses. Unlike earlier fortifications, earth and sand were largely used.

By 1865 it had a mile of sea defenses with 22 guns in 12-foot high batteries, and two on the southern side, 45 and 60 feet high. One small mound became a bombproof hospital, another a telegraph office. The land defenses, including a

above: Troopers stationed at Fort Robinson pose for a photograph in 1898.

Fort Robinson

Camp Robinson in Nebraska was established in 1874 as protection for the nearby Red Cloud Agency, the soldiers there also guarding the Sidney-Deadwood Trail to the Black Hills and surrounding area. The Sioux chief, Crazy Horse, surrendered in May 1877 but was fatally stabbed here on September 5 during a scuffle as soldiers tried to get him into the guardroom. The Agency moved that year and the camp was renamed "Fort" in 1878.

The arrival of the railroad in the 1880s enabled quick dispersal of troops and Fort Robinson expanded as an army post, replacing Laramie as the most important fort in the area. In 1885 the first African-American soldiers of the ninth Cavalry arrived. In 1919 the fort was earmarked as a quartermaster remount depot.

Dogs were trained there from 1942 (till 1945), while a year later it became a prisoner-of-war camp. After the war Fort Robinson was used for beef research by the government until the early 1970s. It ceased to be a military post in 1948.

left: A lone gun stands watch beneath the Confederate flag at the meager remains of Fort Fisher.

Blockhouses and Bunkers

By the 20th century, the awesome power of artillery meant that even fortresses were becoming outdated. Soon too the threat from aerial attack added another dimension to the designers' problems. During the First World War, soldiers on the Western Front in France and Belgium protected themselves in interconnected trench systems with living quarters in underground dugouts or defended by timber and sandbags.

Similarly, fortresses were sunk into the ground. Now they became a subterranean world for soldiers to live in, the forts keeping in contact via radio. On the surface, artillery pieces glowered from cupolas, the dome-like structures set on roofs. Concrete was used in great quantity, with sand in between to lessen the blast of exploding shells. Concrete was also used for some gun emplacements.

The Siegfried Line, a system of strongpoints and pillboxes built in the 1930s on Germany's western frontier, held up the American advance in 1944 for a time, giving the retreating Germans respite until the spring of the following year. Even forts set on legs resting on the bed of the English Channel were used as anti-aircraft batteries.

By the end of the Second World War, guns in fortresses had been made obsolete by missiles and aircraft. In the modern age, "Star Wars" technology may result in space becoming a warzone where defensive missiles are launched to destroy incoming warheads detected by early-warning radar, telescopes, and satellites.

below: A simplified 1930s cross-section of a typical Maginot Line gros ouvrage (fortress) which aims to show the vast scale of France's line of defense.

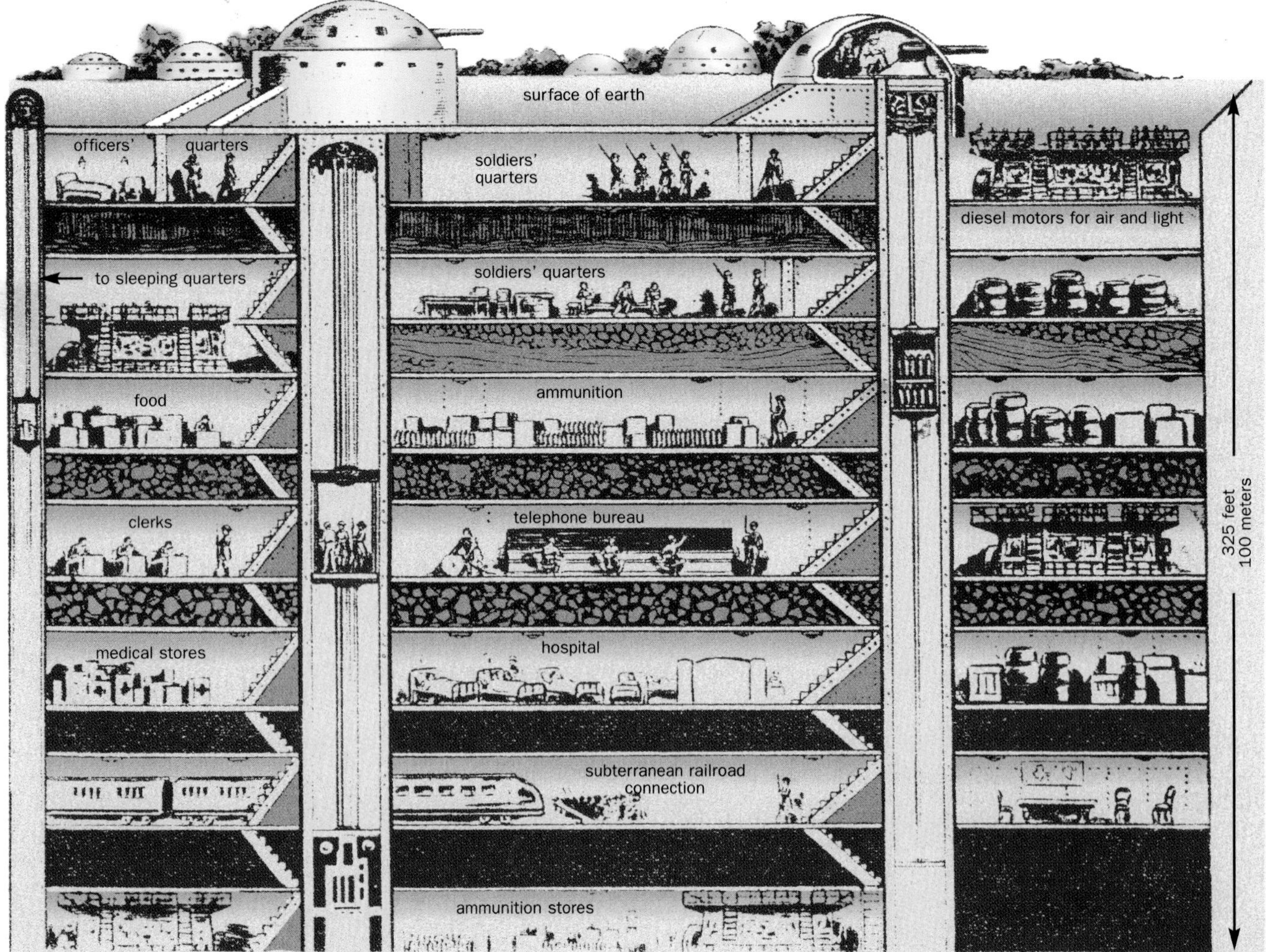

Maginot Line

Named after André Maginot, the French Minister for War who created it, the Maginot Line was constructed in the 1930s along the French-German border in northeast France. Since some First World War fortresses had withstood attack and also saved on manpower, it was decided to employ an improved version of this form of defense.

The line included 58 large forts (*gros ouvrages*) and almost 400 blockhouses (*petits ouvrages*). There were ditches and iron rails rammed into the ground as anti-tank measures, and machine guns to spray advancing infantry. Artillery pieces, of greater power than used previously, were fitted under steel domes (*cupolas*) set in concrete, the rim flush with the ground.

The concrete used was now much thicker, while approximately 2,600 feet behind the forts and 65–100 feet beneath the ground were large underground networks of living and recreation areas and storehouses. Power stations provided electricity for air-conditioning, lighting, ammunition trolleys, and a railway connecting various parts of the line, allowing troops to be quickly transported to strongpoints.

But the defenses did not stretch along the border with Belgium. On May 12, 1940, the Germans outflanked the line, broke through with tanks at Sedan at its northern end, and came around to the rear. Despite gallant resistance in the forts, the French were forced to surrender.

above: Entrance to a Maginot Line *gros ouvrage* (Casemate 353) in the Alsace.

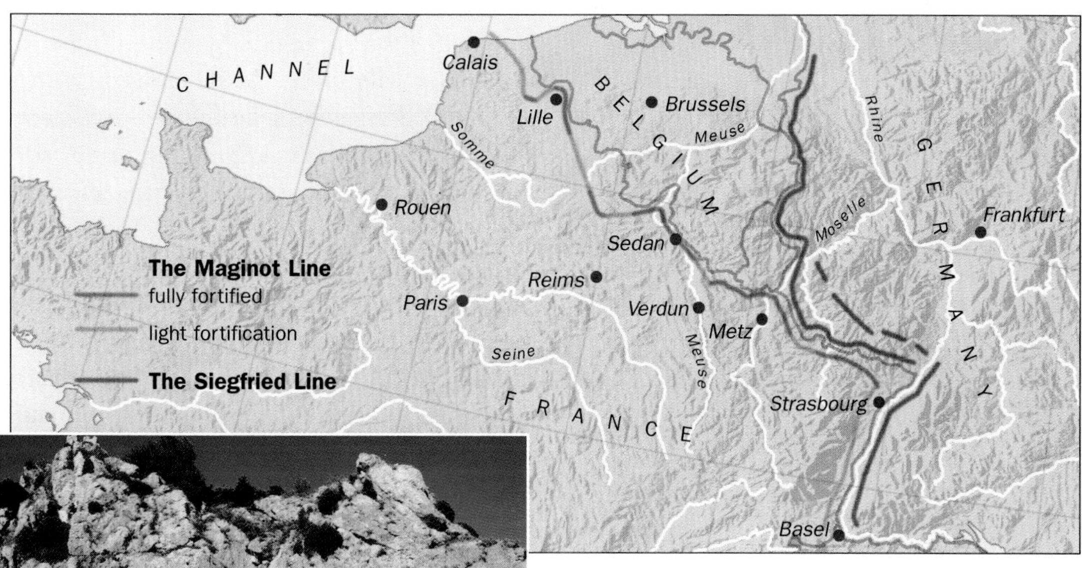

below left: Blockhouse near Menton.

Nuclear Bunkers

The threat of nuclear attack has led some countries to prepare underground refuges from which government officials can direct operations. The devastation from such weapons has meant a ruthless choice of who is chosen to stay in these shelters and who is left outside. In central government bunkers, sometimes set inside mountains, the plotting of incoming missiles and the operation of retaliatory strikes can be conducted.

As with earlier underground defenses, living accommodation is supplied; but dangers from nuclear fallout would preclude leaving after the initial missile impacts had passed, unless people were wearing special protective clothing. All bunkers would need strong, lead-covered doors to protect against blast and radiation, adequate areas for large amounts of food, and a means of recycling air and water, since that outside would be contaminated.

Conclusion

Castles Today

Many castles and fortifications have survived to the present day, despite the best efforts of catapults, shells, bombs, mining, fire, thieves, neglect and over-enthusiastic restorers.

above: Almost synonymous with the British monarchy, over one-fifth of Windsor Castle was destroyed by a fire in 1992, but was fully restored by 1997. The castle remains a popular tourist attraction.

After their military and administrative uses came to an end, many castles have been utilized in a number of new ways, largely depending on the whims of their owners, be they private individuals or a government body. Some are still inhabited as a home, a few are used as offices, several still have a garrison of soldiers (though often more for ceremonial reasons), and until quite recently some still held prisoners. The better-preserved examples form useful backdrops for filmmakers. Even ruins are utilized for costume dramas set in later historical periods, and in some castles interpreters re-enact scenes from the past to publicize the site.

Windsor

Standing on a chalk hill above the River Thames, Windsor Castle is a famous tourist attraction. It was begun by William the Conqueror and is one of the few to remain a royal residence. It has two baileys, with the motte in the center.

The Round Tower, a stone shell keep, was erected on top of the motte by Henry II (1154–89). Edward III (1327–77) added internal buildings during the 14th century. In the reign of George IV (1820–30) the keep was heightened, buttressed, and battlemented, while the state apartments on the north side of the upper ward (bailey), fitted out for Charles II, were also much renovated. Further work was carried out under Queen Victoria.

Windsor castle now houses many fine objects and works of art, including the amazing dolls' house made for Queen Mary in the 1920s. The Chapel of St. George, begun in 1475, houses the tombs of Henry VI, Edward IV, Henry VIII, Charles I, George III, George IV, William IV, Edward VII, George V, and George VI. It is also the chapel of the Order of the Garter, being used for the installation of the knights, whose stall plates and banners line the interior. Adjacent to St. George's chapel is the Albert Memorial Chapel, a shrine of about 1870. Edward VIII's tomb is in Windsor Home Park, and the mausoleum of Queen Victoria is at Frogmore, Windsor.

Blair

Blair castle in the Strath of Garry lies on the Perth-to-Inverness road in the central Scottish highlands. It is a private home to the Duke of Atholl.

The first castle appears to have been begun by John Comyn in 1269 but the fortress was taken over by the monarchs until 1457, when it was conferred on Sir John Stewart of Balvenie, James II's half-brother, ancestor of the present Duke.

The main tower is known as Cummings Tower, restored in 1869. The castle was extended in the 16th century with a new hall range. In the Jacobite rising of 1745 Lord George Murray

left: Due to its role as a high-security prison in WWII, as shown by the plan below, and after many films about the attempts to escape from it, Colditz castle is now a tourist attraction.

returned to his home, which had been taken over by Hanoverian troops, and laid siege to it—Blair was the last castle in Britain to be besieged. His brother, the second Duke, remodeled the castle as a Georgian House. The Duke of Atholl has the distinction to be the only person in Britain allowed a private army.

Colditz

This rugged castle sits high on a steep hill overlooking Colditz town on the River Mulde in Saxony, some 30 miles southeast of Leipzig. A former residence of the kings of Saxony from 1014, it was rebuilt after the Hussite Wars in the 15th century and put into service as a prisoner-of-war camp in 1939; a year later, it was upgraded to a maximum security prison. Despite being 400 miles from the nearest friendly border, 32 allied prisoners managed to reach freedom.

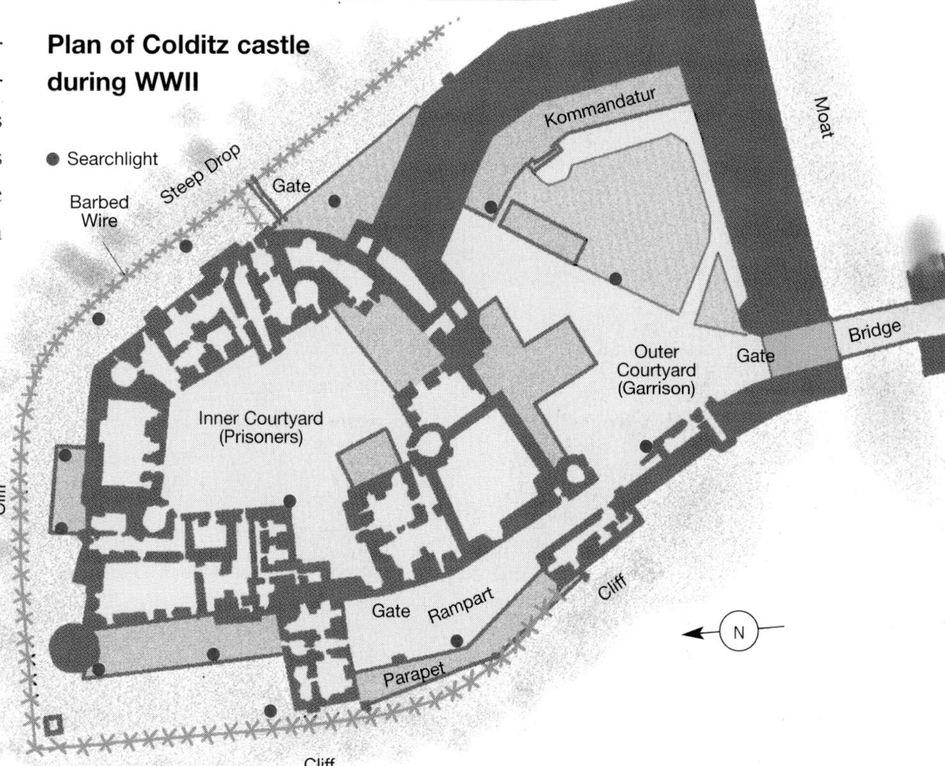

left: Everyone's idea of what a baronial Highlands castle should look like—the many turreted Blair.

Glossary

Ashlar: smooth, well-fitted masonry blocks.
Bailey: a courtyard.
Ballista: a siege engine rather like a large crossbow, for shooting large arrows.
Barbican: forework protecting a gate.
Barmkin: enclosure subsidiary to a pele.
Bartizan: a turret set high on a wall face.
Bastion: a projection that gives a wider firing angle, but can describe any fortification.
Batter: a wall thickened at its base to form a sloping face.
Belfry: a siege tower.
Berm: the space between a wall and ditch or moat.
Bombard: a large siege cannon for destroying walls.
Breastwork: a low defensive wall rapidly constructed in battle.
Bretasche: wooden hoarding on battlements; can also mean breastwork.
Broch: a tall circular refuge tower of dry-built masonry, constructed in Scotland (probably first century AD).
Bulwark: a projecting work usually made from earth.
Burh: earth and timber defensive enclosure used by the Anglo-Saxons and Vikings.
Buttress: a vertical stone reinforcing strip for a wall.
Caponier: a covered passage across a ditch, also used to defend it.
Casemate: a bombproof vaulted chamber built in the thickness of the rampart.
Chemin de ronde: a wall-walk.
Chemise: a skirt wall around a tower.
Concentric: a castle built with rings of mutually supportive walls.
Corbel: a stone bracket.
Counterscarp: a raised rampart on the outer edge of a ditch.
Crenel: the open section of a battlement.
Crenellation: a battlement.
Curtain: a wall that encloses the castle.
Donjon: great tower or keep.
Embrasure: the open area set in the thickness of a wall behind a loophole for archers to stand in.
En bec: a tower beaked or pointed to the field.
En bosse (*en bossage*): cut stone where the outer face is left rough (rustic).
Enceinte: the defended perimeter of a castle.
Escutcheon: a shield-shaped surface decorated with a coat-of-arms.
Fauss-bray: a continuous rampart and parapet in the ditch in front of the main rampart.
Gabion: a tall wicker basket filled with earth.
Glacis: smooth stone incline.
Hoarding: wooden shuttering built out from the battlements to command the space at the foot of a wall.
Hornwork: an outwork.
Keep: a term used from the 16th century to describe a donjon.
Loggia: a roofed gallery on the side of a building.
Loophole: the slot in a wall through which an archer shoots.
Lunette: a detached bastion forming a permanent outwork.
Machicolation: battlement brought forward on corbels to allow material to be dropped through gaps.
Mangon: a catapult, sometimes referred to as a torsion engine, sometimes a traction trebuchet.
Mantlet wall: a secondary defensive wall around a tower of other building.
Merlon: the solid section of a battlement.
Meutrières or "murder holes": holes or slots in a gate passage roof, through which offensive material or water (against fire) can be dropped.
Moat: a ditch, either wet or dry.
Motte: a mound of earth carrying either a tower or shell keep.
Mudéjar: decorative stonework carved by Spanish Moresco craftsmen.
Orillon: a projecting ear that protects the flank of a bastion.
Outworks: a trench or fortification outside the main defenses.
Parallel: a siege trench running parallel to the walls.
Pele (or peel): a tower-house around the area of the Scottish marches.
Petrary: a stone-throwing engine.
Pilaster: a flat buttress with little projection.
Portcullis: iron-shod wooden lattice that could be dropped to block a gate.
Postern: a lesser or private gate.
Putlog holes: square holes in a wall face that secured horizontal scaffolding poles or beams for supporting hoarding.
Rampart: an earthen bank, often on the edge of a ditch, usually topped with a palisade or wall.
Ravelin: an outwork placed beyond the ditch.
Revet: retaining wall or facing, usually of wood, stone, or brick.
Ribat: early Islamic garrison or garrison duty; latterly refers to a fortified frontier or coastal defense.
Ring-work: a ditched enclosure without a motte.
Sap: a covered trench dug when approaching an enemy fortification.
Scarp: the inner side of a ditch.
Shell-keep: a motte in which the palisade around the top is replaced by a stone wall without a tower.
Slighted: to damage a castle so much that it can't be used for defense
Spur: an angular projection from the face of a wall.
Talus: another word for batter.
Tenaille: outwork between two bastions, set before the curtain.
Tenshu: the large main tower of a Japanese castle.
Torre albarrana: an extra-mural tower.
Turning bridge: a counterbalanced bridge in which weights on the inner end allow the outer end to swing up quickly.
Trace: the ground plan of a work.
Trebuchet: a siege engine that works by counterbalance to pivot up the throwing arm.
Ward: a courtyard.

Index